WILDE'S INTENTIONS

WILDE'S INTENTIONS

The Artist in his Criticism

LAWRENCE DANSON

CLARENDON PRESS · OXFORD
1997

Oxford University Press, Great Clarendon Street, Oxford OX2 6DP
Oxford New York
Athens Auckland Bangkok Bogota Bombay
Buenos Aires Calcutta Cape Town Dar es Salaam
Delhi Florence Hong Kong Istanbul Karachi
Kuala Lumpur Madras Madrid Melbourne
Mexico City Nairobi Paris Singapore
Taipei Tokyo Toronto
and associated companies in
Berlin Ibadan

Oxford is a trade mark of Oxford University Press

Published in the University Press
Oxford University Press Inc., New York

British Library Cataloguing in Publication Data
Data available

Library of Congress Cataloging in Publication Data
Danson, Lawrence.
Wilde's intentions: the artist in his criticism/Lawrence
Danson.
Includes bibliographical references and index.
1. Wilde, Oscar, 1854–1900—Criticism and interpretation.
I. Title.
PR5824.D36 1996
828'.809–dc20 96–30317
ISBN 0–19–818375–5

1 3 5 7 9 10 8 6 4 2

Typeset by J&L Composition Ltd, Filey, North Yorkshire
Printed in Great Britain
on acid-free paper by
Biddles Ltd,
Guildford and King's Lynn

Acknowledgements

This book took shape in conjunction with my editorial work on *Intentions* and 'The Soul of Man Under Socialism', a volume forthcoming in the Oxford English Texts edition of *The Complete Works of Oscar Wilde*. Friends and facilitators of that project have also, sometimes unbeknown to themselves, helped with this. I would like to thank some of them here:

Mimi Danson, Jeff Nunokawa, and Elaine Showalter for their encouragement and advice; Russell Jackson and Ian Small, general editors of the Oxford English Texts edition of *The Complete Works of Oscar Wilde*, for getting me into this; Merlin Holland for his generosity and his unparalleled knowledge of all matters to do with his grandfather, Oscar Wilde; the members of my NEH Summer Seminar for School Teachers for sharing their ideas and enthusiasm; my colleagues and friends Victor Brombert, Ronald Bush, Michael Cadden, Patty S. Derrick, Maggie Debelius, Jay Dickson, Linda Dowling, Richard Dunn, Elaine Fantham, Walter Hinderer, William Howarth, Joel Kaplan, Richard Kaye, Uli Knoepflmacher, Mark Samuels Lasner, A. Walton Litz, Idris Magette, Arnold Rampersad, Horst Schroeder, and Susan Wolfson, for help with specific questions or stimulating conversation; Viscountess Eccles, for allowing me to use her superb collection of Wilde and Wildeana; Stephen Fergusson, of the Princeton University Library, Division of Rare Books and Manuscripts, for his unfailing co-operation; Elizabeth Fuller, Rosenbach Museum and Library; Linda Greenwood, Irish and Local Studies Librarian, Belfast Education and Library Board; Gerry Healey, Linen Hall Library, Belfast; and David Utterson, of Gekoski (Booksellers), for answering enquiries; Steve Sohmer for his hospitality; and Jason Freeman, Frances Whistler, Sophie Goldsworthy, and Janet Moth for kindness and good editorial advice.

Portions of this book have previously appeared, in different forms, in the following places, and I gratefully acknowledge permission to reprint: the editors of *Modern Drama* for portions of Chapter 3, which originally appeared in volume xxxviii (1994, special issue edited by Joel Kaplan); the editors of *ELH* for portions of Chapter 5, which originally appeared in volume li (1991).

Contents

Note on Texts and Abbreviations

ALTHOUGH there have in recent years been several excellent editions of individual works or selections, there is as yet no complete edition of Wilde's works which satisfies the needs of this book. (The forthcoming Oxford English Texts edition of *The Complete Works* will eventually make life easier.)

I cite Wilde's essays by individual title, from the following editions: *Intentions* from the first edition (1891), which I describe in the Introduction and Chapter 1; 'The Portrait of Mr W. H.' (expanded) from the edition by Vyvyan Holland (London: Methuen, 1958); 'The Soul of Man Under Socialism' from the volume *Intentions* and *The Soul of Man* in *The First Collected Edition of the Works of Oscar Wilde*, ed. Robert Ross, 14 vols. (London: Methuen, 1908; repr. Dawson, 1969), vol. viii. Wilde's reviews and other occasional works are cited from the volumes in this same edition; his letters, including *De Profundis*, from *The Letters of Oscar Wilde*, ed. Rupert Hart-Davis (New York: Harcourt, Brace & World, 1962), and other writing from *The Complete Works of Oscar Wilde* (London: Collins, 1948; new edn., 1966).

A complete list of abbreviations for frequently cited works follows; most appear parenthetically in the text, by page number only.

CW	*The Complete Works of Oscar Wilde*, introd. Vyvyan Holland (London: Collins, 1948; new edn., 1966)
Ellmann	Richard Ellmann, *Oscar Wilde* (New York: Knopf, 1988)
Heritage	Karl Beckson, (ed.) *Oscar Wilde: The Critical Heritage* (London: Routledge & Kegan Paul, 1970)
Hill	*Walter Pater, The Renaissance: Studies in Art and Poetry, the 1893 Text*, ed. Donald L. Hill (Berkeley: University of California, 1980)
Letters	*The Letters of Oscar Wilde*, ed. Rupert Hart-Davis (New York: Harcourt, Brace & World, 1962)
Misc.	*Miscellanies*, in *The First Collected Edition of the Works of Oscar Wilde*, 14 vols., ed. Robert Ross (London: Methuen, 1908; repr. Dawson, 1969), vol. xiv
More Letters	*More Letters of Oscar Wilde*, ed. Rupert Hart-Davis (London: John Murray, 1985)
Portrait	*The Portrait of Mr W. H.*, ed. Vyvyan Holland (London: Methuen, 1958)
Rev.	*Reviews*, in *The First Collected Edition of the Works*

	of Oscar Wilde, ed. Robert Ross, 14 vols. (London: Methuen, 1908; repr. Dawson, 1969), vol. xiii
'Stage Costume'	Oscar Wilde, 'Shakespeare and Stage Costume', *Nineteenth Century*, 17 (May 1885), 800–18
Trials	H. Montgomery Hyde, *The Trials of Oscar Wilde* (London: William Hodge, 1948)

Introduction

HE'S everywhere again in the *fin de siècle*, on stage, screen, and T-shirt, in books and on bookbags, in Westminster Abbey and, God forbid, classrooms. And still we agree as little about him as when first his ubiquity was the talk of two continents: Whistler's 'aimiable irresponsible esurient Oscar'; Saint Oscar, the Irish outsider, the queer martyr, the spiritual Oscar, the subversive Oscar; Oscar the canonical, Oscar the imposter, the one and only original, the pasticheur, plagiarist, or postmodernist. All this diversity and disagreement despite the fact that (as I once thought of calling this book) Oscar Wilde Tells All! In his prison letter to Lord Alfred Douglas he tells it from the depths, with the result that for some readers he is Christlike in wisdom and suffering, and for others he is an Ancient Mariner of self-pity. In *Intentions*, the book on which his claims as a theorist and critic chiefly rest, he tells it from the heights.

Intentions was published in London on 2 May 1891 by James R. Osgood, McIlvaine and Co., a recently established firm which would also publish *Lord Arthur Savile's Crime and Other Stories* in July and *A House of Pomegranates* in November: about a week, that is to say, after the first book publication of *The Picture of Dorian Gray*. A more expensive large-paper edition of *Dorian Gray* appeared in July. (Wilde presented a copy to his new friend Lord Alfred Douglas.) In February of that year 'The Soul of Man Under Socialism' had appeared in the *Fortnightly Review*. By autumn, Wilde had completed a play he called *A Good Woman*; retitled *Lady Windermere's Fan*, it was running in London shortly after the year's end. And in December he completed the French language version of *Salomé*. When the last decade of the nineteenth century opened, he was Britain's longest-running overnight sensation, with a reputation in excess of real production; by the end of 1891 the body of his work justified the notoriety of his personality.

Beginnings, middles, and endings are surprisingly elusive in the brief drama of Wilde's career, with its extended

overture, painful denouement, and embarrassing richness of
scènes à faire. In this book about Wilde's intentions (to shift for
the first of many times from the titular uppercase to the
biographical lower) I am going to make 1891 the climactic
year. But I want, in the process of introducing my own intentions, to acknowledge another possibility. Most accounts of
Wilde's life take 1895, the year of trials and imprisonment, as
the year that gives shape and meaning to the rest. The result
has often been either a cautionary tale or a hagiography: in *De
Profundis*, Wilde himself set the pattern for both of those familiar narratives. Recent versions, written from the perspectives
of gay criticism and queer theory, have complicated the story
and made it more interesting, because more historically
consequential. It has often been said that Wilde could have
avoided the trials; his critics, I add, cannot.

To the prisoner in the dock came the question, 'What is the
"Love that dare not speak its name"?'[1] To such a question, to
any 'What is?', you can reply with a name, so that the
unknown x becomes a y (which in turn, however, will demand
a 'What is y?' answered by z: and then the alphabet will have
to be extended to give a sum or a name for z). In Chapter 5 I
will look more closely at Wilde's famous answer, '"The Love
that dare not speak its name" in this century is such a great
affection of an elder for a younger man as there was between
David and Jonathan . . . The world mocks at it and puts one in
the pillory for it' (*Trials*, 236); here I simply notice that it pro-
ceeds by examples and encomia, and evades the treadmill of
naming. It refuses to choose from the court's menu of condemnatory words, like sodomy, buggery, gross indecency. But even
Wilde's defiance had to be made out of old linguistic materials, including the resonance of historical names, David and
Jonathan, Plato, Michelangelo, Shakespeare; contested adjectives, like beautiful, fine, noble, spiritual, intellectual; and a
dense allusiveness to putatively Greek and Neoplatonic
philosophy which Wilde, among others, was in the process of
Victorianizing. Everywhere in his life and work, and not only
on the subject of sexuality, Wilde's new meanings pay tribute
to the materials out of which they were created. It was a career
of redefining and transvaluing, by allusion, quotation, or pastiche, or by the quick, hot energy of paradox.

The Wildean paradox unsettles the categorical. It performs the Adamic work of naming in a world where all the names have already been used. It asserts the primacy of the speaker over the word, while recognizing that a new, oppositional meaning can only be accomplished by keeping the old meaning in circulation. The following dialogue from *An Ideal Husband* is a dazzling display of the principle. It enacts its subject-matter, which is the imperial relation of the Wildean self, personified in the dandiacal Lord Goring, to his world, reduced here to the compliant servant, Phipps:

LORD GORING (*taking out old buttonhole*). You see, Phipps, Fashion is what one wears oneself. What is unfashionable is what other people wear.
PHIPPS. Yes, my lord.
LORD GORING. Just as vulgarity is just the conduct of other people.
PHIPPS. Yes, my lord.
LORD GORING (*putting in new buttonhole*). And falsehoods the truths of other people.
PHIPPS. Yes, my lord.
LORD GORING. Other people are quite dreadful. The only possible society is oneself.
PHIPPS. Yes, my lord.
LORD GORING. To love oneself is the beginning of a life-long romance, Phipps. (Act 3: *CW* 522)

Goring begins with the simplest of paradoxical techniques, the directly substitutive. 'Fashion' and 'unfashionable' exchange sites, the former now belonging to the singular self, and the latter, no longer measured by popularity, belonging to the mass of others. It is a joke about bad taste; but putting the one where the many had been, it begins the more complex work performed in Goring's next move: 'falsehoods [are] the truths of other people.' The paradox does not simply assert that when I disagree with other people I am right and they are wrong. What other people possess is still called truth or, better, 'truths', but it is not my truth or truths, and so it is simultaneously 'falsehoods'.

It is not clear where the playwright stands in relation to Goring's relativistic principle: the line reads both as an assertion of the dandy's self-sufficiency and as a satire on the egotism that always assumes its own rightness in the face of overwhelmingly contrary evidence. In the next line, the substitutive technique produces a cheerful solipsism, 'oneself' becoming 'the only possible society'. This makes it less likely that other people's falsehoods can also be truths, but it also makes one's own truth an isolated, incommunicable thing. The final paradox in this sequence draws upon all the instabilities previously generated. The mutual dance of self-effacement previously performed by truth and falsehood becomes now a solo turn for 'love'. Love's negation and its affirmation is 'life-long romance', a sentimental cliché which here becomes the reward of the dandy's icy narcissism. The sexual self-sufficiency the dandy calls 'romance' is not the romance of sentimental literature; but it could not exist as word or idea without the supposedly companionate thing it displaces: to know that he loves himself, the dandy requires all those others who perversely think that their lives of boredom, irritation, and copulation mean 'romance'.

The paradoxes do what the essays in *Intentions* try to do more expansively. They shift from the measure of the many to the measure of the remarkable one, but they also call in question the stability and authority of that One. Wilde tried to rename the world in order to avoid for himself the categorizing which makes us exemplars of the already constructed. And in large measure, I believe, even beyond the measure of two years at hard labour, he failed. Intensely himself, always unassimilable, this fat man floating free became to history a type, even a stereotype; not himself alone, unique, but the representative of a category, a name for a class.

It is a class that in certain ways came to exist because Wilde existed. The film *A Man of No Importance* (1994), directed by Suri Krishnamma, written by Barry Devlin, and starring Albert Finney, dramatizes the point. The unimportant man of the title is a sweet, timid bus conductor in Dublin in the early 1960s, whose two passions are, first, the life and work of Oscar Wilde and, second, the handsome young driver of his bus. In a world in which his desire still had no passable name to speak, not even in the confessional, Finney's character can only realize himself by staging, not only Wilde's work, but himself as Wilde. Modelling himself on Wilde and daring, as Wilde did, to be absurd or grotesque, with self-quotation, green carnation, cosmetics, and cape, Finney's bus conductor creates his life. It is a life that imitates not only Wilde's art but the social idea of Oscar the homosexual. In Wilde's phrase, it 'pick[s] up a brickbat and wear[s] it as a buttonhole', incurring the risks as well as the 'joy' that comes with 'wilfully taking the name given by the common spectators'.[2] It defies but also complicitly accepts the stigma which turns a sexual desire into a social identity.

It was not Wilde's intention to make himself a type; rather, his explicit investment was in what he called 'individualism' or, more often, 'personality'. Those are two of the specific words Wilde submitted, with more or less success, to the refinery of paradox. They are among the Wildean keywords I will be burrowing into at various points in this book: other such words are artist, critic, realism, socialism, sin. Each impinges on the other, and all are related to the issue of sexuality.

Wilde's desire was for a desire of his own fabulating, in a world where only himself—the artist as critic, the frank, fearless, and irresponsible liar—would have the power to name and judge. His utopian voluntarism in the area of sexual desire is related to other intentions he announces in the essays gathered under that title.[3] It is related, for instance, to his intention to decentre the stable, earnest, truth-loving self, and reveal instead a personality always revelling in its own potential incoherence. The intention of a personality which is not always entirely in possession of itself, or is not in certain senses a self to be possessed, puts the very idea of intentions in jeopardy. Hence my decision to make 1891, the year Wilde published his *Intentions*, the focus of this book.

If 1895 made Oscar Wilde what he would become, the face on bookbags, the eponym of a cause, in 1891 he was writing a very different plot for his life. In it he is neither the hero nor butt of a morality play. It is recognizably a comedy of the society sort, but (like the society plays he actually wrote in the few glory years remaining) full of twists and inversions of generic expectations which allow Wilde himself—the Irishman, the sodomite, the social climber who is also, in his liaisons, the leveller of class distinctions—to be the improbable hero of the social drama. And in that plot the year of *Intentions* could be the climax. (For the sake of subplot, 1891 also satisfyingly presents the first appearance of Bosie Douglas in the script.) In *De Profundis* he wrote, 'I was a man who stood in symbolic relations to the art and culture of my age' (*Letters*, 466); amidst a career's-worth of extravagant posing and coruscating paradox, that self-assessment stands, a century later, as a truth, like all Wildean truths, neither pure nor simple. In *Intentions* Wilde expresses and tries to implement his designs upon the age's art and culture. To understand Wilde's intentions, with all their strains and self-contradictions, their impossible aspirations and revolutionary potential, is to understand Wilde's 'symbolic relations' to the society in which he harboured them.

He was making himself, to borrow Pater's phrase, 'the focus where the greatest number of vital forces unite in their purest energy'. *Intentions* announces (sometimes by masking) the aggressive fact: in the book we can read Wilde's intention to secure a powerful position at the centre of the culture whose values he was subverting and whose laws he was flouting; and in its reception we can begin to read the complex fate of that intention. With these essays/dialogues/fictions (destabilizing the genres was part of the plot), Wilde tried to create the conditions for his own social and literary success. They were his boldest attempt to write himself into history by rewriting history. For his intention to succeed, social margin and social centre would have to change places or, better yet, that whole geography of exclusion and inclusion would have to become irrelevant. The Irish son of an Irish patriot would stand at the summit of a newly defined, a revised and perfected, ideal of English culture, the colonial subject outdoing the occupier by capturing the history and future of culture. The sexual dissident would destroy the assumptions that make dissidence a comprehensible category—assumptions about 'nature' and the 'natural', about the sway of the supposedly immutable real over the fantasies and facts of liberated desire. The whole business would take Wildean paradox to is fullest stretch, rewriting history, elevating lies above facts and art above nature, levelling the distinction between creator and critic, questioning the identity of agents who might intend and the stability of results they might achieve.

Even the book's measurables, its shape and date, resist the grip of stability and self-identity. *Intentions*, printed and bound in boards with gilt designs by Charles Ricketts,[4] has a satisfying look of inevitability which disguises the accidents of its coming into being. We get our first glimpse of the incipient book in a letter of 7 July 1889 from Wilde to the publisher William Blackwood. The July issue of *Blackwood's Edinburgh Magazine* carried Wilde's 'The Portrait of Mr W. H.' Blackwood had written to Wilde suggesting that the story be reprinted in a volume of *Tales from Blackwood's*. Wilde's letter contained a counter-proposal. Objecting that 'Mr W. H.' was 'too literary' for the Blackwood's series, Wilde asked, 'Will you compromise and bring it out in a special volume of essays and studies by me? As a frontispiece we will have an etching of the fictitious portrait of Mr W. H. The other studies will be things that have appeared in the *Nineteenth Century* and the *Fortnightly*, and that excited much interest' (*Letters*, 246). The 'other studies' Wilde refers to are 'The Decay of Lying' and 'Pen, Pencil, and Poison', both published in January 1889. But within three days of his original suggestion, and before Blackwood had time to read those other 'essays and studies', Wilde made another proposal: 'What would you say to a dainty little volume of "Mr W. H." by itself? . . . I could add about 3,000 words to the story. Personally I should prefer it to be separate' ([10 July 1889]: *Letters*, 247). Wilde's unfulfilled intention to have a separately bound, enlarged version of 'The Portrait of Mr W. H.' will eventually become part of my narrative. For the moment it is sufficient to note that the book that became *Intentions* had as its first notional contents 'The Portrait of Mr W. H.', 'The Decay of Lying', and 'Pen, Pencil, and Poison'.

In 1890, when Wilde returned to the idea of a 'special volume of essays and studies', he had an exceptionally strong substitute for 'The Portrait of Mr W. H.' The essay eventually called 'The Critic as Artist' had been published, in two parts, as 'The True Function and Value of Criticism' in the *Nineteenth Century* in July and September 1890. A decent-sized volume could have been eked out of the three available essays, 'The Decay of Lying', 'Pen, Pencil, and Poison', and 'The Critic as Artist'. Possibly wanting something more imposing than the slender *Lord Arthur Savile's Crime and Other Stories* and *A House of Pomegranates*, Wilde brought out of the drawer an essay originally published in the *Nineteenth Century* of May 1885, called 'Shakespeare and Stage Costume', which he revised into 'The Truth of Masks'. The contents of *Intentions* were thus apparently fixed.

But never to Wilde's satisfaction. In the summer following publication by Osgood McIlvaine Wilde wrote to William Heinemann with an idea for further publication. Heinemann was issuing a cheap paperback series from Leipzig. Wilde wrote: 'I have sent you a copy of *Intentions*, the copyright of which belongs to me. In case you thought it too large for your series, the last essay might be left out' ([Summer 1891]: *Letters*, 294).[5] The last essay was also expendable in Wilde's plans (not realized until 1914) for a French translation—but for this version of the book he contemplated a strong substitute for the weak 'Truth of Masks'. In a letter authorizing translation by Jules Cantel, Wilde writes, 'Seulement je ne veux pas qu'il traduise le dernier essai, "La Vérité des Masques;" je ne l'aime plus. Au lieu de cela, on pourra mettre l'essai paru dans le *Fortnightly Review* de février dernier sur "L'Ame de l'Homme," qui contient une partie de mon esthétique' ([?Summer 1891]: *Letters*, 295).

Thus *Intentions*, according to Wilde's various plans before and after publication, might have included either 'The Portrait of Mr W. H.' or 'The Soul of Man Under Socialism', and might have excluded 'The Truth of Masks'. The oldest piece in the book as published dates from 1885, the most recent from 1890, but all underwent revision. The revisions could not obscure the fact that the oldest piece argued a position that conflicted with the most recent, nor that each individual piece might contradict itself from one sentence to the next.

Taking advantage of the latitude the publishing history allows, I will consider *Intentions* in its most expansive form, and include in my discussion 'The Portrait of Mr W. H.' and 'The Soul of Man Under Socialism'. And since Wilde's whole career constitutes a running commentary on itself, with frequent revisions and cross-references in the form of extensive self-quotation, I will look elsewhere in the canon, and ask how the intentions of the essays are realized, revised, or refuted in Wilde's other work. But even in its strictest construction, as the volume published in 1891, *Intentions* poses problems and issues enough. Here is a book which contains two dramatic dialogues, the biography of a forger, and an essay about stage realism which concludes with its own retraction: is there a genre for such a book, and if there is, what kind of truth-value or sincerity can it have? It is a genial, amusing book—at least, most Victorian reviewers found it so—but it became one of the key texts of nascent modernism, a movement as earnest in its intentions as Wilde apparently was not.

My title is of course opportunistic. It piggybacks on the title of Wilde's 1891 volume, and lays claim not only to the book but to the intentions of its author. Without quite disowning such presumptuous entitlement, I do of course acknowledge the limits to what can be known about any author's intentions, the limits to the value of knowing it, and the special ironies of claiming to know, of all authors' intentions, those of an author who repeatedly tells us that 'A critic should be taught to criticise a work of art without making any reference to the personality of the author' (27 June 1890: *Letters*, 260), and that 'Art finds her own perfection within, and not outside of herself' ('Decay of Lying', 30).

In *The Picture of Dorian Gray*, a book that never describes an act of physical intimacy between men, many readers think they recognize a particular notion of homosexual identity. Their reading is in various ways impure. It derives from both Wilde's text and Wilde's life, following a hermeneutic protocol used at the Old Bailey, where Wilde's book was judged by the author, and vice versa; it is always a retrospective reading, informed not only by what the author wrote but by how its author came to be written in the history of his culture.[6] Recognizing the extent to which Wilde has become not his own but our text, we might use *The Picture of Dorian Gray* as evidence for 'the death of the author'; and we might read the epitaph of that singular, self-possessed authority in Wilde's cultural fate. It was a fate he helped to make: his own paradoxes, after all, also perform the decentring, of meaning and of its authorizing agencies, which presages the postmodernist author-as-text. But Wilde's paradoxes remain paradoxical in a way that makes 'the death of the author' sound like a truism. At the same time that Wilde banishes the author as self-possessed subject of his or her own intentions, he grounds the author's work in a 'personality' which may not be singular but is still very much alive and kicking and writing its own (however imitable) books.

So my book treats 'Wilde's Intentions' as a complex of personal attitudes, social affiliations, and cultural effects through which we can locate him where he tried to locate himself in the tumultuous world of late Victorian England. It was a world loudly predicting its own death, a degenerate, decadent *fin du monde*; but it also proclaimed its power to be reborn as the modern, the new: the New Woman, the New Fiction, the New Drama, the New Hedonism.[7] *Intentions* is my focus — but it is as riven with contradiction as the age, and as resistant to being brought into focus as anything else in a life and in a series of works which challenge conventional notions of literary and moral shapeliness. I stress the antagonistic discourses — for instance, individual freedom versus the determinism of heredity, the unstable self versus the intensified personality, the amoral autonomy of art versus the critic's prophetic role — which Wilde's language pacified or synthesized. I believe that his intentions were more consciously available to him than some previous narratives have allowed, but that they were also more complex and more surprising. If they put him at odds with majority culture, they also put him at odds with progressive social and sexual reformers who were attempting to define homosexuality as an identity; they allied him with fashionable West End managements against the theatrical fringe where the Englished Ibsen was coming to life; they made him an uneasy fellow-traveller with the philistine rearguard in the debate about realism and 'pernicious literature', at the very moment when his own work was being attacked by the enemies of realism; they made him the dangerous celebrity *du jour* but also the fading remnant of an outmoded aestheticism.

In Chapter 1 I take as my focus *Intentions*, the book itself, literally as an object, a commodity, an indicator of cultural positions and attitudes. I look at the book's reception among contemporary readers — as I will also do, later, for the individual essays. Between what reviewers said and what Wilde says, I try to locate the essays' place in Wilde's social strategies. In this chapter I describe the elusive image Wilde's book created, fractured (intentionally) between seriousness and frivolity; and I notice that this discontinuity is comparable to the discontinuities Wilde's work explores at the level of the individual personality.

Following my discussion of the volume as a whole I devote a chapter to each individual essay. Each of the essays (with the problematic exceptions of 'The Portrait of Mr W. H.' and 'The Soul of Man Under Socialism') underwent revision between first periodical publication and publication in *Intentions*: that textual history makes a chronological arrangement impossible. I have tried to keep repetition to a minimum, but Wilde's essays do comment on, even sometimes contradict, one another; my approach entails a certain amount of circling around similar topics in various contexts. I provide relevant facts about the essays' composition, publication, and reception, because they are necessary for my analysis of the essays' strategies, and because readers will want to have this material available to them for its own sake.

In Chapter 2, for instance, I discuss 'The Decay of Lying', which Wilde put in the first position in his volume. Here I take up, among other things, Wilde's polemic against realism and his position on other elements of a binarized discourse which opposes imitation to creation, nature to form, life to art, realism to romance, and a supposedly 'natural' sexuality to a sexuality which, like art, refuses to be categorized or controlled. The elements of that binary are again a subject in Chapter 3, which deals with 'The Truth of Masks', the first written but probably the last revised of the essays. In this chapter, about an essay on dramatic theory, I discuss a cross-dressed production of *As You Like It* and a novel about cross-dressing (Gautier's *Mademoiselle de Maupin*), both of which affected Wilde's way of thinking about the part of the binary he called 'illusion', and suggest why it mattered offstage as well as on. Chapter 4, about 'Pen, Pencil, and Poison', and Chapter 5, about 'The Portrait of Mr W. H.', both take up ideas of forgery and self-creation. The former, a biographical essay about an art critic who was also a murderer, is elusive in its deadpan satire of aestheticism; the latter, a fiction about the putatively real biographical basis of Shakespeare's sonnets, is elusive in its simultaneous expression and erasure of Wilde's own sexual desire.

'The Portrait of Mr W. H.' enacts Wilde's dictum in 'The Critic as Artist'—my subject in Chapter 6—that for the true critic a work of art is the starting-point for a new work of art. It has not escaped my attention that in taking Wilde's essays as the starting-point for a new work of criticism I am performing the last paradox left to the post-Wildean Wildean critic. This is a work of interpretation, and just the sort of thing Wilde came to stop. 'The Critic as Artist', Wilde's most ambitious, and longest, theoretical essay, discovers a position of refined contempt for the world of fact which non-artist critics continue to inhabit. But it owes its own anxiously unshapely shape to Wilde's polemical concerns at the beginning of the last decade of the nineteenth century; it owes its contempt for history to an urgent need to rewrite his history before others could inscribe it on his behalf. The contest of narratives between Wilde and his critics, including myself, is, inevitably, part of what my book is about.

My final chapter, on 'The Soul of Man Under Socialism', looks at another essay, closely related in time and circumstance to 'The Critic as Artist', where apparent polarities—engagement and disengagement, historicity and its utopian negation, the power of the many and the authority of the one—become the permanently unsettled stuff of Wildean paradox. I set Wilde among the essay's contributory discourses of politics and culture where he imagines a world, adjacent to the imaginative world of *The Importance of Being Earnest*, in which individual desire is fully and joyfully free. I end there, with this last major critical statement before the prison-letter called *De Profundis*, which is another story entirely.

1 Intentions

WHAT were Wilde's intentions? They had always been suspect, from the time of *Poems* (1881), when the word 'plagiarism' was first pronounced against him, to *The Picture of Dorian Gray*, when the word was 'sodomitical'. The trials explicitly raised the question whether his intentions were speakable. In *Intentions*, and in two essays closely related to it, 'The Portrait of Mr W. H.' and 'The Soul of Man Under Socialism', Wilde sets out his aesthetic, cultural, and political positions with all the clarity of his most intensely obscure paradoxes. Wilde's tell-all is contradictory, ironic, masked, unfulfilled: the book of answers is itself a question begging to be interrogated, refusing to be pinned down. And I begin my own questioning with the enigmatic title.

The one-word title seems to suggest more than it discloses; it teases, but in the process it pointed contemporary readers to the book's position in the larger literary milieu of the *fin de siècle*. In most ways, Wilde's title seems to signal an allegiance to the aesthetic preciosity—'aesthetic' here meaning mainly the Gilbert and Sullivan caricature version of that phenomenon, rather than the perplexed set of actual attitudes Wilde's essays uncover—with which he had been associated since his emergence from Oxford. *Intentions* sounds a little like *Whispers*, poems published in 1884 by Robert Sherard and dedicated to Wilde. Or like *Silverpoints* (1893) by John Gray, who in letters to Wilde signed himself 'Dorian'.[1] (Years later, Max Beerbohm parodied this very 1890s tendency in his story about the would-be decadent, Enoch Soames: Soames's first book was called *Negations*; his second 'he rather thought of giving no title at all. "If a book is good in itself— " he murmured, waving his cigarette.')[2] Most suggestively, however, and by design, *Intentions* brings to mind *Appreciations*, Walter Pater's book published the year before Wilde's and reviewed by Wilde in March 1890.

Wilde often brings Pater to mind. Whenever Gilbert, Wilde's spokesman in 'The Critic as Artist', passes into the cool galleries of the Louvre and stands before Leonardo's painting, he murmurs to himself, 'She is older than the rocks among which she sits; like the vampire, she has been dead many times, and learned the secrets of the grave'; and he goes on murmuring Pater's great purple patch until he says to his friend, 'The presence that thus so strangely rose beside the waters is expressive of what in the ways of a thousand years man has come to desire', and his friend answers him, 'Hers is the head upon which all "the ends of the world are come", and the eyelids are a little weary' (140–1). It is one of his cruder demonstrations of the proposition that 'criticism of the highest kind . . . treats the work of art simply as a starting-point for a new creation' (142). 'The Critic as Artist' takes Pater's work as its 'starting-point' so often that it would be tedious to record all its specific echoes or homages, plagiarisms or purposeful distortions. They make *dialogue* not only the name for the sub-genre of the essay but also my name for Wilde's dealings with the world of words that is more often called literary influence.[3]

Wilde's dialogue with Pater, both invocation and revision, begins on the cover of *Intentions*. The title instances in small the essays' astonishing ability to gather up fragments, to call and reply, to be simultaneously themselves and others, like the 'stringed lute on which all winds can play' or the 'twice-written scroll' of Wilde's early poem 'Hélas!' The title of Wilde's book is a portmanteau. It carries the title of Pater's book, but energized from receptive acts of appraising—'in the fine Latin sense of the word' (*Rev.* 539)—to more vigorous acts of stretching out for, aiming at. And it also carries Pater's key-word 'impressions', both words caught up with the original sense of the word 'essays': attempts, trials.

But 'dialogue' cannot be the only or last word on the question of Wilde's allusions, borrowings, plagiarisms, on the whole intricate question of his 'originality'—a word that Wilde transvalues or disables even as we try to use it to judge him. I will occasionally have to call attention to places where Wilde helps himself to a phrase here, a book there. But I will also call attention to ways in which Wilde unsettles our bases for judging such acts by unsettling our sense of history, identity, and agency. Such a place is his review of *Appreciations*—part of which got a second life in 'The Critic as Artist'.

Wilde begins his review retrospectively, recalling his first meeting with Pater, when Pater said, 'smiling, "Why do you always write poetry? Why do you not write prose? Prose is so much more difficult"' (*Rev.* 538–45). That was in Wilde's 'undergraduate days . . . of lyrical ardour'. The invocation of those days brings Pater into the review as he once had been for Wilde, the Pater of *Studies in the Renaissance*, which 'became to me "the golden book of spirit and sense, the holy writ of beauty"'. Those phrases, which Wilde had previously used in 1885 in a review of Shakespeare's *As You Like It*, are quotations from Swinburne's sonnet on Théophile Gautier's novel about cross-dressing and sexual ambiguity, *Mademoiselle de Maupin*. For readers who can excavate the layers of allusion (I will say more about them when I discuss 'The Truth of Masks'), the lyrical epithets invoke an unconventional sexuality, all the more potent for threat or delight because it must be spoken of only by suggestion and indirection; in turn they gesture towards a Pater whose 'beautiful and suggestive essays' were to a generation of Oxford undergraduates what Lord Henry Wotton's 'poisonous' yellow book is to Dorian Gray. In that book, 'Things that [Dorian] had dimly dreamed of were suddenly made real to him. Things of which he had never dreamed were gradually revealed' (*CW* 101). As a result of these self-revealing, self-creating revelations, 'For years, Dorian Gray could not free himself from the *influence* of this book' (*CW* 102; my italics). In *De Profundis* Wilde uses the same charged word to describe *The Renaissance*, 'that book which has had such a strange influence over my life' (*Letters*, 471)—casting against type to put the donnish Pater in the role of Lord Henry Wotton. So, more explicitly, in a conversation recorded by William Butler Yeats, Wilde called *The Renaissance* '"my golden book"' but added, '"it is the very flower of decadence: the last trumpet should have sounded when it was written"'.[4]

His review of *Appreciations* in 1890 seems to swerve from this decadent Pater, the subtle corrupter, to another Pater, the true artist in prose. Like Cardinal Newman (or even, as Wilde will write in *De Profundis*, like Christ), this Pater unites 'personality with perfection'. The sanctified Pater seems to be the subject of the review, but the decadent Pater, the Pater of newly awakened senses who had such a strange influence on

Wilde's life, is also there, and in a less covert way than the allusions I have pointed to. He is there in the typical rhetoric of English decadence: 'exquisite', 'strangeness', 'passionate suggestion'. But most interestingly he is there in a passage about history which Wilde reused in 'The Critic as Artist'. Some of Pater's essays, Wilde writes, are Greek in purity of outline, some are medieval in strangeness and passion, but

> all of them [are] absolutely modern, in the true meaning of the term modernity. For he to whom the present is the only thing that is present, knows nothing of the age in which he lives. To realise the nineteenth century one must realise every century that has preceded it, and that has contributed to its making. To know anything about oneself, one must know all about others. There must be no mood with which one cannot sympathise, no dead mode of life that one cannot make alive. (*Rev.* 539–40; cf. 'Critic as Artist', 169–70)

The passage gives a positive spin to the decadent project in Dorian's 'poisonous book': that plotless novel is 'a psychological study of a certain young Parisian, who spent his life trying to realize in the nineteenth century all the passions and modes of thought that belonged to every century except his own, and to sum up, as it were, in himself the various moods through which the world-spirit had passed . . . ' (*CW* 101). According to *Intentions*, to be modern is to be *not* of one's age, and to know one's self is to know the 'moods' of otherness. According to *Dorian Gray*, to be not of one's age and to be made of moods is to be a flower of decadence. Decadence *is* modernity in this inverted formula.

Wilde's definition of modernity as a turning backward, a rejection of the sufficiency of the moment, runs counter to the great Victorian passion for progress. But he has respectable allies in what would otherwise seem a perverse idea. Matthew Arnold (the other voice, beside Pater's, which is most involved in the dialogue of 'The Critic as Artist') had also urged that 'the function of criticism' was to turn away from the activities of the 'present time' and to look instead both outwards, to Europe, and backwards to the touchstone art of older times. Such a programme requires for its success not the politician or man of action but the contemplative and learned man—in Arnold's definition the critic, in Wilde's the critic as

artist. In either case, one intention of this (potentially) decadent programme is the empowering of the special individual,
the aesthetic critic, whose credentials are his own personality,
burning with a harder, more gemlike flame than others, cap-
able by virtue of learning, taste, sensibility to receive the greatest number of 'impressions' and realize most intensely the
moods and modes that create this dissident modernity.

This redefinition of what it means to be 'absolutely modern'
is, for Wilde, not only socially or politically empowering. In
the same passage we begin to glimpse a kind of self—or as
Wilde will typically call it, again echoing Pater, a 'personality'
—whose potency comes precisely from being not only itself,
not (that is) self-consistent, but rather from being (or accepting
the state of being) the many moods, the masks and poses, by
which it fleetingly makes and remakes itself. If the idea of
modernity as backwardness challenges the Victorian idea of
progress, the idea of personality as multiplicity and surface
challenges the earnest Victorian ideal of the singular and self-
contained individual. And if the idea of a modernity that 'real-
izes' the past owes much to Pater, so too does this idea of a self
that is always also not itself. It is an idea implicit in the
Conclusion to *The Renaissance*, with its scientific-seeming
dissolution of 'what is real in our life' until it is revealed as
a state of 'continual vanishing away, that strange, perpetual
weaving and unweaving of *ourselves*' (Hill, 188; my italics).

Pater omitted the Conclusion in the second edition because
'it might possibly mislead some of those young men into
whose hands it might fall' (Hill, 186). Wilde was avid to be
misled. But Pater is teasingly vague about how the Conclusion
might mislead him. Judith Ryan thinks 'the principal difficulty
may have been the argument that the mind is solipsistic'.[5]
Possibly, but if so the young men were indeed misled, since
the Conclusion is not consistently solipsistic: if it were, there
would be no point in seeking impressions from what is presumably outside the self. Certainly the Conclusion is anti-
idealist, anti-foundationalist, anti-whatever-it-is that would be
necessary to maintain traditional Christianity. It is instead,
as Wilde saw, a fine basis on which to construct a New
Hedonism. John McGowan says that 'In adopting the aesthetic
creed of valuing things "for their own sake", Pater implicitly

attacks one fundamental tenet of bourgeois life: the notion of an accumulative self.[6] Getting and spending rather than slowly accumulating a Christian's capital would be the way of economic wisdom in Pater's world, 'While all melts under our feet . . . on this short day of frost and sun' (Hill, 189). Pater is afraid that his Conclusion might mislead young men into actually believing its demonstration that fleeting impressions, not spiritual essences, are all that is real, and that it is therefore the aesthetic equivalent of a moral imperative to gather as many impressions as possible, as intensely as possible, wherever and from whomever one can find them.

There is more to say about the idea of 'personality' with regard to Wilde's intentions. Here I only want to begin noticing a contradiction, already present in Pater's idea of the impermanent self and omnipresent in Wilde's. On the one hand, Pater (and Wilde) propose a motile, self-creative personality, but simultaneously a personality that is the prison of consciousness, a limiter of freedom but a source of stability. In Pater's Conclusion, 'what is real in our life' is only a 'tremulous wisp constantly re-forming itself on the stream', dissolving into mere 'impressions, images, sensations' (Hill, 188); but against this imagery of dissolution and deliquescence is his assertion that 'Experience . . . is ringed round for each one of us by that thick wall of personality through which no real voice has ever pierced on its way to us' (Hill, 187)—where rocklike stability replaces tremulous wisp.[7]

In Wilde we find similar contradictions between a self-making and an always made self, a creative and a created personality. Such a contradiction is there in the passage about modernity from 'The Critic as Artist'. Having pronounced the liberatory idea that 'There must be no mood with which one cannot sympathise, no dead mode of life that one cannot make alive' (170), Wilde moves immediately to 'the scientific principle of Heredity'. Heredity is, Wilde claims, 'the warrant for the contemplative life', since it shows 'that we are never less free than when we try to act'. So far so good, for the critic–artist who valorizes thinking above doing. But in the very next sentence heredity starts sounding unconducive to the free play of personality: 'It has hemmed us round with nets of the hunter, and written upon the wall the prophecy of our doom . . . It is Nemesis without her mask'. It has made us what we will be from before we ever were.

Here is the dilemma that figures as the two faces of Dorian Gray, the aspiration freely to create one's personality or personalities or masks, versus the fear of fatality.[8] Wilde's attitude towards modernity and its literary expression, realism; his intention to dethrone nature itself and make it only the imitation of what the personality wills; his intention to overthrow by means of paradox the singleness of Victorian heterosexual earnestness, all are emotionally driven by this contest between the personality that weaves and unweaves itself and the personality woven already into the net of its own doom.

Contemporary reviewers of course recognized that Wilde's intentions were related to Pater's. Thus the *Pall Mall Gazette* says that in *Intentions* Wilde shows 'every qualification for becoming a popular Pater. Indeed, if he would condescend to suppress some over-complacent allusions to the artistic value of "sin"—a favourite word of his—he might fairly be described as a Pater-familias.'[9] The attempt to domesticate Wilde's transgressiveness is typical of the response to *Intentions*. Overall, it was a good press: 'entertaining' said both the *Pall Mall Gazette* and *The Times* (7 May 1891), and others chimed in with 'lively', 'brilliant', 'brilliant and amusing'.[10] The geniality is especially remarkable since a very different vocabulary had been in play when the magazine version of *Dorian Gray* appeared only a year before: 'ordure', 'prurience', 'garbage','disgusting','unclean','leprous','poisonous','effeminate'.[11] We should keep that still recent paper war in mind as we consider the contemporary reviewers' response to *Intentions*, and notice that, along with all the praise, most of the positive reviews also had reservations. But where the outraged reviews of *Dorian Gray* read wicked suggestions into all the book's narrative gaps and indeterminate adjectives, the friendly reviews of *Intentions* seem to take the opposite tack: they criticize Wilde for not being really outrageous at all. In the one case he was ostracized for not behaving like a gentleman; in the other he was rehabilitated and assimilated. It is a good question which reviews—the ones that imputed the

dangerous worst to his intentions or the ones that declined to
be subverted—were more accurate or more damning.

Wilde's reputation has always been shot through with contradictions; we see these, for instance, in the reviewers'
remarks about the value of being entertaining, brilliant, and
lively. Repeatedly the reviews of *Intentions* put Wilde's 'matter' at odds with his '[m]annerism' (*Pall Mall Gazette*), his 'substance' with 'the surface of his style' (*Nation*). Grudgingly
attracted by the entertainment value of the latter, most reviewers seem to wish Wilde would get on with the former—with
'the thought itself' which is (they claim) as straightforward as
the style is twisted. Thus, 'The defect of the volume is its
cleverness', since 'this superficial appearance of running
amuck with all sensible people may well conceal the sound
intelligence and acute penetration at the heart of these papers'
(*Nation*).[12] One of the warmest reviews—one virtually
solicited by Wilde as an antidote to the reviews of *Dorian Gray*
—also worries about the manner/matter gap: the book's paradoxical style 'is very readable, even if it is not very real and
only superficially true'.[13] The consensus is that Wilde's style of
paradox and epigram, and his refusal ever to be entirely serious, are the corrigible character defects of an otherwise
promising writer.

The contemporary responses suggest a fractured image of
Wilde, with the fracture self-evidently or tautologically a flaw.
But fracture is, I believe, what Wilde intended his audience to
see: a discontinuity (by contemporary standards), for instance
between seriousness and frivolity, which would correspond at
the level of the work to the discontinuities Wilde finds at the
level of the 'personality'. The critics' difficulty in seeing Wilde
as in himself they presumed he was—objectively (like themselves) continuous, intelligible, and present—served his
strategic purposes. Uncertainty was what he would exploit.
Fracturing presumably stable social, aesthetic, and even sexual categories would create the space for his own stand.
Wilde's comedic refusal to be 'solid and reasonable' is a slap in
the face of Victorian earnestness, and his inconsistency a challenge to common assumptions about the sources and production of meaning. With *Intentions* he achieved a Pyrrhic victory,
which was all that Victorian society would permit. Later gen-

erations have occasionally been more willing to accept that
whatever is not single, whole, or earnest may still be something other than a flaw to be mended by hard labour.

But Wilde was writing for the book-buyer of 1891. The material facts of the book's publication present anomalies—some of
them deliberately contrived by Wilde—in Wilde's relation to
his potential audience. According to the review in the *Graphic*,
Wilde's essays are caviar to the general, so 'Mr Wilde will no
doubt be better pleased if they are read only by the elect'. But
the essays in *Intentions* had previously been published in the
most upmarket of mainstream liberal monthly magazines, the
Fortnightly Review and the *Nineteenth Century*, the latter of
which had a circulation of approximately 20,000. Yet to clinch
its point about Wildean caviar, the *Graphic* concludes that 'in
Messrs Osgood McIlvaine and Co. he has found publishers
after his own heart'. In fact, James Ripley Osgood—the main
partner of the new firm in which Clarence W. McIlvaine was
very much a junior—did not publish *Intentions* (or *Lord Arthur
Savile's Crime* or *A House of Pomegranates*) only for publication's
sake. Osgood, an American, had since 1886 been the London
agent for Harper & Brothers, and had established contacts
with a wide range of English authors. Unlike Elkin Mathews
and John Lane at the Bodley Head—who had cultivated a
reputation as publishers to the elect, printing small runs of fine
books, often by subscription—Osgood, drawing on his connection with Harper's, brought out in his first year of business
a diverse and commercially viable list.[14] On the other hand,
five of the books Osgood published in 1891 were designed by
the artist Charles Ricketts, who had designed *The Picture of
Dorian Gray* and, beginning with his design for the new issue
of Wilde's *Poems* (1892), would work for Mathews and Lane at
the Bodley Head. That is, five of the books in Osgood's initial
list bore on their covers the sign of the aesthetic, the 'fine-
artsy': just the sort of thing the *Graphic* implied. But—a further
twist—the two of the five Ricketts-designed books not by
Wilde were by an author who would be accused of much, but
not of aestheticism or even poor sales: they were *A Group of
Noble Dames* and *Tess of the D'Urbervilles* by Thomas Hardy.

Osgood McIlvaine's press run for *Intentions*—1,500 copies

of the first edition priced at 7*s*. 6*d*. plus an additional 1,000 the following month for a 'cheap edition' at 3*s*. 6*d*.—was several times larger than the typical printings at the Bodley Head.[15] It was larger than their initial printing of Hardy's *Tess*. But for Hardy the presses kept rolling into subsequent editions, and Osgood, with an authentic bestseller on his hands, went ahead with plans for the uniform edition of Hardy's work. The point, of course, is that despite the *Graphic*'s claim that Osgood McIlvaine was publishing only for the elect, Osgood saw Wilde as a marketable author, comparable in sales appeal to Thomas Hardy.[16] Like Wilde, that is, he was banking on turning the appearance of exclusivity into profit. The 'aesthetic' might be a valuable commodity, to artists, to dealers, and to authors and their middlemen—an insight Osgood shared with D'Oyly Carte, who ten years earlier had sponsored Wilde's American tour; and both shared the insight with Wilde himself through all the turns of his career.

The conjunction of Hardy and Wilde in similar bindings on Osgood's list is suggestive. In every obvious way they had nothing to do with each other. But they belonged together because they were two of the most dangerous writers in England. (Yeats, in his *Oxford Book of Modern Verse*, found in *The Ballad of Reading Gaol* 'a stark realism akin to that of Thomas Hardy', but in order to do it he had first to rewrite the poem 'as [Wilde] himself would have done had he lived'.)[17] With *Tess*, Hardy was pushing at the boundaries of the acceptable; magazine editors shied away from it, and he was forced to do much self-censoring to get it into print.[18] With *Jude the Obscure* in 1895, Hardy went too far: 'Jude the Obscene' was burned by the Bishop of Wakefield, and for his part 'Hardy the Degenerate' swore off novel-writing forever[19]. Wilde in the same years was also in the process of outstripping prudence. Charles Ricketts reports an anecdote about this recklessness that curiously links it to Hardy's: Wilde said he was warned by a publisher's reader that 'The Portrait of Mr. W. H.' was dangerous and should not be printed, '"lest it should corrupt our English homes. It seems he and his wife have sometimes asked poor Thomas Hardy to alter his stories!"'[20]

In *Jude the Obscure* Hardy presents a phantasmagorically vivid picture of the death of the old world. It is a novel built on the rubble of ancient ecclesiastical walls and in the shadow of ancient beliefs. But Hardy's novel also points towards a conceivable (and to the conservative a frightening) future: the future of the New Woman and of rational marriage, or love without marriage, in which female and male sexualities would both be satisfied. Hardy's novel was a token of modernity. Wilde's way was unlike Hardy's, although the effect could be similar. To hostile critics, the problem with Hardy was that he left nothing to the imagination: no one has to guess what Arabella means when she tosses a pig's penis at Jude; when Hardy's characters copulate, his readers know it. Wilde, by contrast, was experimenting with the literary uses of the unvoiced vice: 'What Dorian Gray's sins are no one knows. He who finds them has brought them' (*Letters*, 266). The stylistically or morally bothersome surface of his work suggests matters beneath the surface that were even more bothersome; and the silence was in its way as dangerous as Hardy's explicitness.

Modernity of form—to use Wilde's opprobrious term from 'The Critic as Artist'—was another difference. Wilde's way was the 'aesthetic', and in 1891 the aesthetic was associated with the past rather than the future. But it too might be threatening to a bustling Victorian world intent on progress: by turning his back (in disdain, and because the past was more attractive than the present), the aesthete joined with the modern realist in a critique of the present. For Wilde, however, the association with aestheticism, which was the basis of his fame, was a tactical problem. The precocious poet of flowing hair and velvet knee breeches was now looking (in his fleshy person as well as in his literary image) very old very fast. Already famous for more than a decade, with an act now well worn, Wilde in 1891 stood at a crossroads: either he would be relegated to that past he posed as preferring, or somehow he would make the old act new.

The imputation that aestheticism was *passé* had been made in response to *Dorian Gray*: 'Time was (it was in the '70's) when we talked about Mr. Oscar Wilde; time came (it came in the '80's) when he tried to write poetry and, more adventurous, we tried to read it; time is when we had forgotten him ... ' (*St James's Gazette: Heritage*, 68). The charge was renewed for

Intentions. The *Graphic*'s review is especially rich in suggestions both about Wilde and aestheticism. It begins: 'Somehow
or other, there is always a flavour of the early 'eighties' about
Mr. Oscar Wilde, and in opening any book of his a faint odour
of the aesthetic movement, a movement which is of the old
world now, though young a decade ago.' The imagery tells
much: 'flavour' and 'faint odour' suggest the insubstantiality
of aestheticism's too-refined adherents, who lack the firm bodies of healthy English men and women; it also suggests the
danger of aestheticism's doctrine, spreading like a poison or
miasma. Most damning, however, is the imputation that
Wilde, like aestheticism, is ageing into insignificance.

   Nasty intent aside, the imputation contains some fact along
with some wishful thinking. In 1881 Wilde published *Poems*; in
response *Punch* mockingly crowned him the 'Aesthete of
Aesthetes!' (25 June 1881). In 1882, in imitation of his own
satirized image as the aesthete in Gilbert and Sullivan's
Patience, Wilde was telling American lecture audiences that
'the secret of life is in art'.[21] But even in the years of sunflower
and lily, the aesthetic movement was news only to satirists,
journalists, and miners in Colorado. There was already a book
about it, Walter Hamilton's *The Aesthetic Movement in England*,
and Wilde was the culminating figure in its chaotic account of
the figures and forces which 'have helped [the Aesthetic
school] to the position it holds at present, high in the estima-
tion of all true lovers of the ideal, the passionate, and the beautiful'.[22] Wilde was a second generation aesthete; of the first
generation, Rossetti died in 1882, William Morris was active
more as a socialist than an aesthete, Swinburne was living a
temperate life at the Pines in Putney. In 1874, when Wilde was
an undergraduate at Oxford, he joined Ruskin's quixotic effort
to build a road to Ferry Hinksey; however antagonistic Ruskin
would become towards aestheticism, in 1874 his ideal of a
daily life irradiated by art seemed quite in the aesthetic spirit.
And one year before the road-building project, Walter Pater
had published *Studies in the History of the Renaissance*, the book
without which *Intentions* could not have existed.[23]

   So when Max Beerbohm, in the first issue of the *Yellow Book*
(1894), satirically applied to modern England a defence of cosmetics Baudelaire had made in 1863 (in *Le Peintre de la vie*

moderne), part of the fun was watching an aggressively up-to-date 22-year-old posing as an aesthete of days gone by.[24] In 1894 Beerbohm, who was learning his craft by close personal observation of Wilde, also wrote (but did not publish) a satire called 'A Peep into the Past', in which, with more deadly wit than the reviewer in the *Graphic*, he caricatured Wilde as a relic of 'the Early Victorian Era'.[25] Aestheticism—whatever exciting rumour of advanced artistic things it had been in the 1880s—was indeed a fading flower when Wilde for his own purposes revived and revised its attitudes in *Intentions*.

Part of the revision had already been accomplished by, literally, a change of clothes. The costumes and coiffeur and reclining poses had gone. Alfred Douglas, getting even for *De Profundis*, described the change:

He began his notoriety by fantastic dressing, but as he ascended on the rungs of art to the heaven of rank, his great aim was for what he termed 'elegant correctness'. Hence, the Wilde of my time consisted, to a great extent, of silk hat, frock coat, striped trousers and patent leather boots. Add to these a very tall clouded cane with a heavy gold knob and a pair of grey suede gloves, and you have the outward man. On the whole, I believe that he loathed the get-up, especially in the hot weather, but he stuck to it like a Trojan, and nobody ever saw Oscar Wilde in London outside of the regulation harness from eleven o'clock till seven, or outside of the hard white shirt and swallow-tails from seven-thirty till any time you like in the morning.[26]

This is not the received image of the aesthete but of the dandy, who is his own work of art, never *outré* like the aesthete, and always utterly self-contained; not outside of society but so perfectly its embodiment that he puts any actual socialite to shame.[27] The aesthete had been an epiphenomenon; he emerged in mid-century and was disappearing by its end. The dandy, by contrast, was a much longer-lived figure, with a genealogy stretching back to the Regency period. By his genealogy and also by his immutable pose—*always* the striped trousers, *always* the hard white shirt—Wilde as dandy was, in intention, immune to changes of fashion, including, presumably, literary fashion.

'The Critic as Artist' is the only essay in *Intentions* that explicitly continues Wilde's old work of defining 'the mission of the aesthetic movement' (203) and of 'the aesthetic critic'

(153, 183, 191), with his 'aesthetic temperament' (178) and 'aesthetic instinct' (208). Flavour or odour, there certainly is something of the 1880s in this language, which is the language of Wilde's lectures in America. But now, in competition with the lecturer's reformist zeal, the dialogue takes as subtitle the dandy's motto, 'the importance of doing nothing'. The two poses, aesthete and dandy, come together as Gilbert claims that 'Calm, and self-centred, and complete, the aesthetic critic contemplates life, and no arrow drawn at a venture can pierce between the joints of his harness' (174). It isn't easy: Gilbert claims that 'to do nothing at all is the most difficult thing in the world' (167). In his own public polemical life Wilde exhibits the hard work required to maintain a pose of perfect dandiacal aloofness: replying for the *third time* to the *Scots Observer* about its review of *Dorian Gray*, he says, 'by nature and by choice, I am extremely indolent. Cultivated idleness seems to me to be the proper occupation for man' (13 August 1890: *Letters*, 269). The pose signified as much as the work: in the world of muscular Christianity, idleness is sin, and in the world of capitalism it is failure; in *Intentions* it is perfection.

The question of his belatedness dogged Wilde. The Oxford Union refused admission to his *Poems* in 1881 on the grounds of what it called plagiarism—a crude way of naming that volume's derivative poses. Whistler revived the charge in 1890, and 'The Critic as Artist' is, among many other things, Wilde's response to Whistler. Unacknowledged verbatim borrowing —of which Wilde is not much more guilty than many writers who are also omnivorous readers with an ear for a good phrase—is not the real problem. But in the zone of greys that descends from absolute originality of thought through influence to derivation to copy, the matter is more complex. Wilde's style has been called 'anthological', and *Intentions*, which welcomes so many voices into its dialogues, shows why the adjective is apt.[28] The originality of *Intentions*—that distinctive, unmistakable quality we call Wildean—is an originality founded on the already made, a newness that flaunts belatedness.

In 'Pen, Pencil, and Poison', Wilde makes the artist–criminal Wainewright more dandy than aesthete, although a blackly comic failure as either. Wilde's satire of his own image in that

essay suggests one of his tactics for making things new: to cap-
italize on the comedy inherent in his situation, and turn the
critics' accusations of outmodedness to his advantage. The
humour which the critics of *Intentions* commented on lies not
only on the surface of dazzling paradox and epigram, but also
in Wilde's pose as a figure out of his proper time, the dandy in
the new age of realism. Of, as the pose made it seem, the age of
sordid realism. Wilde's polemic against realism is at the very
centre of his book's intentions. Wilde's cultural politics in 1891
are complex: *Intentions* is an attempt to forge a forward-
looking theoretical position by deploying older attitudes to
oppose a theoretical position—realism or naturalism—which
at that moment was laying strong claims to being more politically progressive. The aesthetes of previous decades had as
their antagonist the philistine or bourgeois non-artist. Wilde's
tactical redeployment of aesthetic attitudes in 1891 is as much
directed at other artists as at non-artists; it is a struggle for possession of literary history in order to create a future for his
own art.[29]

Was *Intentions* successful in that cause? The answer supplied
by the reviews is, again, self-contradictory. And they suggest a
danger in Wilde's tactics. They say that Wilde the entertainer
is, to a fault, popular or low, but simultaneously that Wilde the
paradoxical dazzler is the precious possession of a coterie, and
therefore too high (as in high and mighty) for real popularity.
Brilliant, entertaining, lively, and amusing, still *Intentions* is
not for everyone. The *Daily Telegraph* warns 'the novice' that it
'would perhaps be dangerous work to plunge after this
delightfully vagrant *ignis fatuus*', and the *Nation* worries that
the book is beyond 'the commonplace mind'.
    That was a nice way of putting it. The *Graphic* takes us closer
to something not so nice that may be implied by the charge of
exclusivity: Wilde does not write for 'the uninitiated' and 'will
no doubt be better pleased if [the essays] are read only by the
elect'. (Wilde himself supplies the necessary gloss: in 'The
Decay of Lying', Vivian tells Cyril that his essay-within-the-
dialogue was written for 'the elect'; and he defines 'the elect'
as 'The Tired Hedonists . . . [who] wear faded roses in our but-
ton holes . . . and have a sort of cult for Domitian'. Cyril is not

eligible for membership because he is 'too fond of simple pleasures' (7).) The *Pall Mall Gazette* also accuses Wilde of writing
for a 'coterie': 'He has long ago realized that, to the class of
readers among whom his intellectual lot is cast, paradox is the
subtlest form of flattery. . . . [He assumes] our familiarity with
a coterie speech—not to say a jargon—current only on the
highest heights of culture.' The review goes on, apparently in
an assimilationist spirit, to assure readers that 'in truth Mr.
Wilde's perversities are none of them very baffling'. The
immediate reference is to the 'perversities' of his paradoxes,
but another, more dangerous, sense may be available to readers who think they know what goes on among 'the elect' in
Wilde's 'coterie'.

The cultural meanings embedded in the accusation of exclusivity become clearest from a coincidence of reviews in the
Observer (14 June 1891): the brief notice of *Intentions* concludes,
'there are a great many clever paradoxes, a certain amount of
good sense, a great deal of affectation combined with the *sickly
jargon of the aesthetic school*' (my italics). At the top of the same
page is a review of a new book by Alfred Austin, the future
Poet Laureate, which begins, 'Mr. Austin is essentially the poet
of Nature, of Patriotism as *opposed to the sickly, effeminate school*
of versifiers who regard existence from an altogether artificial
and impossible standpoint' (my italics). 'Sickly' and 'effeminate' are the adjectives that divide the aesthete, with his unpa-
triotic belief that nature imitates art, from the truly
representative English writer, for whom love of Country and
love of the country are synonymous. Austin's 'passionate
enthusiasm is infectious', but Wilde's cleverness could make
his readers sick.

With what? Was the critic implying a specifically sexual
sickliness? A year earlier a review of *Dorian Gray* clearly drew
a connection between the novel and criminalized sexual practices: it charged that Wilde's book was written 'for none but
outlawed noblemen and perverted telegraph boys' (*Scots
Observer*, 5 July 1890: *Heritage*, 75). Other accusations are
harder to pin down. When a reviewer accuses *Dorian Gray* of
'effeminate frivolity' (*Daily Chronicle*, 30 June 1890: *Heritage*,
72–3), does he intend his readers to make a connection
between an offensive literary style and an offensive sexual

practice? Does the *Observer* intend that connection when it refers to an 'effeminate school'? To modern readers, with the blindness (in this case) of hindsight, one of the most puzzling questions about Wilde's intentions is whether he expected or wanted his sexuality to figure in his public image. For us, inescapably, it does. Is that because Queensberry outed Wilde, or had Wilde, by his stylistic choices (in person and in print), been doing it himself? For some purposes the question became moot, but for others it was explicitly raised on 25 May 1895 in the Central Criminal Court at the Old Bailey, when Mr Justice Wills, in a fury of 'indignation at the horrible charges brought home' against Oscar Wilde, declared his case 'the worst . . . I have ever tried'; the maximum sentence, he said, was a 'totally inadequate' punishment (*Trials,* 339).

Not just deeds but meanings, which are linked to intentions, repeatedly figured in the three trials of 1895. What did the Marquess of Queensberry mean (questions of orthography aside) by writing on a card that Oscar Wilde was 'posing as a somdomite'? Did he take the view that a pose is the real thing, or did he intend his words to mean (as Wilde's own lawyer in the first trial claimed) 'that there was no guilt of the actual offence [sodomy], but that . . . the person of whom the words were written did appear—nay, desired to appear—and pose to be a person guilty of or inclined to the commission of the gravest of all offences'? (*Trials,* 108).[30] Why would anyone not guilty want to pose as guilty? And what was the intended meaning of Wilde's own writings? Did *Dorian Gray* only 'appear—nay, [desire] to appear—and pose' as a book about 'the gravest of all offences'? In the 'Plea of Justification' against Wilde's charge of libel, Queensberry's lawyer, with grimly comic legal specificity, tried to put an end to literary-critical speculation:

. . . Oscar Fingal O'Flahertie Wills Wilde in the month of July in the year of our Lord One thousand eight hundred and ninety did write and publish and cause and procure to be printed and published with his name upon the title page thereof a certain immoral and obscene work in the form of a narrative entitled 'The Picture of Dorian Gray' which said work was *designed and intended* by the said Oscar Fingal O'Flahertie Wills Wilde *and was understood by the readers* thereof to describe the relations intimacies and passions of certain *persons of sodomitical and unnatural habits tastes and practices.* (*Trials*, 344; my italics)

Sodomy, said the marquess's lawyer, was what Wilde's words meant and were intended to mean.

The trial and imprisonment horribly confirm Wilde's claim that he stood in symbolic relations to the culture of his age. Now it became impossible to consider Oscar Wilde as a person or even as a writer without also considering the symbolizing role he played in a peculiarly modern idea of homosexual identity. (And to the extent that *heter*osexual 'identity' exists in relation to something else which supposedly defines it by difference, Wilde's relation to an idea of homosexuality puts him in symbolic relations to the idea of *any* male sexual identity.) He became not just a remarkable individual but the symbol or type of a certain class of remarkable individual. The class existed before there was a name for it: 'homosexual' was not yet part of the English vocabulary, so other words had to do. Some, like sodomite, were too narrowly specific to take in all the attitudes and attributes that belonged to the class; others, like effeminate, were too general. Whatever the name, this notion of a sexual class is, like the British class system itself, at once immutable and on occasions perfectly permeable. Mr Justice Wills opined that Wilde had 'been at the centre of a circle of extensive corruption of the most hideous kind among young men' (*Trials*, 339): the image suggests that other men might be infected by Wilde and, doing as he did, become like him.

Medico-legal truth is not Wildean truth. The law's attempt at univocality is at the opposite extreme to Wilde's intention to create a freer discourse of widest possibility. At the first trial, Edward Carson for the defence tried to make Wilde confess that 'The affection and love of the artist in *Dorian Gray* might lead an ordinary individual to believe that it might have a certain tendency.' The reticence in the pursuit of full disclosure is remarkable: what, after all, *is* 'a certain tendency', and where would it lead? Wilde replied, 'I have no knowledge of the views of ordinary individuals' (*Trials*, 127). Is anyone sure— even apart from the class superiority implied by Wilde's smart response—that we know the views of other 'ordinary individuals'? In 'The Portrait of Mr W. H.' Wilde made capital out of these kinds of epistemological indeterminacies. But there is also a historical, lexical problem. Recent scholarship impressively shows that the assumptions behind Carson's question were not, in fact, universally shared; that only after, and as a result of, the trials did it become widely understood, with the force of supposed fact, that men whose 'passions' are like those of the witty, indolent Lord Henry Wotton or the artistic, passionate Basil Hallward, or the wicked, beautiful Dorian Gray—or, in *Intentions*, like those of Cyril and Vivian, Gilbert and Ernest, or in 'The Portrait of Mr W. H.' like Willie Hughes and William Shakespeare—belong to the distinct, criminalized class represented by Oscar Wilde.

Both Linda Dowling in *Hellenism and Homosexuality in Victorian Oxford* (1994) and Alan Sinfield in *The Wilde Century* (1994) demonstrate the historical contingency of the large, amorphous set of actions and attitudes designated as 'effeminate'. It is the epithet (as we have seen) which draws other keywords like 'sickly', 'coterie', 'artificial', and 'aesthetic' into a single loose discursive bag. Sinfield and Dowling in their different ways show that in 1891 'effeminate' may have meant something both less and worse than it meant after 1895. On the one hand, effeminacy was less firmly established as a supposed attribute or symptom of homosexuality; on the other hand, effeminacy designated a much wider range of attitudes and practices inimical to a conservative social and political order. In a tradition already deeply rooted in the medieval world, effeminacy was linked not to same-sex desire but to *any* excessively indulged desire that seemed to threaten established political order. The word's semantic spread into social realms far removed from anything we might consider sexual has as much to do with misogyny as with homophobia, since it makes any indulgence in passion (except a passion for abnegation) a weakness, and it makes weakness a quality of the feminine. How moral delinquency by contact with the (supposedly) feminine became delinquency by mutual contact between men is the important, complicated story Sinfield and Dowling, with different emphases, tell.

It is important to get it right because it has so much to do with Wilde's perception of how others perceived him. Was he flaunting it? Or did 'it' exist as something flauntable only after the fact? Sinfield is especially impressive in adducing and weighing evidence to support his claim that only in the 1890s and largely because of Wilde did effeminacy and homosexuality become virtually synonymous. Still, I think he makes the distinction—or newness of association—too absolute. In the Victorian discourse about 'gross indecency' between male persons, what is not quite voiced may be as important as what is, as in Carson's phrase 'a certain tendency', or as in the very statute that made 'gross indecency' (a practice even less localizable than 'sodomy') a criminal offence. The difficulty of voicing what presumably everyone knows is the point of the mock 'missing-word competition' that appeared in an undergraduate paper called the *Ephemeral* at Oxford in 1893:

> To . . . . .
> He often writes of things with brazen candour
> *Non inter Christianos nominanda.*[31]

No one had trouble filling in the blank with 'Oscar Wilde' or supplying 'sodomy' in place of the traditional legal phrase that names it the unnameable.[32] In some of the printed reactions to Wilde the silences must provoke questions. A reviewer of *Lady Windermere's Fan* says that the play could not be a work of art because 'Mr. Wilde is many things needless to enumerate, but he is not an artist':[33] is sodomite one of the things 'needless to enumerate' since the ordinary person already knows it? So too with the other innuendos we hear, including that of effeminacy. The uncertainty was present at the time of the original utterance, not (I think) only retroactively.

Alan Sinfield's important argument about the dissociation of effeminacy and homosexuality begins with a bit of direct, unambiguous, but suspect testimony. Frank Harris, who in 1891 was editor of the *Fortnightly Review*, describes his first meeting with Wilde in a vocabulary ripe with the commonplaces of effeminacy: 'There was something fleshy and fat about him that repelled me. . . . fleshy indulgence and laziness. . . . He shook hands in a limp way that I disliked; his hands were flabby . . . '.[34] Harris's book tells some verifiable truths, including the fact that Harris was helpful to Wilde during the trials. It also contains this bit of dialogue, supposedly spoken

when Wilde was free on bail. Frank is, as usual, trying to moti-
vate the 'weak' Oscar:

> 'Oh, Frank', he said, 'you talk with passion and conviction, as if I
> were innocent.'
> 'But you are innocent', I cried in amaze, 'aren't you?'
> 'No, Frank', he said, 'I thought you knew that all along.'
> I stared at him stupidly. 'No', I said dully, 'I did not know. I did not
> believe the accusation. I did not believe it for a moment.' (167)

Sinfield knows that 'Harris is not altogether reliable', but
thinks 'there is no reason to suppose that he would wish to
appear naïve or ill-informed'; his testimony shows 'that homosexuality was *not* manifest from Wilde's style' (1).

Actually there is good reason why Harris would wish to
appear naïve in this matter. Harris's aggressive heterosexuality was part of his own public story even before he coined it
into *My Life and Loves*. (It is the point of Beerbohm's caricature
of the occasion when Harris loudly denied any knowledge of
'the joys of homosexuality', only to add, 'And yet ... if
Shakespeare had asked me, I would have had to submit.')[35]
Harris was a fabulist but not a fool. He knew enough to see
danger in 'The Portrait of Mr W. H.' He was, apparently, at the
social centre of Wilde's 'circle'. Here we have to weigh the evidence of one Cretan against another: Alfred Douglas, in *Oscar
Wilde and Myself*, describes 'Wilde's own set of friends and
acquaintances' who drank together at the Café Royal. They
were Robert Ross, who had been Wilde's lover, and Reggie
Turner, whose homosexuality was known to his friends; then
'Wilde brought along the late Ernest Dowson ... [and] Mr
Max Beerbohm, who giggled prettily at everything either
Wilde or I said; and Mr Frank Harris, who wore the same
costly furs and roared in the same sucking-dove way as still
continues to delight his troops of friends' (57–8). The friendship between Harris and Beerbohm is well documented.
Beerbohm and Turner were best friends. Turner, whose sexuality was not in doubt, told all to Beerbohm, whose sexuality
was.

In 'A Peep into the Past', his unpublished satire written in
1893, Beerbohm makes Wilde not only old and outmoded: he
makes him both effeminate and clearly sodomitical. Wilde's

'little house in Tite Street' bears 'witness to womanly care and taste'; entering it, a visitor hears 'the quickly receding *frou-frou* of tweed trousers'; the neighbourhood is startled by 'the constant succession of page-boys'.[36] Beerbohm's older brother, the actor-manager Herbert Beerbohm Tree, who produced *A Woman of No Importance* and *An Ideal Husband*, knew what Max knew. When Douglas let one of Wilde's love-letters fall into the hands of the prostitute and blackmailer Alfred Wood, it was through Tree that Wood tried to threaten Wilde. I find it less likely that the centrally placed editor-about-town Harris did not know what Turner, Beerbohm, and Beerbohm Tree knew, than that Harris is as usual doing his prodigious best to stem the decay of lying.

I've been expansive on this small point because it seems to me as important as it does to Sinfield. As actual fact, Harris's statement does not hold up; but that he can expect anyone to believe it—Sinfield is surely right—shows that there was a semantic grey zone between effeminacy and sodomy, between the socially subversive and the merely criminal. That is the zone Wilde publicly inhabited and exploited. He intended people to think something they could not know. And in that zone of provocative indeterminacy, Wilde tried to create a space where the self defines itself, and where artists, in their intensified individualism, might be free from authority, including the authority of stereotype.

Wilde's contrived image of luxury, leisure, refined taste— his 'effeminacy'—would not have had its paradoxical potency (to threaten and attract) if it did not hint at the homosexuality; but 'sodomy' as a proven fact would end the threat of the unknown. Alfred Douglas was already specifying too much with his phrase 'The Love that dare not speak its name'. The unspeakable: that, more precisely, is what Wilde was signifying, in person and in print.[37] Once spoken, whether as love or gross indecency, it is no longer the wonderful or awful thing defined as that which cannot be spoken. As part of his public personality, Wilde's sexuality was strategically deployed to free himself and his audience from the specifying principles of law and science. The evasion of those principles, dear to the regnant realism, is, as we will see in the next chapter, basic to Wilde's critical theory. And later we will see, in 'The Portrait of

Mr W. H.', his story about a deadly search for interpretative certainty, how Wilde takes the indeterminacy principle to its full artistic stretch. But 'The Decay of Lying' and 'The Portrait of Mr W. H.' were victories in a war he could not win. The events at the Old Bailey cruelly proved his failure. Contrary to his every intention he became in the world's eyes not the artist of his own being but the representative of a nature he merely imitated, posing as a sodomite.

2 'The Decay of Lying'

'DIALOGUE ... that wonderful literary form ... can never lose for the thinker its attraction as a mode of expression', says Gilbert, the more expansive of the two speakers in 'The Critic as Artist'. 'By its means he can both reveal and conceal himself, and give form to every fancy, and reality to every mood' (184). Ernest, his interlocutor, breaks frame to add that the writer of dialogue 'can invent an imaginary antagonist, and convert him when he chooses by some absurdly sophistical argument'. Gilbert's reply takes their dialogue-about-dialogues into a realm of fresh paradox where the two dialogues in *Intentions* have their most challenging life: 'Ah, it is so easy to convert others. It is so difficult to convert oneself. To arrive at what one really believes, one must speak through lips different from one's own. To know the truth one must imagine myriads of falsehoods' (185). For Gilbert, 'truth' is, since it can be known; but it exists in close rhetorical quarters with 'what one really *believes*' (which is not necessarily synonymous with objective truth), and it—this truth of the mind—cannot be known apart from the imagining of falsehoods. In *Intentions'* first dialogue, 'The Decay of Lying', Wilde plays seriously with the idea of 'truth' as the belief in what one imagines to be false (call it art, or imagination, or a lie); a 'truth' that can be found by speaking as a self other than the one which believes—as a mask, or a pose, or a character in one's own dialogue.

Writing from HM Prison, Reading, in the early months of 1897, Wilde told Lord Alfred Douglas a story about the coming into being of 'The Decay of Lying'. The story is moralized, even sentimentalized, in a way that suggests deep-dyed role-playing but permits little dialogue. He remembers the sterile profligacy of his life with Douglas—'more than £5,000 in actual money, irrespective of the bills I incurred ... Out of the reckless dinners with you nothing remains but the memory that too much was eaten and too much was drunk'—and contrasts it with the imaginatively rich frugality of his association with his earlier, perhaps his first, lover, Robert Ross:

One of the most delightful dinners I remember ever having had is one Robbie and I had together in a little Soho café, which cost about as many shillings as my dinners to you used to cost pounds. Out of my dinner with Robbie came the first and best of all my dialogues. Idea, title, treatment, mode, everything was struck out at a 3 franc 50 c. *table-d'hôte*. (*Letters*, 428)

Since the essay's 'treatment, mode'—that is, its dialogic form—is so important to its success, it would be nice if we could believe the story of its advent between appetizer and dessert. But the evidence supplied by the extant manuscript tells a different, more interesting story.[1] It reveals that 'The Decay of Lying: An Observation' existed originally, not as a dialogue, but as an essay that, in revision, became Vivian's essay-within-the-dialogue, 'The Decay of Lying: A Protest'. The speakers, Cyril and Vivian (named after Wilde's sons, then $3\frac{1}{2}$ and 2 years old), were the happy afterthought of the dinner in Soho. When Wilde remade his essay into a dialogue he accomplished much: now he could take up and put down the masks by which, according to Vivian, we rise above 'that dreadful universal thing called human nature' (15); he could give his epigrams the kind of dramatic setting he was beginning to create in his society comedies; he could, in the persona of Vivian, take a role like *Dorian Gray*'s Lord Henry Wotton, who 'played with [an] idea, and grew wilful; tossed it into the air and transformed it; let it escape and recaptured it; made it iridescent with fancy, and winged it with paradox' (*CW* 45), while he could also play the part of Cyril, the more conventional man for whose benefit the show is staged.

If the story of the essay's inception in a Soho café is not entirely accurate, it is still appropriate that dinners and lovers figure so largely in it. In revision, becoming a dialogue, 'The Decay of Lying' associated itself with the great original of the form, the Platonic dialogue; and for some of Wilde's readers that would especially call to mind the *Symposium*, a dialogue about love, including Aristophanes' defence of same-sex love, carried on through a long night's dining and drinking. The narrator of 'The Portrait of Mr. W. H.', explaining Shakespeare's love for a beautiful, effeminate boy-actor, draws heavily on 'this wonderful dialogue, of all the Platonic dialogues perhaps the most perfect, as it is the most poetical' (*Portrait*,

42). The *Symposium* and the *Phaedrus* were key texts in which young upper-class Victorian homosexuals could find, as John Addington Symonds did, 'the sanction of [their] love'.[2] And Wilde's Oxford was the centre for the dissemination of Plato. Educational reforms instituted by Benjamin Jowett, Master of Balliol and translator of Plato, had put ancient Greece at the heart of modern Oxford's official intellectual life; as Linda Dowling writes, 'such students of Oxford Hellenism as Symonds and Pater and Wilde would find that Greek *paiderastia* was, through the agency of the Greats curriculum, brought vividly and compellingly to life . . . '[3]

In Wilde's recension of the Platonic dialogue, Vivian adopts the insolent elegance of manner *Punch* regularly caricatured as effeminate—with whatever degree of sexual suggestiveness that pose might have conveyed—and acts the part of a dandified Socrates, corrupting Cyril into an appreciation of 'the lost art of Lying' (52). In the process, Vivian's creator suggests that literary politics may be sexual politics as well. The connection between literature and sexuality will emerge more clearly when I consider the essay's argument against literary realism.

By Christmas 1888 the revised essay was in proof, ready for publication in the January 1889 number of the *Nineteenth Century*. We can be so precise because of another meal connected with the dialogue's inception: in his *Autobiography*, William Butler Yeats recalls that Wilde read to him from the essay's proofs after Christmas dinner with the Wilde family in Tite Street. The occasion's incongruities are worthy of a Beerbohm caricature: under the mistletoe the worldly Wilde reads his wicked essay to the 23-year-old author of *Fairy and Folk Tales of the Irish Peasantry*.[4] But the scene also has an appropriateness, even a symbolic aptness, since it suggests the essay's role in the formation of literary modernism. According to Richard Ellmann,

[Yeats] needed an aesthetic which would take into acccount the intense speculation about the nature and function of art that had been going on in Europe since the pronouncements of the early romantic poets. In the dialogue Wilde summed up the disdain for life and nature of writers from Gautier to Mallarmé, the disdain for common morality of Poe and Baudelaire, the disdain for content of Verlaine and Whistler. (302)

Literary genealogies inevitably oversimplify the complexities of influence and outcome. But 'The Decay of Lying', with its valorization of surfaces and masks over the common-sense notion of sincerity, its elevation of the artistic imagination over the imperializing pretensions of positivistic science, its unresolved interplay between an élitist exclusivity and a redemptivist social ethic, certainly found (as Ellmann says) a 'willing listener' in Yeats.

But Yeats did more than listen, and he was not the only one to dine out on Wilde's essays. Wilde's dialogues would eventually enter into dialogue with a generation of modernists, including not only the Irish Yeats and Joyce, but also Pound and Eliot; Wilde spoke to them, and they replied. Eliot in his phase of Anglo-Catholic orthodoxy tried to distance himself from Pater (in his essay 'Arnold and Pater', 1930), and therefore by implication from Wilde; but the author of 'Tradition and the Individual Talent' is of Wilde's party unawares when he writes that 'Poetry is not a turning loose of emotion, but an escape from emotion; it is not the expression of personality, but an escape from personality. But, of course, only those who have personality and emotions know what it means to want to escape those things.'[5] This is an earnest way of saying, as Gilbert says in 'The Critic as Artist', that 'All bad poetry springs from genuine feeling. To be natural is to be obvious, and to be obvious is to be inartistic' (197). Or that 'To reveal art and conceal the artist is art's aim' (Preface to *Dorian Gray*). It is also Eliot's way of being as divided as Wilde is about the value of 'personality'. In 'Tradition and the Individual Talent', personality is a confining embarrassment of singularity from which we need to escape into the impersonality (whatever that is) of art, while the second part of Eliot's proposition ('only those who have personality . . . know what it means to want to escape [it]') suggests that to be personality-laden is a privilege reserved for the poetically elect. In one clause Eliot-as-artist must 'escape from personality', and in the next he re-erects personality into the artist's distinguishing characteristic.

For Ezra Pound in 1916 the self is experienced as inexpressible evanescence, the sign of our relegation to an always progressive past tense: 'In the "search for oneself," in the search for "sincere self-expression," one gropes, one finds some seeming verity. One says "I am" this, that, or the other, and with words scarcely uttered one ceases to be that thing.'[6] For Pound, the godlike 'I am' is merely the shortest of imagist texts. Pound may be recalling the Conclusion to Pater's *The Renaissance*: 'it may ever be more truly said that [the impression of the individual mind] has ceased to be than that it is' (Hill, 188). That is the sort of frightening or liberating possibility Pater feared would mislead the young men into whose hands his Conclusion might fall. It is a possibility we frequently find, as Pound found it, expressed in Wilde, for instance in 'The Portrait of Mr. W. H.': 'was there no permanence in personality? Did things come and go through the brain, silently, swiftly, and without footprints, like shadows through mirrors? Were we at the mercy of such impressions as Art or Life chose to give us?' (*Portrait*, 81).

The conflicted notion of an unfixed self-creating personality that is also the burdening sign of the artist's distinction or doom appears frequently in *Intentions*, even in the apparently incongruous context of the satirical 'Pen, Pencil, and Poison'. The conflict informs every aspect of Wilde's work. In the society plays, culminating in *The Importance of Being Earnest*, Wilde created a world of characters without depth: the good and the bad alike are exactly the masks they wear and shift. Alacrity of wit, not depth of personality, distinguishes the admirable characters from the less admirable. In his own time and later, critics whose moral or political ideals require an idea of sincerity—the idea, following Wilde, I call earnestness—may find the situation repugnant. Eventually the idea came to frighten Wilde as well. *De Profundis* is, depending on one's point of view, his tired capitulation to or final discovery of the earnest depth-model of a sincere personality.

Regenia Gagnier thinks that Wilde's dramatized poseurs function as satirical images of the audience that bought them: 'Wilde drained his characters of deep psychology to show that the dominant dream of modern society was consumption and the national power to consume the world.'[7] This assumes that a society not dominated by commodity fetishism would be a society of people full (rather than drained) of 'deep psychology'. But for Wilde the replete, deep personality (the personality embraced in *De Profundis*) is also the stuck, the non-creative, personality. The desire for a world where we freely make and remake the surfaces that constitute our most significant subjective reality underlies the positions Wilde takes with respect to current literary and theoretical debates in 'The Decay of Lying'.

Vivian sits in the library of a country house in Notting-hamshire. He is reading the proofs of an article. Cyril enters from the terrace and invites him outdoors to enjoy nature on this lovely afternoon. No last names or titles tell us their social class, but clearly they are to the aristocratic manner born. If so, it is an aristocracy not of nature's, or even of England's, but of Wilde's own creating. Eloquence, indolence, and good taste define this aristocracy. Vivian and Cyril have leisure and wealth, since they seem to know everything and do nothing. Cyril thinks it uncharacteristic that Vivian has written—worked at—an article, but it is an article intended only for 'the elect': even in literary polemics, Vivian keeps his aristocratic amateur's status.

These fantasy-aristocrats are not the kind of aristocrats Matthew Arnold labelled Barbarians. In Arnold's description of the class, 'the passion for field-sports ... and for all manly exercises' as well as 'the passion for asserting one's personal liberty' are among the Barbarians' lovelier qualities, but 'the circumstances of their life' make it impossible for them to have 'a whole range of powers of thought and feeling'.[8] Arnold does not define the aristocracy's missing inward powers; he only wonders whether 'there should perhaps be, for ideal per-fection, a shade more *soul?*'.[9] 'The Decay of Lying', in its two speakers, promotes a fantastically soulful aristocracy to gov-ern (by doing nothing) a utopian England. For the creation of such an aristocracy of aesthetes, a Soho café will do as well as the cloakroom of Victoria Station, or Merion Square, Dublin. It is the first lie 'The Decay of Lying' promulgates.

Even Cyril's tendency toward the outdoors is less barbaric than it is aesthetic. 'The air is exquisite', he says, using the satirical cartoonists' favourite aesthetic adjective. Cyril's 'nature' is already a nature made in the image of art: 'There is a mist upon the woods, like the purple bloom upon a plum. Let us go and lie on the grass, and smoke cigarettes, and enjoy

Nature' (3). The mist in Cyril's metaphor does not imitate a real plum but an impressionist still-life. His enjoyment of nature is accompanied by the characteristically Wildean occupation of smoking cigarettes, 'the perfect type of a perfect pleasure. It is exquisite, and it leaves one unsatisfied' (*CW* 70).[10] Cyril, even before he is enlightened by Vivian, already treats nature as condescendingly as Wilde, appearing before the curtain with cigarette in hand, would treat the first-night audience of *Lady Windermere's Fan*.

As for Vivian, he has 'entirely lost [the] faculty' for enjoying nature, even with cigarettes. Experience teaches him that, contrary to received wisdom, 'the more we study Art, the less we care for Nature' (3). Nature's crude imperfections and unfinished condition, its failure to fulfil its good intentions, is its best point, since it is a cause of art: 'Art is our spirited protest, our gallant attempt to teach Nature her proper place' (4). His language, like Cyril's, shows that we could not go back to nature even if we wanted to, because to think or speak of nature is to be already in the world of art: 'As for the infinite variety of Nature, that is pure myth', he says, turning nature into a failed version of Shakespeare's Cleopatra, whose 'infinite variety ... makes hungry/Where most she satisfies'. He can only describe nature's failure by reference to the work of art, whether it is Shakespeare's play or the character herself, in whom (as in her picture of Venus) 'we see/The fancy outwork nature'. Such 'infinite variety' is precisely not natural: 'It resides in the imagination, or fancy, or cultivated blindness of the man who looks at her' (4). To see the nature that social myth makes infinitely various, we have to look through eyes taught by art, with 'cultivated blindness'.

So Vivian, like Oscar Wilde, has written an article (which he will now read through Cyril's interruptions, interrogations, and emendations); if attended to, it may produce, as Wilde tried to do in his lectures of the 1880s, 'a new Renaissance of Art' (6). It will restore society's lost leader, 'the cultured and fascinating liar', with his frank, fearless disdain for proof of any kind—for any appeal, that is, to the truth of science or economics or sociology or anything not of his own making; the liar, whose very existence, a constant act of self-invention, is a protest against mindless nature.

'The Decay of Lying' was the second article by Wilde to be published in the *Nineteenth Century*. The first, 'Shakespeare and Stage Costume' (revised for *Intentions* as 'The Truth of Masks') had appeared in May 1885; it earned Wilde an invitation to the annual summer party given by the magazine's editor, James Knowles, at his home in Queen Anne's Gate. Another guest was W. E. Gladstone's daughter Mary, who wrote that she 'rather enjoyed sitting out in the garden with unlimited strawberries and cream and the flabby limp figure of Oscar Wilde mooning about'.[11] It is a funny picture and interestingly diagnostic of Wilde's tactical position. At Queen Anne's Gate Wilde was in good company. Tennyson, who had helped Knowles start the magazine, remained one of its stars. Arnold, Ruskin, Swinburne, and William Morris published in the *Nineteenth Century*; so did Beatrice Potter, Prince Kropotkin, Leslie Stephen, and, on a regular basis, both Gladstone and T. H. Huxley, antagonists in the great Victorian debate on the truth of science versus the truth of religion. Acceptance by the *Nineteenth Century* put Wilde at the centre of the British liberal establishment; but, unlike Cyril or Vivian in Nottinghamshire, he stood out—flabby, limp, mooning about, as Mary Gladstone saw it—never quite their sort, by his own choice never quite assimilable. His posture at Knowles's garden party mocks the standards of the society he is trying to conquer. And his second essay for the magazine similarly mocks the customary posture of moral uprightness.

Most of the revisions Wilde made between the magazine version and *Intentions* are a fastidious author's stylistic fiddlings. But the most extensive additions include the essay's most famous passage. In the *Nineteenth Century*, Vivian had proposed four 'doctrines of the new aesthetics' (52), handily summarized in the conclusion: 'Art never expresses anything but itself', 'All bad art comes from returning to Life and Nature, and elevating them into ideals', 'Life imitates Art far more than Art imitates Life', and 'Lying, the telling of beautiful untrue things, is the proper aim of Art'. In revision, Wilde gave Vivian a 'corollary' to the third doctrine:

It follows . . . that external Nature also imitates Art. The only effects that can be shown us are effects that we have already seen through poetry, or in paintings. This is the secret of Nature's charm, as well as the explanation of Nature's weakness. (54)

The corollary recapitulates the longest passage added in revision (39–43): Cyril challenges Vivian to prove 'that Nature, no less than Life, is an imitation of Art', and Vivian, who is 'prepared to prove anything', produces his description of Impressionist fogs, 'those wonderful brown fogs that come creeping down our streets, blurring the gas-lamps and changing the houses into monstrous shadows':

At present, people see fogs, not because there are fogs, but because poets and painters have taught them the mysterious loveliness of such effects. There may have been fogs for centuries in London. I dare say there were. But no one saw them, and so we did not know anything about them. They did not exist till Art had invented them. (40–1)

Vivian criticizes nature for being behind the artistic times: 'Sunsets are quite old-fashioned. . . . Upon the other hand they go on' (41–2).

Nature imitates art: a most ingenious paradox, possibly Wilde's most famous; but, as reviewers of *Intentions* pointed out, it threatens to collapse into a reasonable proposition, or even a tautology. No one denies that culture conditions our way of seeing: that is what culture does, whether in the form of Art (with, as Max Beerbohm put it, a capital H) or advertising. But Wilde's attack on nature as a derivative of culture goes further than this. What we call 'nature' is not natural, not (that is) an inescapable given of existence. Society made what society now worships as the thing which made it: Nature 'is no great mother who has borne us. She is our creation. It is our brain that she quickens to life. Things are because we see them . . . ' (40). So-called nature poses as natural—that is, inevitable —rather than imitative or social, and traps us into imitating it. In quest of the natural we spend our lives imitating an imitation, when (like art) we should 'never express anything but [ourselves]'. Reviewers thought that Vivian's paradox depended on the reversal of 'art' and 'nature'. But the fulcrum, 'imitates', matters most. Vivian's corollary suggests that whatever *is* is wrong (even, perhaps, such a 'natural' fact as universal heterosexuality), because it mindlessly repeats a prior act of imitation. What we take as natural fact (whether we find it outdoors or in society or in the pages of a realistic novel) is someone else's lie—the previously thought or the already created—which we now unwittingly imitate. Not only 'All bad art' but, by implication, all bad social conditions, come 'from returning to Life and Nature, and elevating them into ideals'. The liar heroically refuses to accept the inevitability of conditions that pose as natural facts: the 'beautiful untrue things' he tells are the things that have not entered our repertoire of repetitive, imitative gestures.

In the realm of sexual politics (where Wilde sets himself against nature) as in literary politics (where he sets himself against naturalism), Wilde's position cannot easily be assimilated to the positions taken by his most progressive contemporaries. Jonathan Dollimore has distinguished two modes of 'transgression': one, he writes, operates 'in the name of a desire and identity rooted in the natural, the sincere, and the authentic; Wilde's transgressive aesthetic is the reverse: insincerity, inauthenticity, and unnaturalness become the liberating attributes of decentred identity and desire . . . '[12] André Gide, who insists that his homosexual desire is natural to his authentic identity, represents for Dollimore the first kind of transgression. It is also the kind that was being advocated during Wilde's career by progressive sexual reformers such as John Addington Symonds and Edward Carpenter, who were in the process of defining same-sex desire not as a wilful, aberrant choice but as the attribute of an identity. But the politics of sexual identity are always complicated and often contradictory. *Fin-de-siècle* conservatives like the criminologist César Lombroso and the universal doom-sayer Max Nordau, in his book *Degeneration*, contributed as much to making sexuality 'the subject of scientific discourse controlled by professionals' as Symonds and Carpenter.[13] What Symonds and Carpenter, and in their different way Lombroso and Nordau, wanted to naturalize and thus bring into the world that science can explain, Wilde needed to keep free from the taint of imitation. What they sought to inscribe in the language of science, Wilde wanted to liberate into the free play of artifice. Only the artificial, never the natural, can be true to an identity constituted as a process of always creative change.

On questions of identity, sexual and otherwise, Wilde, like Vivian, writes the Emersonian 'Whim' over his library door. Only once, in the petitionary letter he sent the Home Secretary from Reading Prison (2 July 1896) did Wilde fully entertain, or pose as entertaining, the medical model of homosexuality: '[my] terrible offences ... are forms of sexual madness ... recognised as such by pathological science ... they are diseases to be cured by a physician. ... In the works of eminent men of science such as Lombroso and Nordau ... this is especially insisted on. ... Professor Nordau in his book "Degenerescence" [sic] published in 1894 having devoted an entire chapter to the petitioner as a specially typical example of this fatal flaw' (Letters, 402). This was written under extreme duress, and if it represents a 'mood', it is a very bad mood, badly represented. But traces of a similar mood can be found elsewhere, and by Wilde's own choosing.

So, having dismissed nature in 'The Decay of Lying' as casually as a dandy dismisses a carriage, he will in his next dialogue assert that heredity is an inescapable law. The Picture of Dorian Gray draws much of its power from his conflicting desire for a motile self which is its own invention and his knowledge of a more conventionally Victorian essential self which you can murder but not escape. Dorian is contemptuous of 'the shallow psychology of those who conceive the Ego in man as a thing simple, permanent, reliable, and of one essence. To him, man was a being of myriad lives and myriad sensations, a complex multiform creature ... ' But the sentence, which begins in the liberatory manner of 'The Decay of Lying', continues, without acknowledging any contradiction, to say that this 'multiform creature ... bore within itself strange legacies of thought and passion, and [its] very flesh was tainted with the monstrous maladies of the dead' (CW 112). The 'strange legacies' and 'monstrous maladies' that congregate in Dorian, the rhetoric of 'taint' and 'malady' in the narrative's indirect free discourse, all license the homophobic Queensberry's condemnatory reading of The Picture of Dorian Gray as a 'sodomitical' novel. That rhetoric is the tribute Wilde pays to the society which criminalizes his desires.

In 'The Soul of Man Under Socialism', Christ's message is 'Be thyself'—either deeply, once and for all, or variously, as intensely and often as possible: both readings are available. For a philosopher, such contradictions could be disastrous; for Wilde, the logical difficulties energize the work.

Vivian's advocacy of lying (artifice) over sincerity (nature) begins, it may seem to us trivially, as an attack on the realistic novel, with its 'tedious *document humain*' and 'miserable little *coin de la création*' (8). The question of realism is not a side issue: it is the contemporary polemical context in which the essay has to be understood. The issue seemed as clear in the art world as it did in the literary world. Linda Nochlin writes that 'The premium placed on that most controversial of all entities—truth— rose dramatically towards the middle of the nineteenth century, and the word "sincerity" became a Realist battle-cry. For although the Realist refrained from moral comment in his work, his whole attitude towards art implied a moral commitment, to the values of truth, honesty and sincerity.'[14] To readers not deeply concerned about the reputations of Mrs Humphry Ward or Paul Bourget, this context may have become almost invisible. But in January 1889 literary realism—or naturalism, as it was indistinguishably called—was an explosively hot topic.

Vivian's attack on realism begins with a facetious critique of the fantasists Robert Louis Stevenson and Rider Haggard for falling into habits of accuracy. Vivian moves on to other English novelists—the list expanded between the *Nineteenth Century* and *Intentions*—of whom only Henry James matters any more. With Mrs Humphry Ward's *Robert Elsmere*, the best-selling sensation of the preceding literary season, he gets into deeper waters. Even in the liberal-leaning *Fortnightly Review* a writer diagnosed *Robert Elsmere*'s success as the 'symptom' of a broad social problem: 'a book written to discredit the evidences of Christianity . . . [would not succeed] if the main theme was as offensive to public taste as it ought to be.'[15] But Vivian does not object to the novel's ideology, only its genre, the 'genre ennuyeux' (12): *Robert Elsmere* is not dangerous but boring. His comment on realists who write about conditions in London's East End—'they find life crude and leave it raw' (12) —is the segue to his real target, which had been glanced at in his essay's first paragraph, the great practitioner and theorist of realism, Émile Zola.

Wilde's opposition to Zola and Zolaism comes uncomfortably close to allying him with forces that would eventually destroy him. The moralists were attacking Zola in terms similar to the terms they used to attack *The Picture of Dorian Gray*. On 8 May 1888 Mr Samuel Smith, the Member for Flintshire, rose in the House of Commons in support of his motion deploring 'the rapid spread of demoralizing literature in this country'. He told his fellow members that 'an immense increase of vile literature . . . was working terrible effects upon the morals of the young'. The 'subtle poison of vile and obscene literature . . . corroded the human character [and] sapped the vitality of a nation'.[16] Zola's novels, 'only fit for swine', were bad enough in French but a calamity now that they were being published in English translations—*cheap* Engish translations, which meant that the young, the poor, and the female could acquire them and, by learning about their own lives, be corrupted. Smith quoted many writers in support of his sense of indignation. A writer in *Society* reported '"a brutal change"' that has come about, '"and the name of the worker of the transformation is Realism, and Zola is his Prophet. Realism . . . means nothing short of sheer beastliness . . . filthy ideas . . . dirt and horror pure and simple"'. In the *Sentinel* a writer who had read only two pages of Zola found '"the matter of such a leprous character that it would be impossible for any young man who had not learned the Divine secret of self-control to have read it without committing some form of outward sin within twenty-four hours after"': an uncontrollable outbreak of masturbation would be the least that filthy French realism had to answer for.

In November 1888 Henry Vizetelly was indicted for 'publishing an obscene libel', that is, the English translation of Zola's *La Terre*. The Solicitor-General, characterizing the book as 'filthy from beginning to end',[17] tried to read passages to the jury in support of his claim; the stunned jury begged him to desist. Vizetelly pleaded guilty, promised to withdraw the book from circulation, and was given a suspended sentence. (The following year he was tried again and served three months in prison.) Early in 1889—shortly after the publication of 'The Decay of Lying'—the National Vigilance Society distributed the record of its campaign against dirty books in a pamphlet called *Pernicious Literature*. It urged individuals to bring private prosecutions against obscene literature if the Public Prosecutor failed to act. And when the magazine version of *The Picture of Dorian Gray* appeared the following year, a reviewer, alluding to this pamphlet campaign, suggested that the Vigilance Society might think it worthwhile to prosecute Wilde (*St James's Gazette*, 20 June 1890: *Heritage*, 68–9).

Why, then, in this overheated atmosphere, does Wilde begin the attack on nature with an attack on naturalism, when he himself was so vulnerable and when there are, even to friendly eyes, so many points of affinity between Zolaism and Oscarism—for instance, that nothing should limit the subject-matter of art, that no subject is intrinsically immoral, that 'an artist . . . has no ethical sympathies at all'? (letter from Wilde to the *Scots Observer*, 9 July 1890: *Letters*, 266). Unlike the Vigilance Society, Wilde had actually read Zola, extensively: when his household was auctioned off in the bankruptcy proceedings following his trial, lot 25 was 'M. Zola's Works, &c, 23 vols'.[18] He read Zola, and he must have noticed the similarities.

Some of Wilde's opposition to realism sounds like aestheticized snobbery. Vivian says that 'In literature we require distinction, charm, beauty, and imaginative power' (13). Such qualities cannot be found in 'an account of the doings of the lower orders'. But what sounds like disdain for the larger part of humanity—'Who cares what happens to them?'—transposes the language of social class into a critique of the Zolaist view of 'human nature' itself. In a complex rhetorical move, Vivian adopts the language of social superiority and applies it, not to people born into the lower strata of society but to characters created in the realist's reductive image. Realism produces a democracy of characters with 'dreary vices and . . . drearier virtues' whose lives are 'absolutely without interest' because they all imitate (as presumably their creator does) a nature they should instead be creating. The realist's supposedly scientific objectivity produces the same effect on Vivian as does the nature the realist imitates: 'It is a humiliating confession, but we are all of us made out of the same stuff. . . . Sooner or later one comes to that dreadful universal thing called human nature' (14–15). The French novelist Paul Bourget, for instance, deals not with the lower orders but with the *haute monde* of the Faubourg Saint Germain. Yet Bourget's quest for 'the reality that lies behind the mask' (14) produces characters as uninteresting as Zola's; he analyses them until he 'might just as well write of match-girls and costermongers' (15). Not the commonplace reality but the distinctive mask is what Vivian wants, as he wants the art not the nature; people and characters differ from one another and become interesting in the 'accidentals'.[19]

Some actual comparisons reveal both affinity and opposition between the reductive realist and the decadent romantic. In 'Pen, Pencil, and Poison', for instance, Wilde refers familiarly to *Thérèse Raquin*, the earliest of the novels Zola claimed for naturalism. What Wilde wrote in ironic defence of *Dorian Gray* applies in spades to *Thérèse Raquin*: 'there is a terrible moral in [it]. . . . Is this an artistic error? I fear it is' (to the editor of the *St James's Gazette*, 26 June 1890: *Letters*, 259). Despite Zola's programmatic appeals to scientific objectivity—in his preface to the second edition (1868), Zola says, 'I simply applied to two living bodies the analytical method that surgeons apply to corpses'—*Thérèse Raquin* requites sin with a relentlessness more appropriate to a moral parable than to the theoretical tenets of realism. In other ways, too, *Dorian Gray* recalls *Thérèse Raquin*. In Zola's novel, as in Wilde's, illicit experience, especially the sexual, occurs with heightened, life-transforming intensity; and as in Wilde's the signs of that experience are external and indelible. When Thérèse and her adulterous lover Laurent have their first 'silent and brutal' sex, she experiences a 'passionate abandon' and 'fire leapt from her flesh' as the blood of her African mother 'began to rush and beat furiously. . . . And long spasms ran through her from head to foot.'[20] Laurent drowns Thérèse's sickly, impotent husband, Camille, but as the victim goes overboard he bites Laurent's neck, and 'the bite . . . was like a red-hot brand burning into his skin' (106): the never-healed wound is as remorseless a sign of sin as is Dorian Gray's picture. Thérèse and Laurent never enjoy another moment of love or spasm. They are haunted by the drowned man and finally take poison together; falling at the same moment, 'Her mouth hit her husband's neck on the scar left by Camille's teeth' (256).

In light of this novel alone, one might have expected Wilde to acknowledge Zola a congenial precursor. But two scenes from Zola's later novel *Nana*[21]—conveniently, the first and last scenes —while similar enough to be comparable to *Dorian Gray*, also make clear the sharp ideological differences. The opening chapter of *Nana* is set at the Variétés, an elegant theatre which Bordenave, its owner, insists on calling a brothel. The show is *The Blond Venus*, a broad travesty of classical mythology, with Bordenave's new star, the whore Nana, playing Venus. As the mythological figures on stage are stripped (literally, since Nana appears naked in the final tableau) of any pretence to high cultural meaning, so too Zola's narrative strips the audience of its social covering. The flesh, and the desire of flesh for flesh, is what this theatre, on its stage and in its audience, signifies. The scene, like so much else in the novel, is a stunningly paradoxical feat of reductiveness: its closely observed ornate architecture, its many characters, its careful narrative orchestration, all say (perhaps self-contradictorily) that social acts, even the act of signification itself, disguise the single important fact of a sexual desire that precedes socialization. The narrative energy in the scene comes from Zola's de-creative delight, dressing characters in language only to expose the nakedness which, Zola wants us to feel, is their reality.

Wilde figures theatre very differently in *Dorian Gray*. For Dorian, as for his creator, theatre goes in the opposite direction to *Nana*'s theatre: it is (I will say more about this in the next chapter) definitively the place of illusion. In chapter 4, Wilde pulls out all the conventional stops, even the clichés, to signify a theatre that only begins in the sordid physicality where Zola's ends. Dorian, wandering 'a labyrinth of grimy streets', discovers 'an absurd little theatre' run by a 'hideous Jew' with 'greasy ringlets and an enormous diamond'. (Like Zola's reductiveness, Wilde's depends on prior constructions, here of antisemitism, to convey the sense of supposed emptiness.) In this *ne plus ultra* of sordid reality Dorian discovers—rather, he creates—'the greatest romance of [his] life'. Dorian's energy, like the narrator's, is invested in dressing up the theatre and making it into a theatre of romance. The poor actress Sibyl Vane disappears into Rosalind and Imogen; her flesh is a threat rather than (as in Zola) a goal; symbolization takes precedence over materiality. In response to Lord Henry's question, '"what are your actual relations with Sibyl Vane?"' Dorian—in a moment of great potential comedy—leaps to his feat 'with flushed cheeks and burning eyes', to cry, '"Harry! Sibyl Vane is sacred!"' (CW 51). Dorian cannot bear too much of the realism that kills romance at this first stage in his progress toward experience.

The end of *Nana*, like the end of *Dorian Gray*, transposes moral delinquency into the register of physical degeneration. Throughout the novel Zola tries (again, in a splendid act of self-contradiction) to leave nothing to the imagination: he precedes the reader in specifying Nana's sexual and social crimes and in giving physical shape to, and symbolic judgement on, their consequences. After a career of sexual adventuring that brings ruin upon an entire social order, the Blond Venus, whose 'fiery red . . . pubic hair glowed triumphantly over its [aristocratic] victims stretched out at her feet' (409), is left naked beyond even the theatre manager Bordenave's wildest imaginings:

Now Nana was left alone, lying face upwards in the light of the candle, a pile of blood and pus dumped on a pillow, a shovelful of rotten flesh ready for the bone-yard, her whole face covered in festering sores, one touching the other, all puckered and subsiding into shapeless, slushy grey pulp, already looking like a compost heap. Her features were no longer distinguishable, her left eye entirely submerged in discharging ulcers, the other one a sunken, fly-blown black hole. A thick yellowish fluid was still oozing from her nose. Starting from the left cheek, a reddish crust had overrun the mouth, pulling it into a ghastly grin. And on this horrible and grotesque death-mask, her hair, her lovely hair, still flamed like a glorious golden stream of sunlight. (425)

By contrast, Dorian Gray's unspecified sins are inscribed in his flesh in just a couple of understated sentences: 'Lying on the floor was a dead man, in evening dress, with a knife in his heart. He was withered, wrinkled, and loathsome of visage' (CW 167). Still impeccably dressed, Dorian has aged shockingly, but the only thing that distinguishes his ageing process from anyone else's is the judgement that it makes him 'loathsome'.

Wilde's artistic energy, like Basil's and (before his decline) like Dorian's, is devoted to dressing up rather than stripping away. The rhetorical symptoms are his catalogues of jewellery and other exotica, the starched perfection of his dandies, perhaps even the veils of Salomé which are best not stripped away.[22] But this commitment to the surface depends on knowing and fearing the claim of its opposite, just as Zola's haste to get under the dress depends on his exact knowledge and delight in the couturier's art. Zola's catalogue of Nana's fatal decay is the counterpart of Wilde's catalogues of collectibles. Zola's way is close enough but also alien enough to Wilde's to provoke an opposition where there might equally have been alliance.

But between 1889 and 1895 critics saw less difference than Wilde sees between the 'dreary vices' of characters in realistic fiction and the unspeakably exciting vices of Dorian Gray. In an article in the second *Yellow Book*, in 1894, Hubert Crackanthorpe made fun of the alarmists who cry 'Decadence, decadence: you are all decadent nowadays. Ibsen, Degas, and the New English Art Club; Zola, Oscar Wilde, and the Second Mrs. Tanqueray.'[23] To anyone expecting that the world could end with the century's end, there was not twopence-worth of difference between the realist, the aesthete, and Arthur Wing Pinero. But to Wilde the difference mattered. The unageing Dorian *chooses* his vices: '"I don't want to be at the mercy of my emotions. I want to use them, to enjoy them, and to dominate them"' (*CW* 89). It is sad that the 'nature' inscribed in his picture reveals that his choices were as ugly as Thérèse Raquin's, but it is not necessarily a contradiction of Wilde's position. Dorian's picture, despite Basil Hallward's idealizing efforts, turns out merely to have imitated Dorian's nature.

Theory as much as practice is at the heart of Wilde's opposition to Zola and Zolaism. He opposes in art the professionalization—which naturalizes by disguising law as fact—that he opposes in the realm of identity itself. Zola's novels are 'worked up from life with the same orderly regularity as any other professional is bound to give his business': the words are Mrs Humphry Ward's, praising Zola in 1884; put the same words in the disorderly Vivian's mouth and the ironies resound.[24] What to the scientist or Zolaist is the virtue of accurately observing hard fact is to Wilde the blindness that condemns one to a repetitive imitation of unselfconscious poses. What to the naturalist author is the prestige that comes from membership in a profession is to Wilde the diminution of personality. Realism is a prison, and the bars on its windows are called nature. But we are too much in love—even the artist is too much in love—with the so-called life that realism puts in place of art and form and beauty. The liar's salvific work is to lead us out of nature's prison, to free us from mere reality. To many politically progressive artists of the 1890s, including those interested in sexual freedom for women and homosexuals, realism, with its attention to the grim facts of an inequable social system, was the art of the future.[25] But to Wilde, realism is on the wrong side of a divide that separates imitation from creation, nature from form, life from art, realism from romance, and a supposedly natural sexuality from a sexuality which, like art, disdains any attempt to dictate limits.

Wilde had better company than the Vigilance Society in his opposition to naturalism's programme of art for science's sake. For instance, we get a summary of the doctrine Wilde is responding to, the doctrine of Zola's *Le Roman expérimental* (1880), in an article antagonistic to Zola, written in 1885 by W. S. Lilly, a frequent contributor to the *Nineteenth Century*:

The artist in experimental fiction is . . . merely a specialist, a *savant* who employs the same instruments as other *savants*, observation and analysis. . . . To be master of the mechanism of human phenomena, to exhibit the machinery (*les rouages*) of intellectual and sensual manifestations, as physiology shall explain them, under the influences of heredity and environment . . . —such is the theory of the experimental novel.[26]

Lilly goes on to make a distinction Wilde will also make in 'The Decay of Lying'; and in making it, both Lilly and Wilde are plagiarizing Swinburne—the most passionate anti-Zolaist of them all: 'But there is all the difference in the world between M. Zola's unimaginative realism and Balzac's imaginative reality' (247). In his *Study of Shakespeare* (1879), Swinburne had contrasted Balzac (good) and Zola (bad); and in a footnote he invokes Baudelaire to 'illustrate the distinction . . . between unimaginative realism and imaginative reality'. Wilde liked the phrase so much he used it twice, without acknowledgement, first in a review in 1886 (*Rev.* 78), then again in 'The Decay of Lying': 'The difference between such a book as M. Zola's *L'Assommoir* and Balzac's *Illusions Perdues* is the difference between unimaginative realism and imaginative reality' (17). And in both instances Wilde also quotes, with alterations, the passage from Baudelaire that Swinburne quotes.[27]

In Wilde's defence I could point out that what follows the stolen phrase in 'The Decay of Lying' is original and more interesting:

A steady course of Balzac reduces our living friends to shadows, and our acquaintances to the shadows of shades. . . . One of the greatest tragedies of my life is the death of Lucien de Rubempré. It is a grief from which I have never been able to completely rid myself. It haunts me in my moments of pleasure. I remember it when I laugh. (17)

But this would be a dangerous defence: a reader who does not believe that characters in books have a greater claim than the people in our lives may feel that plagiarism is the least of Wilde's faults in 'The Decay of Lying'. The essay's slipperiest point, the one that can either damn or justify the whole enterprise, is its central one, which keeps it still at the centre of theoretical debate: Is it true that 'Art never expresses anything but itself' (43)? And if it were possible for art to be so thoroughly self-referential, would it have anything worthwhile to express? Realists claim that they refer to a world out there; Wilde claims that the only significant out-there begins in here. The crucial insistence on art's self-referentiality is intended to create a separate, privileged zone where artists are free from moralizing censorship. In fact, however, aesthetics can be as rigidly policed as ethics; or, rather, the distinction between them vanishes at the policeman's knock. According to the Preface to *Dorian Gray*: 'There is no such thing as a moral or an immoral book. Books are well written, or badly written. That is all.' But it isn't: people decide what is well or badly written, and, as Wilde's own response to Zola suggests, subject-matter (what art expresses) easily creeps into the decision.

The essay's radical refusal to let nature take priority leads, not inevitably but problematically, to its radical anti-historicism. If 'Truth is entirely and absolutely a matter of style' (29) and if 'Art finds her own perfection within' (30) and 'never expresses anything but itself' (43), then art in no way 'expresses the temper of its age, the spirit of its time, the moral and social conditions that surround it, and under whose influence it is produced' (43). This anti-historicism is connected to a more modest observation. Vivian will not accept Cyril's proposition that 'the arts of imitation' express the visible aspects of an age. Rather, according to Vivian, 'the imitative arts really give us ... merely the various styles of particular artists, or of certain schools of artists' (45). This is a truth E. H. Gombrich rediscovers, in *Art and Illusion* (1960), when he points out that ancient Egyptian people looked nothing like ancient Egyptian drawings of people. But Vivian goes a step further: 'The Middle Ages, as we know them in art, are simply a definite form of style, *and there is no reason at all why an artist with this style should not be produced in the nineteenth century*' (45, my italics). Wilde's anti-historicism is a subcategory of his anti-realism. Linda Nochlin, writing about painting, says that 'The Realists held that the only valid subject for the contemporary artist was the contemporary world. *"Il faut être de son temps"* became their battle-cry.' And she quotes Courbet: '"I hold the artists of one century basically incapable of reproducing the aspect of a past or future century. ... Each epoch must have its artists who express it and reproduce it for the future ... The history of an era is finished with that era itself and with those of its representatives who have expressed it."'[28]

Vivian and Courbet are both right. Many Victorian artists did adopt a 'medieval' style, and their nineteenth-century medievalism is as rooted in and eloquent of the conditions of its production as is Courbet's realism; and so, by the same token, is Wilde's romantic, aesthetic, anti-historical anti-realism.

Wilde is more successful dealing with the moralism of the anti-Zolaists with whom he potentially allies himself. Vivian neatly turns the tables on them by making them out to be

Zola's allies rather than his. 'From any ethical standpoint [Zola's *Germinal*] is just what it should be. The author is perfectly truthful, and describes things exactly as they happen. What more can any moralist desire?' Moralists approve of truth-telling; Zola tells the truth; therefore Zola is moral— and therefore Zola's 'work is entirely wrong from beginning to end ... on the ground of art' (13). This is the Wildean paradox at its most effective, unsettling categories and revealing unsuspected affinities. A similar tactic is involved in Vivian's co-opting the moralists's language. As he describes them, modern cases of the decay of lying sound like cautionary tales about unnatural vice: 'Many a young man starts in life with a natural gift for exaggeration ... [but] either falls into careless habits of accuracy, or takes to frequenting the society of the aged and well-informed' (9–10). With words most commonly used in the 1890s to condemn 'decadence', Vivian now names a different pathology, the '*morbid* and *unhealthy* faculty of truth-telling' (10, italics added). 'Even Mr. Robert Louis Stevenson', he says, is 'tainted with this modern vice, for we know positively no other name for it' (10). Vivian's outrageous statement, 'We know positively no other name for it', has a real basis: Wilde has no language for moral condemnation—the category does not exist for him—so he must borrow the language of the moralists to whom condemnation comes so naturally. Because Wilde does not stoop to moralize, Vivian can parody the pseudo-scientific language of moral revulsion, which was currently being heard in its non-parodic form in attacks on *The Picture of Dorian Gray* as well as *Nana*.

Standard literary history is also captured and transformed in Wilde's effort to clear a space for his own art. The French novelists Wilde most reveres, Balzac and Flaubert, were often claimed as precursors of realism, but Wilde enlists them in his cause. Balzac especially is the hero of Wilde's (as of Swinburne's) anti-realist aesthetic. Elsewhere he could press even Ibsen into service, characteristically by taking him out of his place and time: watching *Hedda Gabler*, Wilde writes, 'I felt pity and terror, as though the play had been Greek' (letter to the Earl of Lytton [? May 1891]: *Letters*, 293).The idea of decadence itself is transvalued when Vivian traces the decline of art from abstract decoration until 'Life gets the upper hand, and drives Art out into the wilderness. This', says Wilde's persona, 'is the *true* decadence . . . ' (22; italics added).

Contemporary reviewers mostly responded to Wilde's attack on realism with amusement or condescension ('if one can believe [that nature imitates art], there is surely no further need to quote his arguments'[29]). Even Arthur Symons, promoter of decadence and symbolism, says only that 'The Decay of Lying' 'is a protest against realism. . . . It presents certain aesthetic doctrines, which Mr. Wilde partly believes . . . [it is] an old doctrine . . . in which there is . . . a perfectly reasonable view of things' (unsigned review, *Speaker*, 4 July 1891: *Heritage*, 95). An exception to the pat-on-the-back school was the American essayist Agnes Repplier, who nominated *Intentions* 'The Best Book of the Year'. In 'The Decay of Lying' she finds

clearly outlined a great truth that is slipping fast away from us—the absolute independence of art—art nourished by imagination and revealing beauty. This is the hand that gilds the grayness of the world; this is the voice that rings in flute tones through the silence of the ages. To degrade this shining vision into a handmaid of nature, to maintain that she should give us photographic pictures of an unlovely life, is a heresy that arouses in Mr. Wilde an amused scorn which takes the place of anger.[30]

But (as her Wildean pastiche suggests) even she found it difficult to say what, other than the old aestheticism or older romanticism, Wilde's alternative to realism actually *is*.

The reviewer in the *Nation* tried to define it: 'The substance is the old doctrine of idealism', he wrote. 'In characterizing idealism as a mode of "lying", Mr. Wilde, as he takes pains to intimate, starts from a Platonic point of view, or at least maintains analogy with the poet-doctrine of the "Republic".' But this tells us more about the difficulty of fixing Wilde's position than about the position itself. In both 'The Decay of Lying' and 'The Critic as Artist', Wilde does try to enlist Plato in his cause. But he is no Platonist. Platonic idealism posits a world of essential, unchangeable truth beyond the world of appearances; but 'The Decay of Lying' imagines a world in which truth is what we make and unmake, a world where nature pre-

vents us from seeing, not Plato's eternal forms, but the always
new forms of human creation. Platonism, with its ideal reality,
and realism, with its sordid reality, are equally unacceptable,
since they tie us to a nature not of our making.

3   'The Truth of Masks'

THE liar's claim that art refers to nothing but itself and has no relation to brute fact is in stark contrast to the position Wilde had taken in 1882/3 in his American lecture 'The English Renaissance of Art': 'For the artist . . . there is no escape from the bondage of the earth: there is not even the desire of escape. . . . [T]hat work is most instinct with spiritual life which conforms most clearly to the perfect fact of physical life' (*Misc.* 248). It is also in contrast to almost everything in the final essay in *Intentions* except its conclusion:

Not that I agree with everything I have said in this essay. There is much with which I entirely disagree. The essay simply represents an artistic standpoint, and in aesthetic criticism attitude is everything. For in art there is no such thing as a universal truth. A Truth in art is that whose contradictory is also true. And just as it is only in art-criticism, and through it, that we can apprehend the Platonic theory of ideas, so it is only in art-criticism, and through it, that we can realize Hegel's system of contraries. The truths of metaphysics are the the truths of masks. (258)

The calculated mixture of scholarship and cheek is perfect *Intentions*. The repetition of the idea of masks, of the multiplicity of personality, of self-contradiction as a virtue—all make the conclusion of 'The Truth of Masks' an appropriate conclusion to the volume. But the retraction is not just a witty formal gesture: it states a real fact. Between the publication of the essay in its original form as 'Shakespeare and Stage Costume' (*Nineteenth Century*, May 1885) and revision for *Intentions* in 1891, Wilde had changed his mind, or reshuffled his terms. A book that opens with a recently written defence of art's autonomy and a rejection of historicity ends with an older essay in defence of historical accuracy in stage design.

It is forgivable: worrying about the difference between romance and realism, illusion and reality in art is best left for examinations in which (as Wilde has it in 'Phrases and Philosophies for the Use of the Young') 'the foolish ask questions which the wise cannot answer'. Zola claims to work with the detachment of the experimental scientist, and produces a parable that reinscribes folkloristic formulae of sin and retribution. Ideological battles rage over a distinction whose differences vanish in a blink. W. S. Lilly, in an article written in the same year as 'Shakespeare and Stage Costume', distinguishes what he calls the 'Old Naturalism' from Zola's 'New Naturalism' as the difference between idealism and realism: 'The one is dominated by the ideal, and in a true sense is, and cannot help being, religious. The other is strictly materialistic and professes atheism.'[1] Fighting words, which John Addington Symonds, in the year of *Intentions*, easily sets against themselves: 'It is one of the *mauvaises plaisanteries* of the epoch to call M. Zola a realist. Actually, he is an idealist of the purest water; and if idealists are Philistines, then Gath can claim him for her own.' Symonds analyses 'the poetic unity' of *La Bête humaine* and concludes that Zola's novel 'has all those qualities of the constructive reason by which an ideal is distinguished from the bare reality'.[2]

In the same year, 1891, Shaw, in *The Quintessence of Ibsenism*, was wreaking havoc with the counters marked 'idealism' and 'realism'. '[W]e unfortunately use this word ideal differently to denote both the institution which the ideal masks [i.e. a conception of the institution as it ought to be but is not] and the mask itself, thereby producing desperate confusion of thought, since the institution may be an effete and poisonous one, whilst the mask may be, and indeed generally is, an image of what we would fain have in its place'. Shaw himself, like Ibsen, is, he says, an idealist since he sees through the insitution to what 'we would fain have in [the institution's] place'. But that seeing through makes him, like Ibsen, also a realist, and of the two transferable terms Shaw prefers realist over idealist: 'If the term realist is objected to on account of some of its modern associations, I can only recommend to you, if you must associate it with something else than my own description of its meaning (I do not deal in definitions), to associate it, not with Zola and Maupassant, but with Plato' (126–7). In Shavian terms, a realist is someone with enough idealism to reject ideals: 'Unfortunately this is the sort of speech nobody but a realist understands' (128).[3]

And it is the sort of definitional bog Wilde found himself in when he revised the old essay for the new volume. It is a bog that would be worth avoiding except that the problem involves not only definitions but actual plays and productions, where theory and practice meet. The revisionary process maps the evolution of Wilde's polemical relationship with realism, as it became clarified in his relations with one of realism's oddest fellow-travellers. And again, as with 'The Decay of Lying', it suggests a way in which Wilde's literary politics can be sexual politics also, all dedicated to a frankly utopian ideal here associated with the positive state he calls illusion. So I begin a consideration of 'The Truth of Masks' with the problem of revision.

'Shakespeare and Stage Costume' is not a promising title. Its earnestness belongs to a moment when Wilde, recently retired from the lecture platform and newly set up as a reviewer, needed to establish his credentials, and had not yet found the gravity-defying stance he would assume in 'The Decay of Lying' and 'The Critic as Artist'. The titular problem was easily solved: 'The Truth of Masks' is an appropriately paradoxical title that gives the volume's last essay an appearance of symmetry with 'The Decay of Lying', its first. But its contents were more intractable.

'Shakespeare and Stage Costume' is a response to 'the somewhat violent attacks that have recently been made on the splendour of mounting which now characterizes our Shakespearean revivals in England'.[4] In high-dudgeoned particular, it is a response to the attack contained in a single footnote in Lord Lytton's review of Mary Anderson playing Juliet at the Lyceum.[5] Lytton himself was defending Anderson's performance against almost universally bad reviews, like the one in the *Saturday Review* which accused her of (among other crimes) 'occasionally laps[ing] into the American language'. Lytton assures readers that his 'own ear is more sensitive than most men's to the rhythmic sentiment and sound of blank verse properly spoken', and that his superior auditory equipment found few faults in Mary Anderson's delivery.[6] The actress he was defending was an actress Wilde, too, had reason to defend: in New York in 1882/3 he had tried, unsuccessfully, to persuade her to star in *The Duchess of Padua*—it would, he assured her, give her the glory of Rachel, and him the fame of Hugo ([early Sept. 1882]: *Letters*, 125); again in January 1885, possibly still hoping for that great event, he congratulated her 'on the marvellous development of your art' (*Letters*, 167).

So it was not Lytton's treatment of Mary Anderson that galvanized Wilde to retaliate in 'Shakespeare and Stage Costume'. It was, rather, his implied treatment of an unnamed offstage presence. That absent presence is also hinted at in other reviewers' reactions to the production's spectacular, historically accurate sets and costumes, which seemed to them to compete with more important theatrical values. Clement Scott, for instance, wrote that 'Silks and satins, stuffs and tapestry, the shape of a shoe, the cut of a gown, the form of a lamp, the topography of a street are preferred to the interpretation of any one given part.'[7] Lytton chipped in with his offending footnote. He found 'the scenic representation' of Verona 'faultless' but, he added,

I say this without reference to the archaeology of it. The attempt to archaeologise the Shakespearean drama is one of the stupidest pedantries of this age of prigs. Archaeology would not be more out of place in a fairy tale than it is in a play of Shakespeare. This scene is beautiful and animated, and that is all that is wanted. (886)

The unnamed pedant and prig, who in fact had nothing to do with the production, was E. W. Godwin, architect and aesthete, father of Ellen Terry's two illegitimate children, interior designer to both Whistler and Wilde, chief theorist and practitioner of the movement 'to archaeologise' not only the Shakespearean drama but the Greek, the modern historical, and anything else he could get his hands on.

Godwin's career in the theatre has been analysed by John Stokes:

Godwin's position in the Aesthetic milieu was absolutely central but hidden; he was particularly intimate with Wilde, and his undisclosed influence on the man who through his public appearances became more a parody of the movement than its true representative was considerable. The lectures on interior decoration and dress reform that Wilde delivered on his sensational tour of America in 1881 were largely based, unacknowledged, on the teachings of Godwin, who was perhaps too scholarly (or, more likely, too notorious) to receive much publicity himself.[8]

At a time when being an architect meant taking sides in the debate between Gothic revivalists and Classical revivalists, Godwin's interests turned increasingly towards historical research, and from historical research to the theatre where history was staged. Stokes records that 'Between 1874 and 1875, Godwin published thirty-two articles on "The Architecture and Costume of Shakespeare's Plays"' (37). In 1875 he was 'historical adviser' to the Bancrofts in their production of *The Merchant of Venice*, starring his soon to be ex-lover Ellen Terry. It was the first in a series of theatrical involvements leading to Godwin's assuming the kind of power—'one single mind directing the whole production'—which Wilde proposes in 'Shakespeare and Stage Costume': 'Monarchy, Anarchy, and Republicanism may contend for the government of nations; but a theatre should be under the absolute power of a cultured despot' (817). The doctrine Godwin despotically professed was 'archaeology': the doctrine that in order to be aesthetically beautiful a production had also to be historically accurate.

Wilde, responding to Lytton's attack on archaeology in stage design, was defending one of those strong influences, like Pater, Arnold, Emerson, Ruskin, Morris, or Whistler, whose ideas (and sometimes words) he habitually tried to assimilate despite their frequent incompatibility. It was one of the occasions when Wilde seemed to be fighting a historically retrograde cause. Stage archaeology was related to the same pictorial tendency as W. P. Frith's busy realistic canvasses *Derby Day* and *Ramsgate Sands*, which Gilbert makes fun of in 'The Critic as Artist': 'a lady once gravely asked . . . if his celebrated picture . . . was all painted by hand' (100). But it was also related to the aestheticism of the preceding decades. Michael R. Booth points out the connection between theatrical archaeology and the Pre-Raphaelites' 'commitment to the recreation of history' in the shape of medieval legend or biblical tale, the 'painstaking research techniques for the duplication of historical reality' that led Millais to float Lizzie Siddal in a bath to paint her as the drowning Ophelia.[9] And it was related to the succession of great archaeological digs throughout the century: to Wilde, stage archaeology might recapture some of the excitement of the Elgin Marbles or the rediscovered Nineveh.

Taking up the Godwinian cause, Wilde commits himself to at least one aesthetic principle, only accidentally related to historical accuracy, which he could wholeheartedly maintain, the requirement for 'unity' and 'harmony' of effect. His review of *Helena in Troas* (22 May 1886) explains the aesthetic appeal of Godwin's archaeology:

Mr. Godwin is something more than a mere antiquarian. He takes the facts of archaeology, but he converts them into artistic and dramatic effects, and the historical accuracy that underlies the visible shapes of beauty that he presents to us, is not by any means the distinguishing quality of the complete work of art. This quality is the absolute unity and harmony of the entire presentation, the presence of one mind controlling the most minute details, and revealing itself only in that true perfection which hides personality. (*Rev.* 72)

So far so good, except that by committing himself to Godwin's archaeologizing control he also commits himself to defending positions he would stand—or levitate—two-square against in 'The Decay of Lying' and 'The Critic as Artist'.

Wilde begins his essay by demonstrating the obvious, that 'costume . . . is one of the essential factors of the means which a realistic dramatist has at his disposal' ('Stage Costume', 805). Expanding from the claim that Shakespeare ('a realistic dramatist') was interested in costume to the claim that he was interested in the impressive and expressive possibilities of *all* forms of theatrical spectacle, Wilde draws the conclusion that only the technological limitations of the Elizabethan stage kept Shakespeare from employing the full panoply of stage effects available to the late nineteenth-century theatre. Specifically, Shakespeare was an archaeologist *avant la lettre*:

Archaeology . . . was a means by which [Renaissance artists] could touch the dry dust of antiquity into the breath and beauty of life, and fill with the new wine of romanticism forms that else had been old and outworn . . . And this use of archaeology in shows, so far from being a bit of priggish pedantry, is in every way legitimate and beautiful. ('Stage Costume', 807)

Like the nineteenth-century theatrical archaeologist, Shakespeare used historical accuracy for the sake of a higher aim:
'Of course the aesthetic value of Shakespeare's plays does not,
in the slightest degree, depend on their facts, but on their
truth, and truth is independent of facts always, inventing or
selecting them at pleasure. But still Shakespeare's adherence
to facts is a most interesting part of his method of work, and
shows his attitude toward the stage, and his relations with
realism' ('Stage Costume', 811).

Wilde's own adherence to, or contempt for, facts is a most
interesting part of *his* method; it was one of the things he had
to worry about when he revised the essay for *Intentions*. We
have heard Vivian, in 'The Decay of Lying', deploring the
'monstrous worship of facts' that makes art 'sterile' (10). In
'The Critic as Artist' Gilbert tells Ernest that 'To give an accurate description of what has never occurred is not merely the
proper occupation of the historian, but the inalienable privilege of any man of parts and culture' (114). Ernest accuses
Gilbert of rewriting history; Gilbert responds, 'The one duty
we owe to history is to re-write it' (133). So Wilde's use of such
Godwinian terms as accuracy and fidelity in 'Shakespeare and
Stage Costume' was anomalous by the time he revised the
essay for the volume that opened with a defence of lying. Still,
it was not an insuperable problem, since, presumably, the
artist as liar or the critic as artist might use archaeological
accuracy as a means to achieve the imaginative rewriting of
history. But related to *accuracy* and *fidelity* was that other word,
realism—as in 'archaeology is not a pedantic method, but a
method of realism' ('Stage Costume', 818)—and after 'The
Decay of Lying' and 'The Critic as Artist', 'realism' really was a
stumbling-block, even for an author unbothered by the hob-
goblin of a foolish consistency.

In the version of theatre history given in 'The Decay of
Lying', realism is the original sin, always tempting the playwright to bring on 'life' to shatter 'the perfection of form' (24).
Even Shakespeare 'is too fond of going directly to life, and
borrowing life's natural utterance' (24): 'the magnificent work
of the Elizabethan and Jacobean artists contained within itself
the seeds of its dissolution . . . it drew some of its strength from
using life as a rough material, it drew all its weakness from

using life as an artistic method' (25). The present moment in theatre history was the crisis of that long disease called realism:

As the inevitable result of this substitution of an imitative for a creative medium, this surrender of imaginative form, we have modern English melodrama. The characters in these plays talk exactly on the stage as they would talk off it; they have neither aspiration nor aspirates; they are taken directly from life and reproduce its vulgarity down to the smallest detail; they present the gait, manner, costume and accent of real people; they would pass unnoticed in a third-class railway carriage. And yet how wearisome the plays are! They do not succeed in producing that impression of reality at which they aim, and which is their only reason for existing. (25)

In this passage, the terms alluding to social class (dropped aspirates, vulgarity, a third-class railway carriage) allow the possibility that the problem with realism is its subject-matter: realism offends by making visible certain sordid facts of economic and social life. But the passage goes on to claim that the offending plays, though they 'reproduce' life in every detail, fail to produce the 'impression of reality'—a claim about mediation which goes beyond the social particulars to a more sweeping attack on mimesis itself. Not the matter but the method fails: the imitation of reality is self-defeating; realism can never produce the impression of the thing it pretends to be. This more sweeping attack on the failure of realism impugns not only the method of Zola but also that of Wilde's aesthetic mentor, E. W. Godwin: the pursuit of historical accuracy would be just a higher-class version of the suicidal longing to find real life by imitating rather than creating.

In 'Shakespeare and Stage Costume' Wilde is in danger of making Shakespeare an avatar of Zola, and himself a defender of imitation against imaginative creation. And that is how he was understood by the anonymous author of an article called 'Archaeology in the Theatre', an answer to 'Shakespeare and Stage Costume', which damns archaeological productions as 'eminently characteristic of a scientific age' and 'based on what may be called a theory of historical realism'.[10] Wilde's opponent concludes with a plea that Wilde himself could have made, had he not been otherwise engaged—a plea for a non-archaeological 'revival that would assert the supremacy of the imaginative qualities of the drama, and repudiate once for all, as robbing it of half its significance, the pedantic rule of a pretentious and uncertain realism' (134).

Recognizing how far his devotion to Godwin had led him astray, Wilde in revising the essay brazened out the change I have already quoted, the appended sentences of quasipalinode which turned the 'truth' of his defence of archaeology into a demonstration of the relativity of any truth in art. But he also made another, subtler and less well known, revision: wherever the fatally tainted word realism or its cognates appeared, Wilde changed the word to 'illusion'.

Thus in the sentence '[costume] is one of the essential factors of the means which a realistic dramatist has at his disposal', 'a realistic dramatist' became 'a true illusionist' ('Stage Costume', 805; 'The Truth of Masks', 228); '[archaeology] can combine in one exquisite presentation absolute reality with the grace and charm of the antique world' became 'the illusion of actual life with the wonder of the unreal world' (808; 235); Shakespeare's 'relations to realism' became his 'relations to the great art of illusion' (811; 242); 'historical accuracy of costume as a most important adjunct to his realistic method' became 'his illusionist method' (811; 242); costume is 'a most vital element in producing a realistic effect' became 'an illusionist effect' (814; 249); 'archaeology is not a pedantic method, but a method of realism' became 'a method of artistic illusion' (818; 257). Even one of the essay's few good jokes had to suffer the illusion–reality switcheroo: 'The burning of the Globe Theatre —an event, by the way, due to the realism of Shakespeare's stage management' became 'the results of the passion for illusion that distinguished Shakespeare's stage-management' (806; 229).

Realism was banished elsewhere as well: 'the modern realistic spirit' became simply 'the modern spirit' (813; 246); while 'illusion' was inserted at several points: 'his effects' became 'his illusionist effects' (800; 218); 'his plays . . . depend entirely on the character of the various dresses' became 'depend for their illusion on the character of the various dresses' (801; 219); 'Archaeological accuracy is merely a condition of fine stage effect' became 'of illusionist stage effect' (814; 247–8), and the sentence that ended the essay in its original form, warning opponents of archaeology that 'if they will not encourage, at least they must not oppose, a movement which Shakespeare of all dramatists would have most approved; for it has Truth for its aim, and Beauty for its result' ('Stage Costume' 818), obscured its Keatsian echo to become 'it has the illusion of truth for its method, and the illusion of beauty for its result' ('Truth', 257). To finish the affair, Wilde gave the retitled, amended essay a subtitle: 'A Note on Illusion'.

But realism, reality, and all that are not so easy to get rid of. They are especially likely to crop up in the country, where nature's effects can impress the spectator as though they were art itself.

On 6 June 1885—two weeks after the appearance of 'Shakespeare and Stage Costume'—the reviewer for the *Era* wrote that

The battle between the Idealists and the Realists of the stage, between those who hold that the mounting of a play should leave much to the imagination, and those who maintain that the setting of a play should imitate reality with photographic accuracy, has long raged furiously, and is yet undecided. . . . In London we have ranged on one side every dramatic critic of repute; on the other, the managements of the chief West End theatres and the authority, on this point by no means despicable, of Mr. Oscar Wilde.[11]

Even in 1885 it must have been painful for Wilde to see himself allied with the theatrical proponents of 'photographic accuracy' which leaves nothing to the imagination. To make matters worse, the realists (supposedly under Wilde's banner) were, for the moment, victorious.[12] The place was the pleasantly wooded Coombe Park near Kingston upon Thames in Surrey; the production was 'the forest scenes' of *As You Like It*, staged by a mixed cast of professionals and amateurs; according to the *Era*, 'Saturday was certainly the Realists' day out at Coombe. Not only did the mounting leave nothing to the imagination, more even than imitating reality with photographic accuracy, it was reality itself'.[13]

The theatrical event which seemed to the *Era* to be the proof of Wilde's realist pudding was 'Arranged and Produced Under the direction of Mr. E. W. Godwin' in July 1884 and was revived in May 1885. Alfred Austin—'the poet of Nature, of

Patriotism', as the *Observer* called him in 1891—described the genesis and reception of the 1884 production: in his heavy-handed comic account, the triumph of realism begins as the talk of the town at the end of a dull London season. Austin then tells how the *beau monde* went to the country to scoff and stayed to cheer. He himself was present at the third performance, scheduled for 26 July '"by special desire"' of 'the Heir Apparent':

[When] the Heirs to the two most powerful thrones in the world, when Princes and Princesses, Ambassadors and Secretaries of State, fair rulers of society, gifted composers, renowned artists, serious men of letters, popular actors, and yet more popular actresses, with the due sprinkling of notorious nobodies, made their way to the gardens of Coombe Park, once the home of a Prime Minister, and, seventy years ago, the spot where Plenipotentiaries met to decide upon the fate of Europe, they might be surprised when they found themselves in an *al fresco* theatre, the material accessories of which, at least, betokened no prentice hand, and in which, if the trace of the amateur was anywhere visible, it was discerned only in the crowning grace that had been added to the precision of the professional craft.[14]

It is hard to say which is the bigger surprise: that the country turns out to be a place where real (not illusory) power is exercised; or that the powerful socialites did not disgrace themselves by their amateur status as realistic artists.

Austin, like the reviewer in the *Era* the following year, makes much of the *natural* setting. 'One found oneself comfortably seated and shut in'—in, John Stokes explains, 'an "auditorium", some forty feet wide and seventy feet deep ... curtained off with sage-green material and filled with three hundred chairs in tiers'[15]—'with green leaves and blue sky for canopy, and in front of tall, straight-growing elms, whose lower trunks were hidden from view by a loosely-stretched curtain' (128). When that curtain fell, 'you were [wrote Austin] in the Forest of Arden; not a painted semblance of the forest, not a dextrous picture befooling the eye for a moment, but Arden itself, with its sylvan occupants, its green shades, its cool glimpses, its grassy sward, its colouring bracken, its fallen boughs and branches, its fortuitous fagots, its hind's shelter, its twitter of birds and glitter of butterflies, its flocks and distant bleating, all things native and natural, as to the manner born' (128).

Amazing!—as Godwin's good friend Whistler, who was also present, might have said. One of Shakespeare's most sophisticated exercises in literary self-consciousness, with books in its brooks and tongues in its trees and with a cast of characters drawn (and named) from epic, satire, pastoral— calling to mind a Steinberg drawing in which various art-historical styles promiscuously cohabit—is staged in fashion-able Surrey, and that, according to the reviewer, is 'Arden itself', or even, as the man from the *Era* said, 'reality itself'. Victorian society undertakes (in Wilde's phrase) 'an hour's drive to exchange Piccadilly for Parnassus' (*Rev.* 36) and believes that it has outstripped the mediations of art and entered some veritable place called Pastoral. But my point is not to belabour the reviewers' semiological naïvety. I am inter-ested, rather, in what Wilde made of the Coombe Park affair, and in what it tells us about his own theatrical practices and theoretical postures, including especially his intention to dramatize the illusiveness of gender masks and sexual roles.

Wilde reviewed the revival of the Coombe *As You Like It* in the *Dramatic Review* of 6 June 1885.[16] He begins by calling attention to a fact which is totally, even ostentatiously, repressed in Austin's article—that in this production which was 'reality itself', Orlando was a woman named Archie. Or rather, to pay dues both to Illusion and Reality, Orlando was played by a woman, Lady Archibald Campbell, familiarly called (for instance in correspondence between Wilde and Whistler) Lady Archie ([? June 1882]: *Letters*, 121). It was Lady Archie, in fact, who actually conceived the production, enlisted Godwin, assembled the troupe of professionals and society folk called the Pastoral Players, and gave herself the starring male role.

On Shakespeare's stage a boy played the role of the young woman who disguises herself as a man. For at least some members of the Elizabethan audience the convention would have offered not only what Catherine Belsey calls 'the pleasure of a knowingness which depends on a knowledge of sexual difference', but also (as Belsey points out) might have called sexual difference 'in question by indicating that it is possible, at least in fiction, to speak from a position which is not that of a full, unified, gendered subject'.[17] In Victorian Surrey, now, a woman plays the part of a man wooing (an actress playing) a woman disguised as a man. Most of the reviewers treat that production as the triumph of unmediated realism—of nature reconciled with art; and they applaud a mixed cast of professional actors and society people united in an archaeologically accurate aesthetic production under Godwin's benevolent despotism. Wilde's review seems to agree with the consensus, but it differs in one striking particular: it begins with a set of allusions which, for those who want to see it, makes visible the disruption of 'natural' gender roles in Lady Archie's performance.[18]

I have referred to these few lines previously; I do so again because the allusions are worth excavating: text upon text leads to the assertion of a sexual desire which does not follow realism's script, which is playfully creative rather than imitative:

> In Théophile Gautier's first novel, that golden book of spirit and sense, that holy writ of beauty, there is a most fascinating account of an amateur performance of *As You Like It* in the large orangery of a French country house. Yet, lovely as Gautier's description is, the real presentation of the play last week at Coombe seemed to me lovelier still, for not merely were there present in it all those elements of poetry and picturesqueness which *le maître impeccable* so desired, but to them was added also the exquisite charm of the open woodland and the delightful freedom of the open air. (*Rev.* 32)

Wilde's epithets ('golden book of spirit and sense', 'holy writ of beauty') are quotations from Swinburne's 'Sonnet (With a Copy of *Mademoiselle de Maupin*)'. The sonnet is an ambiguous paean to indeterminate sexuality as an endless experience of seeking and losing 'that beauty's excellence / Wherewith love makes one hour of life distraught / And all hours after follow and find not aught'. In Swinburne's version of Gautier's novel, the 'height of all love's eminence' is a place

> Where man may breathe but for a breathing-space
>   And feel his soul burn as an altar-fire
>   To the unknown God of unachieved desire,
> And from the middle mystery of the place
>   Watch lights that break, hear sounds as of a quire,
> But see not twice unveiled the veiled God's face.[19]

Love's eminence is less achievement than frustration, a 'breathing space' while the soul in devotion burns 'To the unknown God of unachieved desire'—a veiled erotic God of 'middle mystery', lord of the not-yet-attained. It is an earnestly ardent description of the prolonged and often comic sexual peekaboo of Gautier's novel.

The Swinburnian phrase Wilde applies to *Mademoiselle de Maupin* in his 1885 review he applied in 1890 to Pater's *The Renaissance*.[20] The two books were always associated in Wilde's mind. Ellmann (268) says that 'Pater had lent [Gautier's novel] to Wilde at the inception of their close friendship'. Both books had, as Wilde was to say of *The Renaissance*, 'a strange influence over my life' (*De Profundis*: *Letters*, 471). The Preface to Gautier's novel was a model for the Preface to *The Picture of Dorian Gray*: 'All art is quite useless', Wilde writes, echoing Gautier's even more brash 'tout ce qui est utile est laid . . .—L'endroit le plus utile d'une maison, ce sont les latrines'.[21] Gautier's preface, because of its status as a source of aesthetic and decadent attitudes, is now better known to many of Wilde's readers than Gautier's novel itself. But it is the novel, which had, like Pater's book, a strange influence over Wilde's life, and which provides the subtext for his comment on Lady Archie's Rosalind.

Gautier's male narrator, D'Albert, goes in search of a love he knows is impossible because any attainable 'real woman, eating and drinking, getting up in the morning and going to bed at night' (23), is only an approximation of the ideal beauty, the 'chimera', men find in works of art, and which nature palely imitates. His actual mistress, the ardent Rosette, 'believes me the most amorous man on earth; she takes this impotent transport for a transport of passion; and to the best of her ability she lends herself to all the experimental caprices that enter my head' (50). But consummated heterosexual desire, however inventive, becomes, for D'Albert, less satisfying the harder he works at it; as he writes in his epistolary narration:

If you knew all that I have done to compel my soul to share in the love of my body, the frenzy with which I have plunged my mouth into hers, and steeped my arms in her hair, and how closely I have strained her round and supple form! Like the ancient Salmacis enamoured of the young Hermaphrodite, I strove to blend her frame with mine. . . . The more she drew me towards her, and the closer our embraces, the less I loved her. (50)

The reference to Salmacis and Hermaphrodite prepares us for the entrance of a new figure in the novel: a young cavalier, whose 'only fault [is] that he is too beautiful, and has too delicate features for a man', arrives at the country house: 'Here, then, is at last one of the types of beauty that I dreamed of realised and walking before me! What a pity that he is a man, or that I am not a woman!' (95).

The narrative shifts out of D'Albert's epistolary voice to give us a teasingly voyeuristic third-person view of the cavalier alone with his young page: the master, on his knees, draws off the sleepy child's boots, kisses his lovely feet and exquisite legs, unfastens his belt. 'It was certainly', the narrator informs us, 'a very graceful picture. . . . The master was as beautiful as a woman, the page as beautiful as a young girl' (97). The scene is titillatingly trangressive however we take it: either both figures are male, or both are cross-dressed females, or an aristocratic adult is sexually abasing himself or herself before a youthful servant. The cavalier, called Théodore de Sérannes, 'will after long narrative dilation be revealed as Madelaine, the eponymous Mlle de Maupin; and the page boy is in fact a girl: but the drawn-out indeterminacy of this scene, opening a range of still veiled, unachieved sexual possibilities, generates its erotic energy.

The reader gets plenty of hints that the object of D'Albert's desire is female; but those hints, possibly like the Elizabethan audience's knowledge of sexual difference in the scenes between Orlando and Ganymede, do not limit the imaginative possibilities; instead, they open a space to experience through D'Albert's flirtation with homosexual desire—and then through the mirroring lesbian desire recounted in 'the cavalier's' own narrative—a dazzling range of polymorphous sexuality. For his part, D'Albert eventually faces up to one of the two now equal facts of his situation: 'I love a man', he writes at the end of chapter 8; and, at the beginning of chapter 9, 'I long sought to delude myself; I gave a different name to the feeling that I experienced; I clothed it in the garment of pure and disinterested friendship . . . but the fact, alas! is only too certain, I love this young man not from friendship but from love;—yes, from love' (131) ('non d'amitié, mais d'amour;—oui, d'amour' (189)).

Briefly, D'Albert throws himself enthusiastically into the possibility of same-sex desire. But certainty proves less appealing than having it both ways: like Swinburne he becomes a devotee of the 'unknown god' who dwells in 'middle mystery'. The hermaphrodite, according to D'Albert, was 'one of the most eagerly cherished chimeras of idolatrous antiquity . . . one of the sweetest creations of Pagan genius':[22]

To an exclusive worshipper of form, can there be a more delightful uncertainty than that into which you are thrown by the sight of the back, the ambiguous loins, and the strong, delicate legs, which you are doubtful whether to attribute to Mercury ready to take his flight or to Diana coming from the bath? The torso is compounded of the most charming monstrosities . . . (146–47)

He continues to agonize over his attitude to Théodore's sexual identity, but concludes, 'It is a singular thing that I have nearly ceased to think about his sex, and that I love him in perfect indifference to it' (147) ('je l'aime avec une sécurité parfaite' (206)).

And so Gautier's characters stage As You Like It. Rosette, D'Albert's indefatigable lover, refuses (because she will not cross-dress) to play Rosalind; instead, we get a situation that might have confused even Shakespeare, or Lady Archibald Campbell: Madelaine disguised as Théodore playing Rosalind playing Ganymede to D'Albert's Orlando. (And Rosette, who has wooed Théodore in 'his' disguise as a man, now plays Phoebe and finds herself attracted to Théodore's Rosalind.) 'Yes', says D'Albert, 'who would not wish to be the Orlando to such a Rosalind, even at the cost of the torments I have suffered?' (198). In Wilde's poem 'The Sphinx'—which he began at Oxford, worked on again in Paris in 1883, and completed in 1894—we can hear echoes of D'Albert's reaction to the enactment of his fantasy, making love under the cover of licit art to a figure of illicit, indeterminate sexuality: D'Albert/Orlando describes his experience as 'a monstrous love that could not be confessed', he is 'devoured by insane longings without excuse even in the eyes of the most abandoned libertines', 'a passion ashamed of itself and hopeless, whose improbable success would be a crime and would cause you to die of shame' (198). What D'Albert calls 'this monstrosity' replaces 'the fresh and chaste illusions of early years'; that innocence is 'metamorphosed into this perfidious sphinx with doubtful smile and ambiguous voice' (198) ('ce sphinx perfide, au sourire douteux, à la voix ambiguë' (266)).

From here until the end of the novel D'Albert refers to the sphinx–cavalier as 'Rosalind'. In 'Rosalind's' own interspersed epistolary narrative, we get the retrospective story of her cross-dressing and her passionate wooing by Rosette. She finds that 'In truth, neither of the two sexes are mine. . . . I belong to a third, distinct sex, which as yet has no name' (282) ('je suis d'un troisième sexe à part que n'a pas encore de nom' (363)). At the novel's end 'Rosalind' comes to D'Albert, dressed as she had been in *As You Like It*, except that now her breasts are bare: '"Well! Orlando, do you not recognize Rosalind?" said the fair one with the most charming smile' (290). She declares herself a virgin, and D'Albert/Orlando plays out the expectedly pornographic script:

The divine moment approached. A final obstacle was surmounted, a supreme spasm convulsed the two lovers, and the curious Rosalind became as enlightened as possible on a matter which had so deeply perplexed her. Still, one lesson, no matter how intelligent one may be, cannot suffice; D'Albert gave her a second and a third. (295)

Sexual difference and a preference for heterosexuality seem to be reasserted as pedantically as possible; but in the next moment, as D'Albert sleeps, the 'prodigiously apt' Rosalind slips from the room and 'Instead of returning to her own room she entered Rosette's' (296). The coy narrator claims to be unable to say what happened here, but Rosette's maid tells him that 'the bed was disturbed and tossed, and bore the impress of two bodies. Further, she showed me two pearls, exactly similar to those worn in his hair by Théodore when acting the part of Rosalind. She found them in the bed when making it' (296).

So Rosalind/Théodore/Madelaine slips out of the lives of D'Albert and Rosette, leaving only an epistolary trace declaring that once was enough. Neither D'Albert nor Rosette will see (as Swinburne has it) 'twice unveiled the veiled God's face'.

When Wilde saw 'the real presentation' of *As You Like It* at Coombe, then, he saw Gautier's praise of illusion as well as Godwin's triumph of historical accuracy; he saw a production in which some of the actors were aristocrats who (like Vivian and Cyril) lord it over nature; he saw staged the anxiety as well as the pleasure of belonging to what Mlle de Maupin calls 'a third, distinct sex, which as yet has no name' (282);[23] he saw the 'poetry and picturesqueness' of a novel which defers realism's accurate differentiation in favour of a prolonged erotics of illusion, with that illusion made 'lovelier still' by 'the exquisite charm of the open woodland and the delightful freedom of the open air':

[A]nd Lady Archibald Campbell's Orlando was a really remarkable performance. Too melancholy some seemed to think it. Yet is not Orlando lovesick? Too dreamy, I heard it said. Yet Orlando is a poet. And even admitting that the vigour of the lad who tripped up the Duke's wrestler was hardly sufficiently emphasised, still in the low music of Lady Archibald Campbell's voice, and in the strange beauty of her movements and gestures, there was a wonderful fascination, and the visible presence of romance quite consoled me for the possible absence of robustness. (*Rev.* 34–5)

Wilde praises this aristocratic amateur whose social and financial resources could prove useful to him; but his apology for her epicene performance has traces of a characteristic vocabulary—'strange beauty' and 'wonderful fascination'—which points towards the subversive romance of Gautier's golden book and even towards the temptations Dorian Gray finds in Lord Henry Wotton's merely yellow book. In Coombe Park's 'delightful freedom', Wilde finds a nature in which sexuality is unconstrained by the realism that, purporting to imitate it, delimits and polices it.

Two years after writing this review he became editor of *The Lady's World*—a title he changed to *The Woman's World* to remove the 'taint of vulgarity' from a magazine intended to be 'the organ of women of intellect, culture, and position' (*Letters*, 203). The first article in his first issue is called 'The Woodland

Gods', written by Lady Archibald Campbell under the name Janey Sevilla Campbell. On the first page is an illustration labelled 'Orlando': the figure lies in melancholy repose at the base of a large tree; on the next page, a smaller drawing shows 'Orlando' standing. The Coombe Park trees are prominent in the third and most striking illustration, a photograph of a scene from a subsequent Pastoral Players production, of John Fletcher's *The Faithful Shepherdess*: it is entitled *Perigot and Amaryllis*, and this time Lady Archie, as the pastoral hero, looks directly at the viewer, her slightly hooded eyes suggesting not only melancholy but defiance, as Perigot holds and comforts a cowering and very conventionally feminine Amaryllis.

In a helpful article on Wilde's editorship of *Woman's World*, Laurel Brake says that Wilde's project 'included not only the construction of the cultivated, new woman but the introduction of male, homosexual discourse into female space'; 'in the first number [she writes] is a piece on a theatrical subject, "The Woodland Gods", heavily illustrated with plates of comely young men in costume'; a 'languorous Orlando . . . greets the reader'; and this 'Orlando is able to function as an image (akin to a pin-up) which cultured women and aesthetic or gay men consume'.[24] Brake is apparently unaware that the 'comely young men in costume' are all of them Lady Archibald Campbell, or that Lady Archie is the article's author, Janey Sevilla Campbell. Much of the article is devoted to obituary praise of Godwin, who had died in 1886, and to the history of their joint efforts in the Pastoral Players: the identity of the author is, in effect, part of the article's subject. Still, Laurel Brake's confusion is understandable, since there is nothing in Lady Archie's article—as there had not been in Alfred Austin's 1884 review—which would alert her to the fact that Orlando was played by a woman.

Instead, Lady Archie's article—commissioned by Wilde and placed at the front of his first editorial effort—plods, as earlier reviews did, over the boggy ground of illusion and reality. When she 'first thought of open-air plays it was repeatedly said to me that art and Nature could not be brought into contact without destroying dramatic effect'; but she replied 'that there were certain plays, of which the chief elements and sur-

roundings were so eminently natural, that open-air representation would . . . strengthen their dramatic effect'.[25] With the
meaning of 'natural' so firmly reduced to the out-of-doors,
Lady Archie can promulgate Godwin's doctrine, which
'assimilated art to Nature, and Nature to art' (3), while simultaneously distancing herself from 'the realism of the common-
place, the every-day life which, whether sensational or not,
appeals in no way to our sense of beauty' (2). Now, nature is
associated with things-that-palpably-are (like real trees in real
forests), but this unmediated nature is the setting of romance
and beauty, while realism is associated only with 'the
common-place'.

Lady Archibald Campbell knows that 'the drama can never
be strictly said to be imitative of Nature, but only representative' (1). She herself, the patroness of 'actual pastoral life' (4),
might be said to descend to us in a circuit of representations,
the perfect image of life imitating art. According to John
Stokes, 'the idea [for the Coombe Park production] originated
with Lady Archibald, after she had painted the actress Eleanor
Calhoun as Rosalind, using for background the woods of
Coombe Warren in Surrey'.[26] Lady Archie herself was
famously painted by Whistler: she is the *Arrangement in Black:
The Lady in the Yellow Buskin* (1882–4), whose attractively disdainful face, turned back towards the viewer over a shoulder
which, enigmatically, is either warning us off or inviting us
hither, now hangs in the Philadelphia Museum of Art. Originally, Whistler's portrait was exhibited at the Grosvenor
Gallery, and it was there that this painter whose portrait they
had come to see met Godwin and suggested the outdoor performance of the forest scenes from *As You Like It*, featuring as
Rosalind the actress whose portrait she had already painted in
that role and in that setting. Her own Orlando now looks out
at us from the pages of Wilde's *Woman's World*, an English
Mlle de Maupin who the modern scholar can mistake for a
'comely young m[a]n . . . able to function as an image (akin to
a pin-up) which cultured women and aesthetic or gay men
consume'.

At Coombe Park in 1884/5 town and country went Bunbury-
ing together and the critics called it 'the Realists' day out'. Ten

years later, in *The Importance of Being Earnest*, Wilde would in effect return to the scene of the crime. There, he could get away with lots. Historical accuracy is an irrelevant standard where, like the diarist Cecily, we write the romance of our life before we live it, and where those 'delightful records', the Army Lists of patriarchal authority, confirm that Jack's name 'naturally is Ernest'. Wilde reinvents Arden at the Manor House, Woolton, Hertfordshire. In that pastoral spot, you can have your cake, or cucumber, and eat it, and for a breathing space, at least, the examinee's famous illusion-versus-reality distinction dissolves.

What Wilde calls 'illusion', I have been suggesting, is associated, by him, with an escape from constricting definitions of personal identity, including those of gender and sexuality. *Salomé* is, as Wilde conceived it, an archaeologist's nightmare of historical inaccuracy. Wilde told the designer Graham Robertson, 'I should like everyone on stage to be in yellow'. Charles Ricketts, for his 1906 production, 'could not remember whether it was he or Wilde who had planned "masses" of colour for the original design, with the Jews all in yellow and Herod and Herodias in blood-red. The stage floor was to have been black to show up Salome's white feet, moving "like doves"; the sky "a rich turquoise blue, cut by the perpendicular fall of gilded strips of Japanese matting, forming an aerial tent above the terraces".'[27] *Salomé* is faithful to archaeology's ideal of unity and harmony, but the historical road to the ideal has been abandoned. But of course it is neither biblical historicism nor even historical inaccuracy that appalled the Lord Chamberlain. It is, rather, the image of a woman kissing the lips of the dead prophet and taking possession of the white phallus of Christian power.

Wilde's so-called 'society comedies', *Lady Windermere's Fan*, *A Woman of No Importance*, and *An Ideal Husband*, need no archaeologist to dress their stages: the time is 'the present'. But the society comedies do not record 'the return of art to life', as Wilde in one of the unrevised Godwinian moments of 'The Truth of Masks' defines the purpose of playing. Their melodramatic plots and appurtenances—the lost letters, fans, brooches, and parents—may come from the theatrical trunk of so-called realism, but Wilde's upper-crust characters could not 'pass unnoticed in a third-class railway carriage'. Other deep-dyed social markers, however, including those having to do with gender, Wilde uses as transformable props in his illusion-ist's kit. In *Lady Windermere's Fan*, for instance, he turns a woman with a past into a dandy with a future. On the Victorian stage, a woman acquires a past when she assumes the male prerogative of extramarital sex; she has allowed her sexuality to become scandalously part of her social definition, and thus by having been inordinately feminine she has in effect become inappropriately masculine: a variation of the ratio that feminizes the male dandy. Her punishment typically requires an abject acceptance of the ideology of womanly, and especially motherly, self-sacrifice. But in *Lady Windermere's Fan* the woman with many pasts is becoming socially acceptable:

LORD AUGUSTUS (*puffing a cigar*). Mrs. Erlynne has a future before her.
DUMBY. Mrs. Erlynne has a past before her.
LORD AUGUSTUS. I prefer women with a past. They're always so demmed amusing to talk to.
CECIL GRAHAM. Well, you'll have lots of topics of conversation with *her*, Tuppy. (Act 3: *CW* 415)

In the *scène à faire* with Lord Windermere, Mrs Erlynne revises the convention even further by refusing to play her role's last act: 'Oh, don't imagine I am going to have a pathetic scene with her [the daughter], weep on her neck and tell her who I am, and all that kind of thing. I have no ambition to play the part of a mother' (Act 4: *CW* 425).

Mrs Erlynne's metadramatic knowingness introduces the next surprise: she refuses to play her part as woman-with-a-past because she intends instead to act a more liberating part. She takes over the epigrammatic style: 'London is too full of fogs and—and serious people, Lord Windermere. Whether the fogs produce the serious people or the serious people pro-duce the fogs, I don't know . . . ' (Act 4: *CW* 422). The words in which she admonishes Lord Windermere—'manners before morals!' (Act 4: *CW* 423)—originally belonged to the indirect free discourse of *Dorian Gray*. Most daringly, Mrs Erlynne rejects 'a mother's feelings' because she will be, by choice, unproductive, feelingless, and attractive:

... how on earth could I pose as a mother with a grown-up daughter? Margaret is twenty-one, and I have never admitted that I am more than twenty-nine, or thirty at most. Twenty-nine when there are pink shades, thirty when there are not. So you see what difficulties it would involve. No, as far as I am concerned, let your wife cherish the memory of this dead, stainless mother. Why should I interfere with her illusions? I find it hard enough to keep my own. I lost one illusion last night. I thought I had no heart. I find I have, and a heart doesn't suit me, Windermere. Somehow it doesn't go with modern dress. (Act 4: CW 425)

'Dandyism', according to Wilde's 'Maxims for the Instruction of the Over-Educated', 'is the assertion of the absolute modernity of Beauty', and Mrs Erlynne's assertion that feeling and modern dress do not go together is the assertion of a re-gendered dandy.[28] In Wilde's drawing-room she claims for herself some of the transgressive privilege Mme de Maupin claims in the bedroom of illusion.

Lord Windermere is filled 'with horror—with absolute horror' by the liberty Mrs Erlynne takes on stage; some, at least, of the opening night audience were similarly horrified by the liberty Wilde took. The story is well known: Wilde enlisted his friends in the audience to wear green carnations, as did Ben Webster, the actor playing the part of Cecil Graham on stage, to create, as Ellmann puts it, 'The suggestion of a mysterious confraternity enigmatically binding one of the players with some of the members of the audience' (365). Wilde made his curtain speech holding a lit cigarette, congratulating the audience 'on the great success of your performance, which persuades me that you think almost as highly of the play as I do myself'.[29] The conservative critic Clement Scott was not amused by the behaviour of Wilde's characters, Lady Windermere, who contemplates leaving her husband and child, and Mrs Erlynne, the insufficiently repentant fallen woman. But he was equally appalled by Wilde's own behaviour. Wilde's gesture spoke aloud and at length to Scott; it said

'I will show you and prove to you to what an extent bad manners are not only recognized but endorsed in this wholly free and unrestrained age. I will do on the stage of a public theatre what I should not dare do at a mass meeting in the Park. I will uncover my head in the presence of refined women, but I refuse to put down my cigarette. The working-man may put out his pipe when he spouts, but my cigarette is too "precious" for destruction. I will show no humility, and I will stand unrebuked. I will take greater liberties with the public than any author who has ever preceded me in history.'[30]

The cigarette said that the person holding it felt himself to be at leisure, although supposedly in a place, for him, of work. It made an occasion for humility into an act of insolence. It said that the smoker takes 'liberties' with the rules. And in Clement Scott's world, where there's smoke there's fire.

In *An Ideal Husband*, which opened at the Haymarket in January 1895, a month before *The Importance of Being Earnest* opened at the St James's, the dandy, this time nominally male, is turned from a marginalized figure of social inutility into a social and political arbiter. Lord Goring is the sphinx made non-perfidious. For the dandy, 'The condition of perfection is idleness' ('Phrases and Philosophies': *CW* 1206): he is not an artist but art itself, since (as Wilde and Gautier both have it in their prefaces) 'All art is quite useless.' The useless is the decorative, and the decorative (in the equation that provides the *Punch*-line to innumerable Victorian cartoons and satires) is the effeminate—here an attribute of gender, not sexuality.[31] Lord Goring's father calls his son 'good-for-nothing. . . . [b]ecause he leads such an idle life' (Act 1: *CW* 483). But *this* artful good-for-nothing has a woman (a New Woman posing as an *ingénue*) to defend him. Mabel Chiltern transvalues Lord Caversham's charge of idleness:

How can you say such a thing? Why, he rides in the Row at ten o'clock in the morning, goes to the Opera three times a week, changes his clothes at least five times a day, and dines out every night of the season. You don't call that leading an idle life, do you? (Act 1: *CW* 483)

Conventionally productive Victorian masculinity is amply represented in *An Ideal Husband* by its politically active men, from the earnest Sir Robert Chiltern to the comic Lord Markby —and it is not a pretty sight:

. . . since Sir John has taken to attending debates regularly, which he never used to do in the good old days, his language has become quite impossible. He always seems to think that he is addressing the House, and consequently whenever he discusses the state of the agricultural labourer, or the Welsh Church, or something quite improper of that kind, I am obliged to send all the servants out of the room. It is not pleasant to see one's own butler, who has been with one for twenty-three years, actually blushing at the sideboard, and the footmen making contortions in corners like persons in circuses. (Act 2: CW 516)

By contrast, the idle Lord Goring, who will not be accompanying his father to Downing Street because it is not the Prime Minister's day to see the unemployed, assumes the dandy's privilege of acting like an 'ideal' woman, devoted to self-adornment and display.

In Wilde's revisionist version, the dandy is not (as Regenia Gagnier calls Lord Goring's position in the play) only a 'frill to catch the audience'.[32] This dandy, by being a work of art, creates the age that imitates him; as Wilde writes in a stage direction: 'One sees that he stands in immediate relation to modern life, makes it indeed, and so masters it' (Act 3: CW 522). Lord Chiltern, by contrast, works at politics in public, and at insider trading and repentance in private; but his continued success both in public and private depends on Lord Goring. The idle Goring determines the play's after-curtain future. He saves the Chilterns' marriage and Lord Chiltern's career. Conventionally feminized by his abstention from manly professionalism and his indulgence in self-ornamentation, he manages both to be the girl and get her, in the person of Mabel Chiltern. Wilde bends the convention by making his effeminate man also society's leading man. As the play's *raisonneur*, Lord Goring tells Lady Chiltern her proper role as a woman; the speech (which she will repeat verbatim) disturbingly reinscribes the most rigidly masculinist idea of gender difference:

Women are not meant to judge us, but to forgive us when we need forgiveness. Pardon, not punishment, is their mission. . . . A man's life is of more value than a woman's. It has larger issues, wider scope, greater ambitions. A woman's life revolves in curves of emotions. It is upon lines of intellect that a man's life progresses. (Act 4: CW 548).

This sexual asymmetry (female curves and male lines), economic disparity ('A man's life is of more value than a woman's'), and unequal division of labour (female emotion and male intellect) would be even more offensive than it is were the speaker himself not a figure of social androgyny.[33] For all the conventional 'realism' of its plot and staging, *An Ideal Husband* gives us in Lord Goring a figure—at once an effeminized man and a newly defined masculine ideal—as fantastically overdetermined as Rosalind/Théodore/Madelaine, or as an Orlando that Lady Archibald Campbell might play.

4 'Pen, Pencil, and Poison'

FROM the praise of lying and the truth of masks to the aesthetic appreciation of forgery and murder: a dangerous declension. But the few reviewers in 1891 who commented on the second essay in *Intentions* dismissed it as 'merely quite admirable' (*Nation*) or, in the harshest censure, wondered whether 'the joke has gone far enough' when, in an otherwise 'clever' essay, 'the reader is gravely asked to believe that "there is no essential incongruity between crime and culture"' (*Literary Opinion*). Modern readers are not more easily shocked than Victorians but they do have more Wildean texts available to them, including the records of a trial which the presiding judge pronounced 'the worst case I have ever tried'. Superimposed for us on the image of the cigarette-smoking, green-carnationed dandy of *Lady Windermere's Fan* is another image, unimaginable to the first readers of *Intentions*, of the prisoner who stood from two o'clock to half past two 'on the centre platform of Clapham Junction in convict dress and hand-cuffed, for the world to look at . . . in the grey November rain' (*Letters*, 491). So Wilde's essay on the congruity of crime and culture, the efficacy of 'sin' in the creation of 'personality', and the relation between the hidden life and the public reckoning may actually seem more daring now than it did when it appeared in January 1889 in England's most distinguished liberal journal, the *Fortnightly Review*. The *Fortnightly* (published monthly) had been founded in 1865 by G. H. Lewes. In the same issue as 'Pen, Pencil, and Poison', it carried Swinburne on Victor Hugo, John Addington Symonds on Victorian poetry, Edmund Gosse on Ibsen. Its editor was the incredible Frank Harris.

Harris entangles himself frequently in Wilde's story, from 1884 when they met, through the trials when Harris learned to his 'amaze' that Wilde had sex with boys, through the years in France when he bought the scenario for Wilde's unwritten play *Mr and Mrs Daventry*, to 1916 when he published *Oscar Wilde: His Life and Confessions*. Only Harris's two interventions

in 1889 are relevant here. The first was his decision to publish
'Pen, Pencil, and Poison'. Writing much later about the essays
in *Intentions* Harris says, 'They were all . . . conceived and written from the standpoint of the artist, and the artist alone, who
never takes account of ethics, but uses right and wrong indif-
ferently as colours of his palette.' He describes the book's
reception: '"The Decay of Lying" seemed to the ordinary,
matter-of-fact Englishman a cynical plea in defence of men-
dacity. To the majority of readers, "Pen, Pencil, and Poison"
was hardly more than a shameful attempt to condone cold-
blooded murder.'[1] But the readers of the *Nineteenth Century*
and the *Fortnightly Review*, like the reviewers of *Intentions*,
were as likely to be amused as shocked by Wildean paradox.
Harris's *Life and Confessions* of Wilde is single-mindedly the
narrative of a Fall: it requires that 'Pen, Pencil, and Poison' be one
of the articles which 'helped to injure [Wilde's] standing and
repute'; yet in the first month of 1889 Harris considered the
essay publishable in his great magazine. A few months later,
however, Wilde offered him 'The Portrait of Mr W. H.' for publication. This time Harris (or, as he claimed, his deputy editor)
rejected the offer.

Harris's *Life and Confessions* is a version of the familiar narrative of a wilful and (to use Harris's repeated word) 'weak'
Oscar Wilde intent on sinning in order to make his sins
known, trangressing in order to be punished. In Wilde's own
writing, the raw material for such a narrative (which would
include this essay about the aesthete as criminal) extends from
the homoerotic hints in the poem 'Hélas!' through the daring
self-exposure of 'The Portrait of Mr W. H.', and the scandalous
hinting at unspeakable sin in *The Picture of Dorian Gray*. In this
life-narrative, *An Ideal Husband* is Wilde's plea to be
unmasked; and the best evidence, finally, when all the other
evidence is collected, will be the West End laugh-riot about the
double life, *The Importance of Being Earnest*. It is a compelling
narrative, with much that rings true. But the presumption of
Wilde's unconscious wish to punish himself by exposing his
secret guilts (a common enough motive in 'that dreadful universal thing called human nature' ('Decay of Lying', 15))
underrates the complexity of his conscious intentions in all
these works, including 'Pen, Pencil, and Poison'.

The essay tells the story of Thomas Griffiths Wainewright, who was 'not merely a poet and painter, an art-critic, an antiquarian, and a writer of prose, an amateur of beautiful things, and a dilettante of things delightful, but also a forger of no mean or ordinary capabilities, and as a subtle and secret poisoner almost without rival in this or any age' (60). Tone is all in this essay: Wilde's pose of restrained, scholarly judiciousness allows the smallest touches of incongruity or excess to unsettle the obvious ironies and leave the object of the satire perfectly unclear. Literary tradition—the example of Swift's 'Modest Proposal' most strongly, and De Quincey's 'Murder Considered as One of the Fine Arts' more distantly—suggests that the reader's job is to invert the initial shocking assumption, that there is no significant difference between art and murder. More local contexts, for instance Wilde's unironic insistence elsewhere that the spheres of art and of ethics are entirely separate, suggest that we should leave the initial assumption exactly as we found it. The second strategy is supported by a common (and inadequate) biographical reading: 'Wilde adopted Wainewright as a kindred spirit, a precursor of aestheticism, and a dandy.'[2] Poisoning relatives is not much different from feasting with panthers, and (in this reading) 'Pen, Pencil, and Poison' is more about Wilde than Wainewright. Regenia Gagnier reverses the satiric ratio: not, Crime is equal to culture, but Culture is a crime. In her reading, Wilde only poses as a man of 'culture' who takes 'Wainewright's gaudy career as the object of art' instead of seeing 'the larger movements of history (like the colonial deportation of 300 starving convicts) . . . '. In Gagnier's reading, 'Pen, Pencil, and Poison' satirizes the narrator's aestheticism as 'a limited conception of social life and a dangerously isolated egotism'.[3]

In fact, Wilde's narrative is poised two-square for both of these readings, and more. Like its author, it refuses simply to mean. The author's pose as a dandy pays homage to Wainewright, and it mocks dandyism as a fraud. Wainewright's failed aestheticism is the foil for Wilde's successful aestheticism, and it subverts the very idea of aestheticism. Throughout his career Wilde was more self-mocking than his English or French precursors in aestheticism had been; his masks acknowledged the absurdity (and in *Dorian Gray* the tragedy) of self-knowledge in a world of surfaces. In the early 1880s he had dressed like a clown to preach beauty in America, and risked the audience's laughter; the dissonance of his performance, absurdly sublime, was a calculated effect. By the time of *Intentions*, the dissonance was even more extreme; the perfect farce of *The Importance of Being Earnest* was shortly to come, but *Salomé* had already been written. Yet those extremes could coalesce or even exchange places—the comedy revealing the seriousness of his intentions, the high-falutin becoming strategically comic—as Aubrey Beardsley recognized with his illustrations for *Salomé*. In 'Pen, Pencil, and Poison' Wilde practises a dizzying double consciousness for which 'camp' is the anachronistic name. As Susan Sontag writes, 'Camp involves a new, more complex relation to "the serious." One can be serious about the frivolous, frivolous about the serious.'[4] In 'Pen, Pencil, and Poison' Wilde camps both ways.

'Pen, Pencil, and Poison' was Wilde's second attempt (and 'The Portrait of Mr W. H.' would be his third) to write about forged art and forged life, about the art of forging a personality. The first, in 1886, took for its subject Thomas Chatterton (1752–70), the Bristol boy who at the age of 16 'found' a chest of manuscripts by a fifteenth-century monk named Thomas Rowley. In 1770 Chatterton brought his forgeries to London; four months later, frustrated in his desire for quick literary success, he committed suicide. The fame that eluded him in life came spectacularly in his posthumous career as Romantic icon. Keats dedicated *Endymion* to his memory and called him 'the purest writer in the English language'.[5] Wordsworth, in 'Resolution and Independence', made him immortal in two lines: 'I thought of Chatterton, the marvelous Boy, / The sleepless Soul that perished in his pride.' His 'unrecorded face' is beautifully present in Henry Wallis's fanciful painting (1856) *The Death of Chatterton*.[6] But despite all these memorials, there was in 1886 no monument to Chatterton in his native city, and Wilde—who had a special affinity for the young self-fabricator—was one of a group of admirers who sought (unsuccessfully) to correct the oversight.

Wilde planned to use all the media to spread the Chatterton message. He returned to the lecture platform. On 7 December

1886 he told Herbert Horne, another member of the Chatterton group, about his recent appearance at Birkbeck College: 'To my amazement I found 800 people there! And they seemed really interested in the marvellous boy!' (*Letters*, 192). Horne was editor of the arts-and-crafts magazine the *Century Guild Hobby Horse*, which in October had carried the announcement that 'Mr. Oscar Wilde's article on Chatterton has been unavoidably postponed until the January number'.[7] The article, which would have been a version of the lecture, never appeared. Possibly Wilde wanted to save it for future lecture occasions. But there was a more compelling reason for its indefinite postponement: print would have exposed the fact that at least two-thirds of the lecture was outright plagiarism.

To plagiarize the biography of a forger is an amusing conceit: it is the only amusing thing about Wilde's 'Chatterton'. The manuscript, approximately seventy pages in a quarto exercise book, is at the Clark Libary, UCLA. Most of it is cut-and-paste from two published books, Daniel Wilson's *Chatterton: A Biographical Study* (1869) and David Masson's *Chatterton: A Story of the Year 1770* (1874). It would be nice to think that this was merely a source-book, but Wilde's finicky alterations of a word here or a phrase there suggest that it is the text of the lecture pretty much as he delivered it, with notes to himself about subjects to elaborate either extempore during delivery or later in revision.

As a prelude to 'Pen, Pencil, and Poison', 'Chatterton' is interesting for two reasons: how unimaginatively Wilde's own contributions fall in line with his untransformed 'sources', and how earnestly he takes the enterprise. He begins with a discussion of the impersonality of art, then acknowledges cases where art and artist are so bound up that biography cannot be ignored, which leads him to his subject, 'Thomas Chatterton, the father of the Romantic movement in literature, the precursor of Blake, Coleridge and Keats, the greatest poet of his time . . . ' —which begins the biography he soon leaves his co-authors to complete. With the issue of forgery he does almost nothing; and when the issue does arise, it does so only to be put firmly in its place:

Was he a mere forger with literary powers or a great artist? The latter is the right view. Chatterton may not have had the moral conscience which is truth to fact, but he had the artistic conscience, which is truth to Beauty. He had the artist's yearning to represent and if perfect representation seemed to him to demand forgery, he needs must forge. Still his forgery came from the desire for artistic self-effacement.

In the one phrase 'he needs must forge' is the potential for 'Pen, Pencil, and Poison', with its playful destabilization of the ideas of sincerity and authenticity, and of the divide between forgery and art. It is the idea that actually does begin 'The Portrait of Mr W. H.', where the argument that Chatterton's 'so-called forgeries were merely the result of an artistic desire for perfect representation' launches the search for an always receding ground of narrative certainty, and calls into deadly question the proposition that 'to censure an artist for forgery was to confuse an ethical with an aesthetical problem' (*Portrait*, 3). But the potential realized in those two essays is derailed in 'Chatterton' by the insistence on a conventionally 'right view'.

Wilde was trying on a style that we find in some of his reviews from this period, and that we still find in 'The Truth of Masks': the mode of the Man of Letters, only slightly dandified as Professor of Aesthetics. It is measured and scholarly and it wins its way by assuming the authority that comes with the acquisition of many facts. Wilde could speak to an audience of 800 at Birkbeck College in a voice compounded of Masson's, Wilson's, and his own, yet the mode seemed so natural, so authoritative that as far as we know nobody noticed the impersonation. Later, in 'The Portrait of Mr W. H.', he transformed that mode by speaking (as Vivian puts it in 'The Decay of Lying') through different lips than his own, giving dialogical form to the proposition that 'To know the truth one must imagine myriads of falsehoods' (185). And in 'Pen, Pencil, and Poison' he transformed the mode by making it work self-consciously as a pose which, like his other public poses, was potentially its own parody. As a potentially self-parodic pose, it became the appropriate style to explore the ambiguous relations of forgery and art, criminality and personality.

Wilde's ventriloquism in the 'Chatterton' lecture was an

attempt to revive a role, that of the independent but influential man of letters, which was, even apart from the plagiarism, already a phantom. Both Regenia Gagnier and Ian Small have diagnosed what Small calls the period's 'crisis of authority' caused by the disappearance of the 'sage' who spoke to society at large with the prestige of the special individual, and the emergence of the specialized academic who speaks to almost no one.[8] Arnold and Pater were remnants of the old order, the cultural critic in the original signification of the phrase. Ian Small suggests that Wilde, 'in a typically iconoclastic strategy', tried in his essays and reviews to revive that 'virtually defunct' tradition (112). But he tried to revive it, I suggest, with the difference that now it was a self-conscious pastiche which acknowledged its belatedness, as Wilde's aestheticism acknowledged its belatedness by self-mockery. It was a transformation he effected at the level of rhetoric, in (for instance) the epigrammatic mode which reduces sage-like wisdom to a turn of phrase. Reciprocally it was a transformation he effected at the level of his public persona. In 'The Critic as Artist' we hear the voices of Arnold and Pater, not plagiarized and not merely cited (as the specialized academic would cite them), but made full participants in the dialogue, and therefore susceptible to parodic subversion at the very moment when they are also the sources of authority. A similar transformation occurs in the narrative voice of 'Pen, Pencil, and Poison'.

For 'Pen, Pencil, and Poison' Wilde appropriates several dissonant voices. One is the voice not of a sage, not an Arnold or Pater, but of a quintessentially, even congenitally belated man of letters, William Hazlitt's dull grandson, W. Carew Hazlitt. Hazlitt the younger (1834–1913) was an assiduous bibliographer, editor, and compiler. S. Schoenbaum, in *Shakespeare's Lives*, calls him an 'antiquarian bumbler': his last book, *Shakespear: Himself and His Work* (1912), is written, says Schoenbaum, in 'unspeakably bad prose', a 'thoroughly bad [book], without interest or influence'.[9] But that would be too harsh a judgement for Hazlitt's edition with biographical introduction of *Essays and Criticisms by Thomas Griffiths Wainewright* (1880). Hazlitt is occasionally witty in his introduction (where Wilde got most of the facts and some of the words for 'Pen, Pencil, and Poison'): he recognizes the story's comic potential; but more typically he is a heavy-handed moralizer, as in: '[Wainewright] was a heartless and callous voluptuary, who was prepared to trample on the noblest and tenderest feelings of humanity in the unpitying pursuit of his own selfish purposes' (p. lxxvii). In 'Pen, Pencil, and Poison' Wilde puts a dandy's *sang froid* in place of Hazlitt's righteous indignation. And in place of the conventional condemnation of 'selfish purposes' he conducts a comic interrogation of what it means to have a self or to be a personality.

A second source, much slighter in extent but crucial to Wilde's design, was Swinburne's *William Blake: A Critical Essay*.[10] Swinburne gave him not only the alliterative title with its suggestion that pens, pencils, and poison are members of a single category, but the model for a style of such impenetrable earnestness that a reader can neither trust nor dismiss a word of it. In fact, Swinburne out-deadpans Wilde. His five pages about Wainewright appear without warning in the course of his brilliant, inordinate, utterly engaged (and engaging) exposition of Blake:

Another [friend of Blake's] worthy of notice here was, until our own day called forth a better, the best English critic on art; himself, as far as we know, admirable alike as a painter, a writer, and a murderer. In each pursuit, perhaps, there was a certain want of solid worth and fervour, which at times impeded or impaired the working of an excellent faculty; but in each it is evident there was a noble sense of things fair and fit; a seemliness and shapeliness of execution, a sensitive relish of excellence, and exquisite aspiration after goodness of work, which cannot be overpraised. With pen, with palette, or with poison, his hand was never a mere craftsman's. (67–8)

Only the repeated triplets give away his game of conflating incommensurate categories, and the first one ('a painter, a writer, and a murderer'), lacking the alliteration which signals comic intent, almost slips by.

Swinburne's digression satirizes the idea that art can be judged according to utilitarian standards. He pretends to defend Wainewright against detractors on the basis 'that in accordance with the modern receipt he "lived his poems;" that the age prefers deeds to songs; that to do great things is better than to write; that action is of eternity, fiction of time . . . ' (69). Wilde's essay also takes up this congenial line, but the directness of Wilde's assertion makes it oddly more ambiguous in intention than Swinburne's strong irony: 'This young dandy sought to be somebody, rather than to do something. He recognized that Life itself is an art, and has its modes of style no less than the arts that seek to express it' (65). For Wilde, unlike Swinburne, the artist–forger–murderer can pass from being a true aesthetic hero, the dandy who is his own best work of art, to being a sordid, unimaginative criminal or, worst of all, a person with a bad prose style; and he can make the transition, or occupy all the positions, within a single sentence. This instability derives partly from Wilde's extensive quotation of Wainewright's hectically comic but unfunny prose (which he sometimes praises and at other times condemns as a model for the worst excesses of modern journalism); and partly it derives from a narrative opacity that is the rhetorical equivalent of the masking, disguising, or forging through which, the essay tells us, a 'personality' is made.

In revision for *Intentions*, Wilde added two sentences which, like the longer additions to 'The Decay of Lying', crystallize what had been in suspension in the magazine version: 'A mask tells us more than a face. These disguises intensified his personality' (64). The revision brought the satirical 'Pen, Pencil, and Poison' into the same discursive universe as the polemical 'Critic as Artist', and as the revised title of 'The Truth of Masks': 'Man is least himself when he talks in his own person. Give him a mask, and he will tell you the truth' (182). It is a vitally important but a also a characteristically conflicted proposition. The problem (which I have already glanced at in relation to 'The Decay of Lying') is that two incompatible ideas of 'personality' are being asked to cohabit. If 'personality' is (as Dorian Gray says of 'the Ego') *not* 'a thing simple, permanent, reliable, and of one essence', if there is (as the narrator of 'The Portrait of Mr W. H.' suspects) 'no permanence in personality', then where *is* the personality that the masks intensify? In 'The Critic as Artist' masks do not intensify; instead they multiply: 'insincerity is simply a method by which we can multiply our personalities' (188). In 'Pen, Pencil, and Poison' the possiblity of depth rather than number is acknowledged: 'One can imagine a strong personality being created out of sin' (88). In either case, whether the mask disguises an absence or whether it is the surface to an unusual depth, the superior personality (more intense or more diverse) is measured by its deviance from the norm—by insincerity and sin.

The funniest and, with hindsight, most chilling line in 'Pen, Pencil, and Poison' is the one in which Wilde acknowledges the difficulty: of Wainewright's imprisonment for a crime committed thirteen years earlier, Wilde writes, 'The permanence of personality is a very subtle metaphysical problem, and certainly the English law solves the question in an extremely rough-and-ready manner' (85). In *De Profundis*, having experienced that English legal solution, Wilde completes the thought in a less humorous vein:

But we who live in prison, and in whose lives there is no event but sorrow, have to measure time by throbs of pain, and the record of bitter moments. Suffering—curious as it may sound to you—is the means by which we exist, because it is the only means by which we can become conscious of existing; and the remembrance of suffering in the past is necessary to us as the warrant, the evidence, of our continued identity. (*Letters*, 435)

As in his earlier writing, existence is measured in Paterian units, except that now the 'counted number of pulses . . . given to us of a variegated, dramatic life' (Conclusion to *The Renaissance*: Hill, 188) are 'throbs of pain' measuring the unvariegated, undramatic life of sorrow. And now, rather than the fleetingness of impression leading to a need for constant renewal in fresh sensation, there is 'the remembrance of suffering' which, like English law, asserts 'the permanence of personality'.

This 'subtle metaphysical problem' is already inscribed in the wide semantic range of the word *personality* in Victorian culture. At one linguistic extreme of stability and presence is what Maude Ellmann calls 'the unified transcendent consciousness that the nineteenth century had understood as "personality"'.[11] As the century drew towards its end, its transcendence was under threat from various quarters, for instance, from the science of the mind. The distinguished psychologist Dr Henry Maudsley, in *The Pathology of Mind* (1879), defines personality as the 'physiological unit of organic functions'.[12] Noting that in sleep and dream 'our conscious functions are in the greatest distraction', Maudsley none the less believes that 'the organism preserves its identity' by virtue of 'something deeper than consciousness [which] constitutes our fundamental personality'. Here we seem to have the essentialized Victorian personality etherized upon the clinician's table. But the word's entrance into Maudsley's vocabulary also suggests a less transcendent possibility: the personality 'deeper than consciousness' must be susceptible to change if the clinician is to be a therapist rather than merely a taxonomist. Similarly from the physical sciences: Herbert Spencer, in his *Principles of Biology* (1864–7), describes 'the unceasing change of matter which oxygen and other agents produce throughout the system', so that 'by ceaseless integration and disintegration it gradually undergoes an entire change of substance without losing its individuality'.[13] The rhetorical reassurance that 'individuality' is preserved despite 'disintegration' seems a frightened afterthought to the striking image of a 'system' subject to 'unceasing change'.

Every personality, according to Maudsley, is distinct from every other and continuous with itself; functionally they are all the same. But not qualitatively. The slippage from 'personality' designating mere personhood to 'personality' designating a special person with qualities different from those who, while demonstrably persons, are not quite personalities, has clearly happened by the time of *Intentions*. And it has happened not only in the culture of science but of the commodity. Thus we find in the *Pall Mall Gazette* (30 January 1891, p. 3) descriptions of Bradlaugh as 'one of the most unique personalities' and (16 January 1891, p. 1) of Rossetti 'as a grand man . . . with a magnetic personality . . . '. Bradlaugh and Rossetti share a distinction with Sir Robert Chiltern in *An Ideal Husband*, described in Wilde's stage direction as 'A personality of mark'.

This is the personality whose portrait sold copies of *Vanity Fair* in the late nineteenth century as it still does in the late twentieth. It is the media personality who is more intensely organized, more distinctly itself than other less personified persons, yet who (and here we find a contradiction in this emergent notion of personality) depends for its existence upon the perceptions of the less personified consuming others. This personality is outstanding by virtue of some 'strong or unusual character' it personally possesses, yet its existence as personality depends on its being the 'focus . . . of public interest'.[14] The strength or distinctiveness of the public personality is the product of the public interest it produces; yet for those whose interest confers that status, this commodified personality is the real thing which can give substance to their own more tenuous personalities. Wilde himself was such a 'personality'. One result, for some critics both friendly and hostile, is the relegation of his writing to a secondary place, the epiphenomenon of the personality. Richard LeGallienne put it that way in 1909 when he wrote that the work 'is but the marginalia . . . of a striking fantastic personality'.[15]

It is only a step from the commodified realm of the public personality to the aesthetic realm inhabited by the 'engaging personality presented in life or in a book' that Pater celebrates in the Preface to *The Renaissance* (Hill, p. xx).[16] The fifteenth century in Italy, according to Pater, was a time especially 'productive in personalities, many-sided, centralised, complete' (Hill, p. xxiv). Therefore fifteenth-century Italy 'can hardly be studied too much': eliding the space between the 'personality presented in life or in a book', Pater specifies among the Quattrocento's curricular claims 'its concrete works of art, its special and prominent personalities, with their profound aesthetic charm' (Hill, p. xxiii). The 'aesthetic charm' that in a book takes the form of literary character or style exists equally in the personalities outside of books—equally in the 'work of the artist's hands, or the face of one's friend' (Conclusion, Hill, 189). The conflation of life and book implies one of the dangers Pater saw when he suppressed the Conclusion from the second edition. The aesthete becomes a consumer of personalities; he seeks out those fair personalities 'in life or in a book' to give 'the highest quality to [his] moments as they pass' (Hill, 190).

Under the pressure of Pater's analysis, individuality becomes an always vanishing, unspeakable thing, 'gone while we try to apprehend it, of which it may ever be more truly said that it has ceased to be than that it is' (Hill, 188). In its original form, as an essay in the *Westminister Review* of 1868, Pater took this deconstruction a melancholy step further:

Such thoughts seem desolate at first; at times all the bitterness of life seems concentrated in them. They bring the image of one washed out beyond the bar in a sea at ebb, losing even his personality, as the elements of which he is composed pass into new combinations. Struggling, as he must, to save himself, it is himself that he loses at every moment. (Hill, 273)

The personality that receives the impressions that are all we know of life, and is itself (in life or in a book) the impression above all others that it is our privilege to receive, is 'at every moment' losing itself.

Wilde's personality too—the man and the word—is often torn by contradiction. But in the early 1880s, lecturing in America and reviewing in London, Wilde used the word in counterpoint to the word 'perfection' in a way that makes personality a virtually quantifiable quality, simply half of the equation which equals art. Thus Henry Irving is 'a great actor because he brings to the interpretation of a work of art the two qualities which we in this century so much desire, the qualities of personality and perfection' (9 May 1885: *Rev.* 17). The former quality, belonging to the artist, brings the stamp of individuality; the latter, belonging to the medium, turns what would otherwise be mere idiosyncrasy into the universality of art. A few years later, he makes Pater himself exemplify the balance: 'in Mr. Pater, as in Cardinal Newman, we find the union of personality and perfection' (*Speaker*, 22 Mar. 1890: *Rev.* 545). Then, from prison, it is his own turn: he describes himself to Alfred Douglas as 'an artist . . . the quality of whose work depends on the intensification of personality' (*Letters*, 425); and he associates himself with another artist: 'we can discern in Christ that close union of personality with perfection . . . [T]he very basis of his nature was the same as that of the nature of the artist . . . ' (*Letters*, 476).

But in 'Pen, Pencil, and Poison' it is not the union of personality with perfection that interests Wilde; rather, 'His crimes . . . gave a strong personality to his style'; and again, 'One can fancy an intense personality being created out of sin' (88).

Rodney Shewan comments, 'To the moralist, Wainewright is a citizen; to the artist-as-critic, a personality. Personality creates the artist, and while genius separates him in quality from ordinary people, personality separates him in kind'.[17] There are problems with this otherwise fine formulation: personality may create the artist but (as we have seen) the artist also creates the personality; and for another thing Wainewright did not have genius. *His* personality is really the personality of his biographer. Wainewright is not only a forger but, as an artist, he is himself a forgery. He commits crimes against prose style, and as a criminal he is prosaic: his crimes were of the ordinary, speakable sort, which is why he can be a figure of fun. But latent as a possibility in the satire's unstable irony are other cases (possibly the biographer's own) of personalities that really are created 'out of sin'. Though Wainewright may be a dubious example, the satire admits the possibility that 'crime' can give 'personality' to the style which (in circular fashion) creates the personality. In Wilde's proposition, the rhetoric moves from 'crime' to 'sin', from the stupidly illegal to the numinously transgressive, from the definable to the unspeakable. It suggests that the criminal life really may be a vale of personality-making; and in doing so it adds another nuance to the word 'personality'.

We hear it most clearly in *Dorian Gray*, the melodramatic complement to Wainewright's comedy. When the painter Basil Hallward first meets the eye of Dorian Gray across a room crowded with 'huge overdressed dowagers and tedious Academicians', 'A curious sensation of terror', he tells Lord Henry Wotton, 'came over me. I knew that I had come face to face with some one whose mere personality was so fascinating that, if I allowed it to do so, it would absorb my whole nature, my whole soul, my very art itself.' Hallward's hostess intercepts him as he struggles toward the door to escape; she introduces him 'to Royalties and people with stars and garters and elderly ladies with gigantic tiaras and parrot noses', until 'Suddenly I found myself face to face with the young man whose personality had so strangely stirred me. We were quite close, almost touching. Our eyes met again' (*CW* 21–2).[18]

What is so fascinating, stirring, and terrifying about Dorian's amazingly projective personality? We may not want to wield the Marquess of Queensberry's hermeneutic sledge-hammer: according to his Plea of Justification, *The Picture of Dorian Gray* 'was designed and intended . . . to describe the relations and intimacies of certain persons of sodomitical and unnatural habits tastes and practices' (*Trials*, 334). But readers more sympathetic than Queensberry may also think that what passes between Basil and Dorian is a glance of sexual recognition. At the first trial, Edward Carson cross-examined Wilde about the magazine version of that passage. He asked whether the feeling described was 'a proper or an improper feeling?' Wilde replied that 'it is the most perfect description of what an artist would feel on meeting a beautiful personality that was in some way necessary to his life and work' (*Trials*, 127). Carson then asked Wilde about a later passage, again in the magazine version, in which Basil tells Dorian 'from the moment I met you, your personality had the most extraordinary influence over me. I quite admit that I adored you madly, extravagantly, absurdly':

> 'Do you mean to say that that passage describes the natural feel-ings of one man towards another?'
> 'It would be the influence produced by a beautiful personality.'
> 'A beautiful person?'
> 'I said a "beautiful personality". You can describe it as you like. Dorian Gray's was a most remarkable personality.' (*Trials*, 129)

Carson's intention is to close the distance between the 'remarkable personality' and its legally proscribed habitation in the male body. Wilde's intention, although beginning to waver in his answer to Carson, is to keep that numinous, over-determined personality free from the reductive grip of real-ism's misreading.

Thomas Griffiths Wainewright is no Dorian Gray: he is not one of the elect. Still, affinities are noticeable. Wainewright is, or aspires to be, like Dorian, a member of the leisured or dandy class; his dilettantism brands him with effeminacy; and he lives a secret life of crime. His end—alone, drug-addicted, compulsively drawing portraits of his victims—also associates him with Dorian. So do the instruments of his craft. In Wilde's own rhetoric, as in Vigilance Society polemics, pens and poison go together. Books spread ideas that poison the mind (or intensify the personality), as does the 'poisonous book' Lord Henry gives to Dorian Gray: 'For years, Dorian Gray could not free himself from the influence of this book' (*CW* 102). Pen and poison initiate Dorian into his career of unnameable sins, and Basil Hallward's pencil draws the picture. 'One can fancy an intense personality being created out of sin': in both the satirical essay and the melodramatic novel, the personality intensified by sin may be its own punishment. Self-fabrication is in conflict with fatalism, art with nature, romance with realism.

5 'The Portrait of Mr W. H.'

LIKE Shakespeare's sonnets, its purported subject, 'The Portrait of Mr W. H.' offers a key but withholds the heart it might unlock. It is Wilde's most extensive exploration into the art of forgery. The material facts of its composition as well as its form and rhetoric contribute to the sense that here mysteries begin with their solution. He published its original version the same year as 'Pen, Pencil, and Poison', and tried unsuccessfully for the rest of his life to publish an expanded version. That unfulfilled intention is emblematic: the story or essay or hoax— one is not sure how to name the kind of thing it is—seems, in its textual imperfection, still to be growing, still trying to achieve itself; to be, that is, alive in a way that would be Borgesian if it had not previously been Wildean. No piece associated with *Intentions* seems to speak more daringly about his sexual intentions or come closer to giving a name to his numinous sin, and no piece more ingeniously questions the very idea of intentionality by withholding the personality that could intend, or the stability of results that a personality might achieve.

It—or rather, a version of it—was published in *Blackwood's Edinburgh Magazine* for July 1889. 'Maga', as it was familiarly known, was an eminently respectable, family-valuing monthly. 'The Portrait of Mr W. H.' ran at the front of the issue, and the editor, William Blackwood, proposed reprinting it in a new series of *Tales from Blackwood*. Wilde's counter-proposal was that Blackwood publish 'a special volume of [his] essays and studies'. The frontispiece would be an etching of the fictitious portrait, and the other studies (as we've seen) would have constituted a premature version of *Intentions*. Blackwood objected to the proposal on economic, not moral or prudential, grounds: 'as a rule these volumes of reprinted stories and essays are not remunerative to either publisher or author' (*Letters*, 243–6).

Yet the story which the cautious Blackwood published, Frank Harris's magazine had rejected, after publishing 'Pen, Pencil, and Poison' earlier in the year. Harris said 'Pen, Pencil, and Poison' had hurt Wilde's reputation, but it was nothing compared to the damage done by 'The Portrait of Mr W. H.' According to Harris, 'The Portrait of Mr. W. H.' 'did Oscar incalculable injury', because it 'appear[ed] to justify the peculiar rumours about his private life'. To the reckless author that was just fine: 'Oscar seemed to revel in the storm of conflicting opinions the paper called forth.'[1] Charles Ricketts, who was intended by Wilde to design a book version of 'Mr W. H.', seems to confirm Harris's account. Wilde told Ricketts, apparently just after the *Fortnightly* rejected the story, '"Already I have been warned that the subject is too dangerous." Again he laughed and mentioned the reader of a famous firm. "This *gardien du serail* (such people should ever be mute) advises me not to print it, lest it should corrupt our English homes."'[2] Press reaction goes some way toward justifying these editorial fears: the *Scots Observer*, which was going to have a field day with *Dorian Gray* the following year, said that one article in the July *Blackwood's* 'is out of place . . . in any popular magazine', and the *World* said that 'The subject is a very unpleasant one, and it is dilated upon in the article in a peculiarly offensive manner.'[3] Andrew Lang, in an unsigned leader in the the *Daily News*, described Wilde's character Cyril Graham as 'one of the pretty undergraduates who used to act girls' parts in College plays. This class of young man is not universally "respected in the parish" . . .'[4]

Here is that hinting around the contested notion of effeminacy—and 'effeminate' is Wilde's own word for his character Cyril Graham—which I mentioned in Chapter 1. But now the hints predict the problem I find in Wilde's story. If we are uncertain what Wilde really intends to say on the subject of his own or his characters' sexuality, the critical response—'out of place', 'very unpleasant'—closes the circle by forcing us to read one silence or indeterminacy in terms of another.

The full extent both of the danger and the elusiveness of 'The Portrait of Mr W. H.' did not appear until 3 April 1895. The critic was Edward Carson, counsel for the Marquess of Queensberry:

Carson: I believe you have written an article to show that Shakespeare's sonnets were suggestive of unnatural vice?

Wilde: On the contrary, I have written an article to show that they were not. I objected to such a perversion being put upon Shakespeare. (*Trials*, 129)

It was one of Wilde's most daring paradoxes, the idea of a love between men that is not 'unnatural', not 'a perversion'. In 1895 it was a contradiction almost beyond the reach of language. What *could* Wilde call it? Words that made sense in the Old Bailey, 'sodomy', 'buggery', 'unnatural vice', 'gross indecency with another male person' implied 'disgust, disgrace, vituperation'.[5] They were words of legal condemnation, and the prison house of language was not all Wilde had to fear in those names. There were other possibilities. The word 'homosexuality', for instance, had been coined by a Swiss writer in 1869. But in Engand in the 1890s, 'homosexuality' belonged to the discourse of science; it named a medical problem or a scientific situation, a supposed *fact* which belonged on the wrong side of the divide that separates imitation from creation, nature from art, realism from romance. 'Urning', 'inversion', even Whitman's term 'adhesiveness' were neologisms; they 'were suggestive of' something strange and new.[6] But the desire they tried to name was as familiar and old as the world. Was there any language that would not falsify Wilde's desire—and Shakespeare's and Michelangelo's and Plato's—in the process of speaking it?

Carson wants 'The Portrait of Mr W. H.' to state what it is 'suggestive of' down to the last forensic detail. In 'The Critic as Artist', Wilde in effect responds by saying that a work of art is suggestive only of another work of art: it is a suggestion yielding a suggestion, not a diagnosis or sentence. The question that 'The Portrait of Mr W. H.' poses about the representation of homosexual desire is only partly bound to the particular circumstances of Victorian reticence and fear. If we intend to take Wilde seriously we still need to play with the problem of the 'suggestive', the unnameable. At the start we need to ask what 'The Portrait of Mr W. H.' is all about, what it is 'suggestive of', because the obvious answer (it is about Shakespeare's love for 'the onlie begetter' of his sonnets) is radically undercut by the very narration that proposes it.

Wilde creates a daisy-chain of converts and sceptics to tell his story. Their self-subverting narrative enlists a tale of scholarly detection in the service of the indeterminate. Wilde's narrator hears from his friend Erskine the story of Cyril Graham, the beautiful boy who as an undergraduate acted to perfection the part of Rosalind and who later solved the mystery of Shakespeare's sonnets. According to Cyril Graham, the 'Mr W. H.' of the sonnets' dedication was Willie Hughes, a boy player in Shakespeare's company. The sonnets tell the story of their love. Erskine is unconvinced by Graham's theory: he wants 'some independent evidence about the existence of this young actor'.[7] So Graham gives him ocular proof, the portrait of Mr W. H. But Erskine quickly discovers that the portrait is a forgery. Erskine loses his belief, and Cyril Graham commits suicide, a martyr to his theory about Shakespeare's love. Now the narrator, having heard Erskine's story of faith and fraud, inherits Graham's belief in the theory, and despite Erskine's warning that 'there is nothing in the idea of Willie Hughes' (21) he takes up the cause. After further research he writes a letter to Erskine in which he puts 'all my enthusiasm . . . all my faith', with the result that immediately 'It seemed to me that I had given away my capacity for belief in the Willie Hughes theory of the Sonnets, that something had gone out of me, as it were . . . ' (80–1). Erskine, however, is reconverted by the very letter that drains the narrator of conviction. He writes to the narrator that he intends to commit suicide as a sign of his faith. The narrator rushes to stop the martyrdom but is too late: Erskine is dead, but not, it turns out, by his own hand. He has died of consumption, his last evidence of faith another fraud.

In form, then, 'The Portrait of Mr W. H.' denies as much as it affirms the theory it creates. It demonstrates Gilbert's point in 'The Critic as Artist': 'Ah it is so easy to convert others. It is so difficult to convert oneself. . . . To know the truth one must imagine myriads of falsehoods' (185). Truth and falsehood here are positions in a social dialectic. What Wilde's story really says or means to say about Shakespeare's love remains inaccessible. Or does it? Most of Wilde's readers, then and now, think they know exactly what it says: that Shakespeare, like Oscar Wilde, loved boys and acted on that love. Every narrative denial is converted to affirmation in a reading process that we can also see at work in the proceedings of Wilde's trial.

More famously, of course, such a process was at work in the reception of *The Picture of Dorian Gray*. In the novel, the negatives of direct statement—for instance, that Basil Hallward's love for Dorian 'had nothing in it that was not noble and intellectual. It was not that mere physical admiration of beauty that is born of the senses and that dies when the senses tire' (*CW* 97)—can easily be subverted into sexual affirmations.[8] For many of Wilde's readers, both before and after the trials, this 'rationalization of homosexual desire as aesthetic experience' (in Elaine Showalter's phrase)[9] was a verbal fig-leaf bulging with phallic reality. Wilde's refusal to heed editorial cautions suggests that he was complicit with those readers. Yet he was not lying when he told Carson, 'I objected to such a perversion being put upon Shakespeare.'

Where, then, or what, was the truth in Wilde's speaking about a desire he called 'noble and intellectual' and the law called criminal? Do Wilde's verbal gestures in 'The Portrait of Mr W. H.' point to heart and soul, or to penis and anus? Not that these are exclusive choices, except in linguistic situations like the one I have just created. But in 'The Portrait of Mr W. H.' Wilde very elaborately creates just such a situation, and adds this further twist: his language demands a choice, but it also makes either choice seem inadequate or wrong. If we decode Wilde's denials into affirmations we deliver his text into the hands of Mr Justice Wills; and even if we do not share that jurist's 'utmost sense of indignation at the horrible charges brought home' to Wilde (*Trials*, 339), still we have agreed with judge and jury about the facts that Wilde's text is at pains to deny. But if we accept Wilde's denials we not only convict ourselves of naïvety; ironically, we still condone the court's judgement, by agreeing in effect that a sexual reading must be a peccant one. Any attempt to stop the play of Wilde's narrative and to say what it is *really* about will either demonize or neuter it.[10]

In 'The Portrait of Mr W. H.', then, Wilde tried to speak about sexual desire by withholding the language of his own speaking—always deferring the revelation the language promises, because that revelation, being *in* language, would necessarily falsify his truth. But Wilde's representative reader was Queensberry's lawyer, Edward Carson, and Carson was not much interested in narrative indeterminacy or utopian individualism.

Queensberry had also published an ambiguous text. On 18 February 1895 he entered Wilde's club, the Albemarle, and handed the hall porter the widely reprinted visiting-card 'For Oscar Wilde posing as somdomite', or as Wilde's counsel, Sir Edward Clarke, interpreted it, 'Oscar Wilde posing as a sodomite'. Clarke provided his own exegesis of the offensive text. He found a 'suggestion' in it that made Queensberry, despite himself, a master of the indeterminate: Queensberry's words 'are not directly an accusation of the gravest of all offences—the suggestion is that there was no guilt of the actual offence', only (Clarke suggested) the appearance or 'pose' of such an offence (*Trials*, 108). Queensberry had chosen his words, if not spelled them, as carefully as Wilde habitually chose his. Between the signifier (Wilde's pose) and the signified ('the abominable crime of buggery with mankind'[11]) there was a loophole big enough to drive a libel through.

What may seem surprising, then, is that Carson largely ignored the loophole. He chose not to let his client slip through the gap between seeming and being, signifier and signified; instead he brought them violently together. Where Wilde's lawyer, Clarke, read Queensberry's accusation symbolically, or as a medieval exegete might say, *in bono*—Wilde *posed* in the sense of seeming to be something he was not—Carson read it literally, or *in malo*—Wilde *posed* in the sense of extravagantly displaying what in fact he was. When Wilde was forced to withdraw his prosecution, Clarke tried to get Carson to accept a verdict of not guilty of libel 'having reference to the word "posing", and to *Dorian Gray* and the epigrams in the *Chameleon*. Nothing would then be conceded about Wilde's acts of sodomy . . .' (Ellmann, 452). The defence would not co-operate. In order to imprison Wilde, Carson chose first to imprison language itself; he would capture language—not only Queensberry's but Wilde's too—within the court's strict construction, stripping it of its subversive indeterminacy.

So Carson's questioning of Wilde was a contest of hermeneutic principles, a battle over the protocols of reading. Carson appealed to the 'common sense' of the 'ordinary individual' who knows that where there's smoke there's fire.

Wilde countered from the radically antimimetic and subjectivist position of 'The Decay of Lying' and 'The Critic as Artist', proposing that language is its user's personal creation, not a common denominator, and that it creates its truth, rather than mimicking a truth that precedes it. In Carson's forensic reading, the Wildean text is transparent: Wilde posed as a sodomite; only a pervert would pose as a sodomite; the pose told the truth, and the truth was available for all to read. And books? Carson wants to know whether 'A perverted novel might be a good book?' But Wilde does 'not know what you mean by a "perverted" novel':

'Then I will suggest *Dorian Gray* as open to the interpretation of being such a novel?'
'That could only be to brutes and illiterates. The views of Philistines on art are incalculably stupid.'
'An illiterate person reading *Dorian Gray* might consider it such a novel?'
'The views of illiterates on art are unaccountable.' (*Trials*, 124)

From Carson's point of view, illiterates can read perversion as well as anyone else. The truth of Wilde's text is open to all, and it is identical to the truth of Wilde's life.[12]

Carson asks if it is not true that 'The affection and love of the artist of *Dorian Gray* might lead an ordinary individual to believe that it might have a certain tendency?' (*Trials*, 124). The author of *Dorian Gray*, however, says that he has 'no knowledge of the views of ordinary individuals'. Indeed Wilde repeatedly disclaims knowledge of the very language Carson is speaking: these words are not his. Did Wilde think that the story 'The Priest and the Acolyte' was 'blasphemous'?

'I think it violated every artistic canon of beauty.'
'That is not an answer.'
'It is the only one I can give.' (*Trials*, 121)

Carson demands, repeatedly, that Wilde speak the court's language; repeatedly Wilde refuses any language except his own:

'I wish to know whether you thought the story blasphemous.'
'The story filled me with disgust. The end was wrong.'

'Answer the question, Sir. Did you or did you not consider the story blasphemous?'

'I thought it disgusting.'

And once again: 'Do you consider that blasphemous?' 'I think it horrible. "Blasphemous" is not a word of mine' (*Trials*, 121–2). 'Blasphemy', like 'sodomy', is a word that carries with it a whole vocabulary and a whole system of values that are not part of Wilde's system. More than verbal fastidiousness is at stake in Wilde's attempt not to be imprisoned in Carson's literalizing hermeneutics.

Why did Wilde charge Queensberry? Why, against the good advice of all his friends except Douglas, did he put himself in the legal arena where language is policed as the preliminary enforcement to all others? Wilde seemed to believe that his romance would actually triumph over the lawyers' realism. He brought the imperial claims of personality to counter the claims of that worst of all authorities, the one (as we'll see in 'The Critic as Artist') created when the People join with the Government to suppress the Individual. His faith included an optimistic belief in the power of his language to name his desire, precisely by its privacies, its silences, its refusals of determinate meaning. What Wilde tried to get away with in court, telling his own truth in his own words, he had tried already in 'The Portrait of Mr W. H.'

But not to his perfect satisfaction. By summer 1893 at the latest, he had revised and expanded the published story to more than twice its original length, approximately 14,000 additional words. On 28 February 1895, on his way to the Albemarle Club where he would find the card left for him ten days earlier by the Marquess of Queensberry, Wilde visited Charles Ricketts and C. H. Shannon at their studio in Chelsea.[13] For over a year the manuscript of the expanded story had been in Ricketts's and Shannon's possession: they were supposed to design a new edition, complete with a frontispiece that would purport to be the (forged) portrait of Mr W. H. The designers' dilatoriness was not Wilde's only problem in getting the book into print. In late August through September 1894, his recent publishers, Elkin Mathews and John Lane, were dissolving their partnership, and in the process dividing up Wilde's work.

'The Portrait of Mr W. H.' became a hot potato between them. Wilde proposed that Lane retain rights to the plays and that Mathews publish 'Mr W. H.' Mathews refused: he would not publish 'The Portrait of Mr W. H.', he said, 'at any price'. But Mathews did want the plays; only Lane 'pointed out that if he takes the plays he must also take "Mr W. H."' — with the result that 'he declines both'. Lane finally agreed to publish the plays and 'Mr W. H.', but with a proviso: 'I am sure that you as a man of the world would not expect me or any other publisher to issue a book he had never seen' (7 September 1894: *More Letters*, 124–5). He had not seen the book because Ricketts and Shannon had the manuscript in Chelsea; but it sounds as though he hoped he would never see it. After all, 'as a man of the world', he had seen enough in the earlier, unexpanded version. More of the same could only make things worse.[14]

In fact Wilde's judgement in expanding the story is questionable on various grounds. The added freight of Shakespearean scholarship tips a sharp, ingenious parable in the direction of heavyweight exegesis. Wilde runs the danger of replicating Cyril Graham's fatal error, bringing a fine theory down to the level of forensic (if forged) evidence, this time in the form of further quotations and more summarized scholarship. The added section III, for instance, under the pretence of fleshing out the biography of Willie Hughes, draws on an impressive range of nineteenth-century scholarship to tell us more than we may want to know about the history of boy actors in the Elizabethan theatre.

To complete the 'Willie Hughes theory', Wilde worked out a solution to the other part of the sonnet puzzle, the story of the Dark Lady. In the added section IV he gives her a shape if not a name: 'The woman that came between Shakespeare and Willie Hughes was a real woman, black-haired, and married, and of evil repute' (61). Her actual identity is less interesting than her function. She becomes for the narrator not only a heterosexual impediment to the homoerotic love-story, but an instance of the inevitability and danger of forgery in real life. Using the sonnets as his ostensible evidence, the narrator decides that Shakespeare entered the triangular affair only to 'shield [Willie's] purity' by interposing his own body: 'To compass this end he abandons himself to her, feigns to be full of an absorbing and sensuous passion of possession, forges false words of love, lies to her, and tells her that he lies' (12). Forgery and feigning are not in themselves culpable acts: the narrator begins his story by proposing 'that all Art being to a certain degree a mode of acting, an attempt to realise one's own personality . . . to censure an artist for a forgery was to confuse an ethical with an aesthetical problem' (3). Cyril Graham, who forges a portrait of Willie Hughes to prove his theory about Shakespeare's love, is an avatar of the Shakespeare who forged false words to the Dark Lady to protect Willie Hughes.

Shakespeare's involvement with this bad woman shows that personality is a thing we create, or forge, to recreate ourselves as something (however briefly) new. With more sublimity than the wisecracking mode of 'The Decay of Lying', the narrator explains the precedence of language. Both Shakespeare and Cyril Graham learn that

It is never with impunity that one's lips say Love's Litany. Words have their mystical power over the soul, and form can create the feeling from which it should have sprung. Sincerity itself, the ardent, momentary sincerity of the artist, is often the unconscious result of style . . . (expanded version, 63; not in *Blackwood's*)

Acting as if he desired her, Shakespeare comes in fact to desire; forging a passion, he discovers the 'many maladies' of desire, and 'Lust that makes one love all that one loathes, and Shame, with its ashen face and secret smile' (64). Wilde's narrative energy in the story's heterosexual interlude is invested not in the passion between lovers but in the eroticism of artistic creation. And in the more extensive additions that explain the nature of Shakespeare's love for Willie Hughes words are also the issue: words which can be forged, which can create the thing they are supposed to imitate, and which are always subject to interpretation.

So John Lane's fear—that the expansion would make the story's 'tendency' more explicit—is only partly realized, for the expanded version simultaneously hides more than the original, by creating more spaces into which interpretation must pry. In both versions the narrator asks, 'Who was that young man of Shakespeare's day who, without being of noble birth or even of noble nature, was addressed by him in terms of such passionate adoration that we can but wonder at the strange worship, and are almost afraid to turn the key that unlocks the mystery of the poet's heart?' (12): additions elsewhere in the revised text do nothing to remove the teasing vagueness ('*strange* worship') and hesitancy ('*almost* afraid') of the briefer original. Wilde's apparent explicitness always leaves the impression of something more to be said; hence there is a regress of revelations, each one provoking the need for another.

The deferrals invite the reader to go beneath the surface into the suggestive spaces created by the story's absences; but (as Wilde puts it in the Preface to *Dorian Gray*), 'Those who go beneath the surface do so at their peril', for 'It is the spectator, and not life, that art really mirrors.' Carson's 'ordinary individual' thinks that art is a window on reality; Wilde's narrator knows that 'Art, even the art of fullest scope and widest vision, can never really show us the external world. All that it shows us is our own soul, the one world of which we have any real cognizance' (expanded version, 76; not in *Blackwood's*). But even that 'cognizance' is partial, unstable, for the 'one world' of the soul turns out to be multiple and shifting. The revelation of the self to itself in art also changes, creates, and recreates, the self. The proof is this very narrative of gained and lost belief.

In Cyril Graham's theory and in Shakespeare's sonnets the narrator finds his personal truth:

The soul, the secret soul, was the only reality. How curiously it had all been revealed to me! A book of Sonnets, published nearly three hundred years ago, written by a dead hand and in honour of a dead youth, had suddenly explained to me the whole story of my soul's romance (expanded version, 79; not in *Blackwood's*).

But almost immediately with the revelation comes the change: the narrator wonders why his passionate belief in Willie Hughes left him as soon as he expressed it:

Had I touched upon some secret that my soul desired to conceal? Or was there no permanence in personality? Did things come and go through the brain, silently, swiftly, and without footprints, like shadows through a mirror? Were we at the mercy of such impres-

sions as Art or Life chose to give us? (expanded version, 81; not in
Blackwood's)

The work of art—Shakespeare's sonnets, Wilde's 'The Portrait
of Mr W. H.'—tells us what we are and in the process makes
us something different. Its meaning is as elusive as personality, from which it derives and which it creates and in which it
can never rest.

So how is the reader of Wilde's story to know what Wilde's
story means? Or, perhaps, since 'It is the spectator, and not life,
that art really mirrors', *who* it means? When the narrator tells
us that Shakespeare's sonnets (in the Cyril Graham version)
had 'suddenly explained to [him] the whole story of [his]
soul's romance' are we to understand that the sonnets had
revealed to him the homosexual nature of his genital desire?
Or does the phrase 'soul's romance' imply something more
sublimated or sublime, to which genital sexuality is irrelevant? What in fact was the nature of Shakespeare's love for
Willie Hughes? Did they sleep together? Who did what to
whom? At Wilde's second trial, a chambermaid testified that
the sheets in Wilde's room at the Savoy Hotel 'were stained in
a peculiar way' (*Trials*, 220): was that the stain of truth, at last,
or an irrelevant accident of the body? 'The Portrait of Mr
W. H.', a fiction in the form of a theory denied in its making,
invites the reader to 'go beneath the surface' to explore an
absence ('There is nothing in the idea of Willie Hughes'); what
a reader finds is a reflection of his or her own interminable
quest for meaning.

Wilde's additions to the published version tempt the reader
deeper into its illusory depths. In the *Blackwood's* text, the narrator says, 'I did not care to pry into the mystery of [Willie
Hughes's] sin'—in a context that makes the sin seem to be
Willie's desertion of Shakespeare for a rival playwright. The
expanded version has: 'I did not care to pry into the mystery of
his sin *or of the sin, if such it was, of the great poet who had so dearly
loved him*' (35; my italics)—where the effect is to make the
reader ask *what* sin ('if such it was') Shakespeare may have
been guilty of. The expansion is richer in reticence: still the
narrator will not pry into the mystery he has created, but now
he has nominated it a 'sin' only to wonder if in fact it was a sin,

and added the phrase 'so dearly loved him' which may lead us to suppose either a sexual sin or a sin against art. Like Queensberry accusing Wilde not of being but of posing as a sodomite, Wilde's addition opens the text to interpretation. The 'ordinary reader' may find 'a certain tendency' in it, a tendency Carson will designate 'unnatural' and 'perverted'. But Wilde will protest that the meanings of 'brutes and illiterates' cannot be his.

In revision, Wilde added long passages about Hellenism, Platonism, and Neoplatonism. These are the passages that most precisely describe the nature of Shakespeare's attachment to Willie Hughes. Or seem to: in the narrative context they can only tell us the precise nature of the narrator's belief (now disavowed) about the nature of that attachment. But the indeterminacy of the added passages derives not only from the self-subverting narrative context. In the last decades of the nineteenth century, the invocation of Hellenism, Platonism, and Neoplatonism was richly ambiguous in ways Wilde knew well and exploited brilliantly.

I mentioned in a previous chapter the recently achieved centrality of Plato in the Oxford curriculum of Wilde's time. (Cyril Graham and the narrator of 'The Portrait of Mr W. H.' lack Wilde's advantages: they went to Cambridge, where they avoided 'a sound commercial education' only because they played more than they worked (6).) Richard Jenkyns in *The Victorians and Ancient Greece* (1980) and Linda Dowling in *Hellenism and Homosexuality in Victorian Oxford* (1994) recount the influence of this renascent and reconstituted Hellenism, which gave a small but influential group of young men a way to name—indirectly, and in Greek—a love for which English had no acceptable name. Richard Jenkyns has little patience for what he sees as the interpretative inaccuracies of Pater and Wilde. Privileging his own classical scholarship over the purposes of the Victorians, he concludes that they are simply wrong when, like Pater, for instance, they transmute Plato's advocacy of 'a temperance entirely freed from the tyranny of the senses . . . into an aesthetic cult of sensuous austerity' (257). According to Pater, Platonism 'is not a formal theory or body of theories, but a tendency, a group of tendencies—a tendency to think or feel . . . in a particular way'; according to Jenkyns,

'These words can scarcely be read without amazement and indignation' (259). Jenkyns's indignation arises partly from offended professionalism, but his repeated use of the anachronistic epithet 'invert' to characterize the offending writers suggests another area of aggravation. A century after the fact, that is, the Paterian or Wildean appropriation of the language of Hellenism can still seem a sexual as well as a scholarly affront.

In 'The Portrait of Mr W. H.' Wilde Victorianizes his Platonic discourse by introducing it with a version of Matthew Arnold's distinction between Hebraism and Hellenism: '"The fear of the Lord is the beginning of Wisdom", said the stern Hebrew prophet: "The beginning of Wisdom is Love", was the gracious message of the Greek' (expanded version, 42; not in *Blackwood's*). This is the gracious message the Renaissance ('which already touched Hellenism at so many points') learned to read, but by no ordinary process of reading: it was only by 'catching the inner meaning of this phrase and divining its secret' that the Renaissance 'sought to elevate friendship to the high dignity of the antique ideal' (42). Already, the suggestion of a hidden meaning or sub-cultural code, presumably unavailable to 'brutes and illiterates' (in court, read 'ordinary persons'), begins to press the Arnoldian distinction into the service of a liberated erotic desire.

Ficino's translation of the *Symposium* is for Wilde's narrator the near-magical link between ancient Greece and Renaissance England. The description of the translation itself and of its effects is marked by the numinous words—strange, curious, subtle; colour, influence, passion—that also describe the 'poisonous' yellow book that Lord Henry Wotton gives Dorian Gray. But it is not only the decadent keywords that give the passage its illicit spice:

this wonderful dialogue, of all the Platonic dialogues perhaps the most perfect, as it is the most poetical, began to exercise a strange influence over men, to colour their words and thoughts, and manner of living. In its subtle suggestions of sex in soul, in the curious analogies it draws between intellectual enthusiasm and the physical passion of love, in its dream of the incarnation of the Idea in a beautiful and living form, and of a real spiritual conception with a travail and a bringing to birth, there was something that fascinated the poets and

scholars of the sixteenth century. Shakespeare, certainly, was fascinated by it . . . (expanded version, 42; not in *Blackwood's*)

The 'subtle suggestions of sex in soul' and the analogies
'between intellectual enthusiasm and the physical passion of
love' might, in another context, for all their apparent explicitness, pass as unexceptionable. But the fact that the dialogue
'exercise[s] a strange influence over men', colouring 'their
words and thoughts, and manner of living', is almost a parody
of what the homophobe most fears about the freemasonry of
sexual perversion. Plato's book, like Oscar Wilde himself,
seems to beckon from—here I quote Mr Justice Wills's words
to Wilde—'the centre of a circle of extensive corruption of the
most hideous kind among young men . . . ' (*Trials*, 339). On this
reading, Plato's 'strange influence' passed to Ficino who
passed it to Shakespeare who infected little Willie Hughes; the
sonnets to Willie infect the already effeminate Cyril Graham,
who lures first Erskine and then the narrator into the secret
circle; Erskine dies—nominally of consumption—but the narrative that records it all, 'The Portrait of Mr. W. H.', carries the
pernicious influence into the future.

According to Wilde's narrator, 'it is only when we realise the
influence of neo-Platonism on the Renaissance that we can
understand the true meaning of the amatory phrases and
words with which friends were wont, at this time, to address
each other' (expanded version, 43; not in *Blackwood's*). So to
understand 'the true meaning' of Shakespeare's language we
must understand the true meaning of Neoplatonic language;
but to understand that we must understand the true meaning
of Wilde's story—a story that purports to elucidate the languages, Platonic and Shakespearean, on which it in fact
depends. On the question the forensic reader finds most
urgent—is the sort of love designated by these discourses
criminally culpable? is it in fact fully sexualized?—Wilde
makes the mutual elucidations perfectly self-cancelling. 'There
was', he writes, 'a kind of mystic transference of the expressions of the physical sphere to a sphere that was spiritual, that
was removed from gross bodily appetite, and in which the
soul was Lord' (expanded version, 43–4; not in *Blackwood's*). Is
this 'transference of expressions' only a linguistic dodge, a

code that directs us to go on understanding *body* where mystically it seems to put *soul*? Or would such a coded reading merely reproduce the error of those 'who find ugly meanings in beautiful things' (Preface to *Dorian Gray*)? Wilde's next sentence is heavy with the language of mystic meaning: 'Love had, indeed, entered the olive garden of the new Academe, but he wore the same flame-coloured raiment, and had the same words of passion on his lips' (44). This Love that looks and sounds like sex—what would it call itself if it dared to speak its name? Or would there be a name for it to speak?

Wilde's intentions were conceived with an audience in mind —to an extent an audience of his mind, an audience of most unordinary persons. We know what the prosecutorial reader found in the hollows and hints created by Wilde's discourse of Platonism and Neoplatonism. Here I want to speculate beyond the published record to ask about another class of potential readers, the scholarly experts.

No one knew more about the key texts in that discourse than the Reverend J. P. Mahaffy (1839–1919), the man who had been Wilde's tutor in Classics at Trinity College, Dublin, and in whose company Wilde travelled to Greece in 1877. When the first edition of Mahaffy's *Social Life in Greece from Homer to Menander* appeared in 1874, its preface acknowledged the help of 'Mr Oscar Wilde of Magdalen College'. But a second edition, in 1875, no longer carried that acknowledgement. And Wilde's name was not the only thing missing: 'In one direction . . . this [second] edition is partially rewritten', Mahaffy explained:

There were certain phases in Greek morals, which had hitherto not been fairly discussed and which had been consequently misunderstood, and upon these I wrote freely what I thought due to the Greeks and to their culture. I see no reason to retract one word I have written, and refer scholars interested in the byways of Greek society to my first edition which will thus retain for them an independent value. But there are things which ought to be said once, and which it is nevertheless inexpedient to repeat. I have therefore substituted for my discussions in Greek morals, new matter, which will, I hope, prove interesting, and which will be suited to all classes of readers; so that the book in its present form can be made of general use for school and family reading.[15]

In the section thus banished from 'school and family reading', it is not hard to spot Wilde's contribution in a single sentence: 'As to the epithet unnatural, the Greeks would answer probably, that all civilisation was unnatural . . . '[16] The rest sounds pure Mahaffy.

Ten years after their trip to Greece, Wilde wrote a devastating (unsigned) review of a later Mahaffy book, taking his former teacher to task for blatant imperialism and provincialism. Mahaffy not only wrote as a Unionist Irishman, but as if Greece *were* Ireland: 'in his attempts to treat the Hellenic world as "Tipperary writ large", to use Alexander the Great as a means of whitewashing Mr Smith, and to finish the battle of Chaeronea on the plains of Mitchelstown, Mr Mahaffy shows an amount of political bias and literary blindness that is quite extraordinary' (*Pall Mall Gazette*, 9 November 1887: *Rev.* 209). Writing about Greek love in the first edition of *Social Life in Greece*, Mahaffy reveals as much about the anxieties of an Anglo-Irish heterosexual as he does about Greek homosexuality.

Mahaffy's historical imagination extends only to seeing himself in fancy dress: 'I can . . . easily imagine a modern Irishman transplanted to an old Greek symposium, and there observing that in spite of the romantic feelings existing between the men present, nothing was done, or even hinted at, inconsistent with the strictest taste and propriety.'[17] Mahaffy gets around the embarrassment of genital sexuality, whether Greek homo- or Irish hetero-, not exactly by denying its existence, but by relegating it to the aberrant. He admits that in Greek society there were exceptional 'cases' where 'sentiment . . . did ally itself with passion, and lead to strange and odious consequences', but Mahaffy asks us to remember 'the modern parallel': 'in the midst of all the romantic and chivalrous respect with which ladies are treated in society, there are also cases where sentiment allies itself with passion . . . '. Who are we to judge? After all, in heterosexual society the aberrant alliance of sentiment with passion 'leads to consequences socially more serious, though less revolting (of course) to our tastes'.

In its normative form, then, Greek love was as innocent of sexuality as the modern love experienced by 'Every English gentleman, who has not gone in search of low philosophy to palliate bad morals . . . '. Such a gentleman knows 'that though there is a distinct difference in his sentiment as regards friends of the opposite sex, yet to him, consciously at least, any physical cause is not only rare, but abhorrent':

His sentiment takes the form of brighter conversation, or increased politeness, of voluntary slavery, of keenness in argument or in teaching, and stops there in almost every case, giving him no trouble or thought when the hour passes, and is nowise related to that strong want with which the Darwinians identify it. (307–8)

The ancient-modern parallel almost breaks down when Mahaffy confronts the institution of heterosexual marriage; but that too is salvaged by being relegated to the aberrant and even then only grudgingly allowed any taint of sexuality: 'Even in the exceptional case where this [modern] sentiment leads to the longing for a permanent union, it is held separate from the lower passion, so much so that a modern gentleman who married for the reasons admitted by St Paul, would be justly stigmatised as a low and brutal creature, who was dishonouring the so-called object of his affections' (308).

Thus Mahaffy can look at Greek homosexuality only by modelling it on heterosexuality, and he can look at heterosexuality only by seeing it as no sexuality at all. But the fact that Mahaffy suppressed even this sterilized account from his second edition suggests that his prophylaxis was unsuccessful. The problem lay not in the ancient but the modern world, where it proved impossible to represent homosexuality without the emphasis falling on the *sexuality*. The scandal of love between men is that it makes sexuality itself visible, and thereby infects even the love between men and women with the taint of a 'strong want'. The modern sexual invert—as opposed to the ancient asexual Greek lover of boys—must be 'a low and brutal creature' (like the heterosexual who marries for sex) not because males are the object of his genital desire but simply because he desires.

Mahaffy's opinion of *The Picture of Dorian Gray* and 'The Portrait of Mr W. H.' is not on record, but his efforts to clear himself of the taint of Wilde are. He expunged Wilde's name from *Social Life in Greece*, and in 1896 he refused to sign a petition for Wilde's release from prison, saying that Wilde was 'the one blot on my tutorship' (Ellmann, 29). Inevitably, when Mahaffy read the vagueness of *Dorian Gray* or the precision of 'Mr W. H.', the classical scholar, like Carson's 'ordinary person', would find the allusions to Hellenism and Platonism 'perverse' and 'unnatural'. He would read the author in the text in order to avoid reading himself, because for him sexuality itself is perverse and unnatural.

There was another classical scholar whose understanding of the transaction of desire between reader and text was closer to Wilde's, and who was more prepared—eager, indeed—to find himself mirrored in the ancient texts. John Addington Symonds (1840–93) was as learned in the Classics as Mahaffy; but he was also a leading theorist, as well as indefatigable field worker, in the developing discourse of English homosexuality. In the expanded version of 'The Portrait of Mr W. H.' Symonds actually makes an appearance: he is the narrator's authority for the opinion that 'the Platonic conception of love [is] nothing if not spiritual . . . ' (44). In fact, however, Symonds's understanding of Platonic love, on the page and elsewhere, mixed spirit and flesh more complexly than that.

In his *Memoirs*, Symonds writes that 'Our earliest memories of words, poems, works of art, have great value in the study of psychical development. They indicate decisive points in the growth of personality.'[18] Two texts, one Shakespearean and one Platonic, stand as especially vivid indices of Symonds's personality. 'Venus and Adonis' is the Shakespearean text. Symonds thinks he was less than 10 years old when he read it: 'It gave form, ideality, and beauty to my previous erotic visions' (63). Where his earlier fantasies had been of 'adult males . . . shaggy and brawny sailors', he now found the 'adolescent Adonis' a more complex and satisfying form for identification and projection:

In some confused way I identified myself with Adonis; but at the same time I yearned after him as an adorable object of passionate love. Venus only served to intensify the situation. I did not pity her. I did not want her. I did not think that, had I been in the position of Adonis, I should have used his opportunities to better purpose. No: she only expressed my own relation to the desirable male. She brought into relief the overwhelming attraction of masculine adolescence and its proud inaccessibility. Her hot wooing taught me what it was to woo with sexual ardour. I dreamed of falling back like her upon the grass, and folding the quick-panting lad in my embrace. (63)

It is a remarkable passage of introspection; its analysis of the narcissistic element in sexual desire and its acknowledgement of sexuality in childhood seem historically prescient, until we remember how much of Freud's work was also done during Victoria's reign. For the moment, however, I only want to emphasize the role that Symonds gives to *reading*: it was the Shakespearean work of art, seen by his unique personality, that made that personality know itself, and gave it form.

Thus taught by Shakespeare at 10, Symonds went on at 13 to pursue his education at Harrow. For someone else it might have been the ideal place, but Symonds describes it as a sexual hell. Here in horrible abundance were parodies of the physical acts that might have gratifed his sexual desires, mocking rather than fulfilling his personality:

Every boy of good looks had a female name, and was recognized either as a public prostitute or as some bigger fellow's 'bitch'. Bitch was the word in common usage to indicate a boy who yielded his person to a lover. The talk in the dormitories and the studies was incredibly obscene. Here and there one could not avoid seeing acts of onanism, mutual masturbation, the sports of naked boys in bed together. There was no refinement, no sentiment, no passion; nothing but animal lust in these occurrences. They filled me with disgust and loathing. (94)

Amidst Harrow's pullulating adolescent sex, Symonds 'remained free in fact and act from this contamination' (95).

It was a dangerous period for Symonds, not because of the easy availability of sex but because its avoidance tempted him to think that he 'had transcended crude sensuality through the aesthetic idealization of erotic instincts' (96). Like the Reverend J. P. Mahaffy, the young Symonds 'did not know how fallacious that method of expelling nature is' (96). But Symonds outgrew the belief that 'crude sensuality' could be transcended. What saved him from the twin dangers of 'aesthetic idealization' and 'the animalisms of boyish lust' was 'the gradual unfolding in [himself] of an ideal passion which corresponded with Platonic love' (96)—a Platonic love, it should already be clear, which does not exclude the flesh to gratify the spirit.

He was 17 when he read the *Phaedrus* and the *Symposium*. Here was 'the true *liber amoris* at last, the revelation I had been waiting for, the consecration of a long-cherished idealism. It was just as though the voice of my own soul spoke to me through Plato, as though in some antenatal experience I had lived the life of a philosophical Greek lover.' In Plato he 'had obtained the sanction of the love which had been ruling [him] from childhood' (99). Symonds's revelatory reading of the *liber amoris* inevitably brings to mind Dorian Gray's reading of the poisonous yellow book: 'Things that [Dorian] had dimly dreamed of were suddenly made real to him. Things of which he had never dreamed were gradually revealed' (*CW* 101). Like Symonds, Dorian finds in the book a prescient portrait of the self he now knows he is destined to become: 'the whole book seemed to [Dorian] to contain the story of his own life, written before he had lived it' (*CW* 102).[19] In 'The Portrait of Mr W. H.' too—where Wilde uses the trope of 'the fatal book' even more centrally and ingeniously—the narrator, like Symonds, reads his way to self-revelation:

As from opal dawns to sunsets of withered rose I read and re-read [the sonnets] in garden or chamber, it seemed to me that I was deciphering the story of a life that had once been mine, unrolling the record of a romance that, without my knowing it, had coloured the very texture of my nature, had taken the place of personal experience. . . . A book of Sonnets . . . had suddenly explained to me the whole story of my soul's romance (77, 79).

In Wilde's own life, as in Symonds's, the *Symposium* was the text that gave sanction to sexual desire. In exactly the sort of circular reading process I have been describing, it allowed him to interpret, or revise, the text of his own history and in turn give meaning to Plato's text. Writing to Douglas from prison, Wilde describes the degrading progress of a letter in which he 'compared [Douglas] to Hylas, or Hyacinth, Jonquil or Narcisse. . . . ' Because of Douglas's negligence, the letter passes to blackmailers, who pass it around London where 'every construction but the right one is put on it', and it ends in the Old

Bailey where it is denounced as the epistolary equivalent of 'gross indecency'. Wilde's explanation that the letter is a prose-poem, 'like a passage from one of Shakespeare's sonnets', is unavailing because (as he now tells Douglas), 'It can only be understood by those who have read the *Symposium* of Plato . . . ' (*Letters*, 440). To understand Wilde's Shakespearean prose-sonnet to A. D. one must understand Plato, and to understand Plato one must understand that 'The Portrait of Mr W. H.' is not 'suggestive of unnatural vice'.

Symonds's discovery of himself in Plato's text seems to differ from the discoveries in 'The Portrait of Mr W. H.' in one important respect: in Wilde's story the texts bring death, while Plato's text points Symonds the way to life. In fact, however, Symonds's attitude towards the book that saved him is interestingly ambiguous. Following the passage that describes his reading of the *Symposium*, Symonds includes in his *Memoirs* the text of a letter he wrote in 1889 to Benjamin Jowett, warning the man responsible for introducing Hellenism into the curriculum against the danger of 'making Plato a textbook for readers in a nation which repudiates Greek love, while the baser forms of Greek love have grown to serious proportions in the seminaries of youth and in the centres of social life belonging to that nation' (101–2). Thus Symonds warns others against the very book that ratified his own identity. But there is no necessary contradiction in Symonds's position. What is involved is precisely the interpretative issue I find in 'The Portrait of Mr W. H.': Symonds fears that readers 'in a nation which repudiates Greek love' will interpret Plato not as licensing *his* desire but, instead, its parody, which the court designates by the words buggery or sodomy or gross indecency. One phrase—'Greek love'—has to do for two antithetical things, itself and the 'baser forms' of itself. The true Greek love, for Symonds, is what Symonds feels and does, an entirely different thing (however much it may outwardly resemble it) from the baser things the boys at Harrow do.

Symonds was perfectly aware how difficult it was to maintain the distinction between Harrovian animalism and his own version of Platonized sexuality: scholarship as well as personal experience taught that difficulty, and here too the *Symposium* was a key text. Pausanius' speech on the 'two loves'—the higher and the lower Aphrodite, different in essence yet so identical in appearance that any lover might be excused for mistaking the one for the other—is a confusing and turgid passage. What is lawful in one place, Pausanius says, is censured in another; distinctions here do not exist there. In Athens and Lacedaemon 'the rules about love are perplexing', but in Elis and Boeotia, where there are men of few words, 'they are very straightforward'; in Ionia 'the custom is held to be dishonourable', but liberty-loving Athenians know the political value of strong friendships, except that nowadays those friendships are in ill repute because of 'the evil condition of those who make them to be ill reputed'—and so on.[20] In a brief footnote in *A Problem of Greek Ethics* Symonds explains why Pausanius' speech is so difficult. He notes that 'Mr Jowett censures this speech as sophistic and confused in view'. Symonds agrees about the confusion but not about the censure: 'It is precisely on this account that it is valuable. The confusion indicates the obscure conscience of the Athenians. The sophistry is the result of a half-acknowledged false position.'[21]

Symonds's understanding both of the need to idealize sexuality and the sophistry of that idealizing made him the best-qualified person in late nineteenth-century England—including Wilde, who went to trial because he gave more weight to the idealizing than the sophistry—to understand the problem of naming homosexual desire. In his century, wrote Symonds (in a phrase I have already alluded to), 'The accomplished languages of Europe . . . supply no term for this persistent feature of human psychology, without importing some implication of disgust, disgrace, vituperation.'[22] But in the *Laws*, Symonds writes elsewhere, Plato had explained why *no* single term could be adequate: 'There are three distinct things, Plato argues, which, owing to the inadequacy of language to represent states of thought, have been confounded.' Symonds continues with an analysis of Plato's distinctions between 'friendship, desire, and a third, mixed species'.[23] But the analysis is less important for my point than the phrase I have already quoted: 'the inadequacy of language to represent states of thought'. It points me back to the language of 'The Portrait of Mr W. H.'

Under cross-examination at his second trial, Wilde was asked by the counsel for the Crown, Charles Gill, about the meaning of Douglas's poem 'Two Loves':

'There is no question as to what it means?'
'Most certainly not.'
'Is it not clear that the love described relates to natural love and unnatural love?'
'No.'
'What is the "Love that dare not speak its name"?' (*Trials*, 235–6)[24]

Wilde's eloquent answer to this interpretative impasse threatens to reproduce the problem of 'The Portrait of Mr W. H.' There is the definition by reference to texts that can go, as it were, in either direction: '"The Love that dare not speak its name" in this century is such a great affection of an elder for a younger man as there was between David and Jonathan, such as Plato made the very basis of his philosophy, and such as you find in the sonnets of Shakespeare and Michaelangelo.' Again there is the assertion of a spirituality that may rule out the sexuality it seems simultaneously to affirm: 'It is that deep, spiritual affection that is as pure as it is perfect.' But here Wilde confronts the problem of naming as such:

It is in this century misunderstood, so much misunderstood that it may be described as the 'Love that dare not speak its name', and on account of it I am placed where I am now. It is beautiful, it is fine, it is the noblest form of affection. There is nothing unnatural about it. (*Trials*, 236)

The bold transvaluation of terms in Wilde's answer suggests that his tactic in 'The Portrait of Mr W. H.' is neither a tease nor an evasion but an effort (in Blakean terms) not to be trapped in another man's system. The story's structure of self-subverting narratives and its deferral of determinate meaning are not on this account shirkings of authorial responsibility. In a century that could not name Wilde's love without making it 'unnatural', the deferral of naming could be an act of resistance. But other accounts are possible. Six years after Wilde's death—six years into the twentieth century—James Joyce, writing to his brother Stanislaus, said of *The Picture of Dorian Gray*,

It is not very difficult to read between the lines. Wilde seems to have had some good intention in writing it—some wish to put himself before the world—but the book is rather crowded with lies and epigrams. If he had had the courage to develop the allusions in the book it might have been better.[25]

Wilde's expansion of the original version of 'The Portrait of Mr W. H.' may show him hankering to speak the unspeakable with the kind of courage Joyce wishes for his countryman. But it also shows him cannily negotiating the danger (not only legal) of representing homosexual desire in Victorian England. In the Neoplatonic language of spirit and intellect, male homosexual desire could both declare itself and efface itself. In his implicit dialogue with Plato, Ficino, Shakespeare, even with J. P. Mahaffy and John Addington Symonds, Wilde could (in Joyce's phrase) 'put himself before the world' yet keep it a world of his own making. In the case of *Regina* v. *Wilde* the law tried to stop this subversive doubleness of representation and to reclaim Wilde's world for itself.

6 'The Critic as Artist'

'[M]EN are the slaves of words,' says Gilbert in 'The Critic as Artist'. And Wilde is the emancipator:

[People] rage against Materialism, forgetting that there has been no material improvement that has not spiritualized the world, and that there have been few, if any, spiritual awakenings that have not wasted the world's faculties in barren hopes, and fruitless aspirations, and empty or trammelling creeds. What is termed Sin is an essential element of progress. Without it the world would stagnate, or grow old, or become colourless. By its curiosity, Sin increases the experience of the race. Through its assertion of individualism, it saves us from the monotony of type. In its rejection of the current notions about morality, it is one with the higher ethics. (130)

The passage begins in paradox, as 'material' and 'spiritual' change places in the supposedly mechanical shuffling that Wilde's reviewers took to be the essence of his method. But the shuffle produces more than the inverse of its more familiar original. Gilbert's propositions try to do what they advocate; they try to make him 'a lord of language' (*Letters*, 458), and master of the world it creates. As Gilbert knows, it is a mastery possible only in Utopia ('England will never be civilized till she has added Utopia to her dominions' (176)). But in Utopia there is no need for mastery because there is no authority.

Art, another way to 'increase experience', is not an alternative to sin, since 'All art is immoral' (166) and the artist is guilty of 'the gravest sin of which any citizen can be guilty': 'For emotion for the sake of emotion is the aim of art, and emotion for the sake of action is the aim of life, and of that practical organization of life that we call society.' The Utopian name of this gravest sin is 'contemplation' (167), but in England men call it indolence, effeminacy, aestheticism. Society demands work, action, results, but the artist provides sterility and uselessness. To say so requires either the acceptance of society's slavish language, hence the condemnation of the artist as sinner, or the recreation of that language by Wildean paradox.

Such recreation is one of the 'true function[s] and value[s] of criticism', the anti-work of 'the critic as artist'.

Between July 1890 and May 1891, when *Intentions* appeared, Wilde was just where he seemed to like to be: in trouble. In the previous year he had published 'Pen, Pencil, and Poison', 'The Decay of Lying', and 'The Portrait of Mr W. H.' Frank Harris claimed that the first two 'helped to injure [Wilde's] standing and repute', and his magazine rejected the last, which would later be used at the trials as evidence of Wilde's perverse intentions. Then, on 20 June 1890, *Lippincott's Magazine* published *The Picture of Dorian Gray*. Attacks on Wilde's novel about nameless sin and its gaudy retribution began immediately in the press, and immediately Wilde took to the letters columns to reply. He had gone the same route earlier in the year when Whistler revived another old charge, the shaming crime of plagiarism. (Whistler proleptically linked the two charges when he imagined Wilde 'criminally prosecuted, incarcerated, and made to pick oakum, as he has hitherto picked brains—and pockets!')[1] In the midst of these controversies Wilde published 'The True Function and Value of Criticism', in issues of the *Nineteenth Century* for July and September 1890, which, revised for *Intentions*, became 'The Critic as Artist'.[2] It is his longest and most ambitious theoretical text, and his most embattled. A dialogue which sublimes the dandy's insolent languor, promoting the contemplative life and the virtue of doing nothing, was not only born amidst controversies but literally shaped by them.

Wilde continued his counter-attacks against journalists and other opponents with 'The Soul of Man Under Socialism', published in February 1891. I will discuss the essays separately and in that order, but in this chapter I will also notice where they echo, amplify, or contradict one another on the subject of Wilde versus the Press. The two essays measure, both in scope and tone, the extent of Wilde's trouble. It would be wrong to say that they are more in earnest than his previous work; they are, if anything, as defiantly irresponsible, as carefree of the shibboleths of consistency, accuracy, and sincerity, as anything he ever wrote. But the stakes are higher than in the other essays of *Intentions*. 'The Critic as Artist' recreates the dubious aesthete of 'Pen, Pencil, and Poison' and the irresponsible liar of 'The Decay of Lying' as the sublime critic who looks out upon the world and knows its secret and becomes divine (212). In both 'The Critic as Artist' and 'The Soul of Man Under Socialism', aesthetic concerns are inescapably also political concerns, and explictly they involve questions of real power. Who will judge artists and who will control their products?— a question posed not only in the rarefied context of aesthetic discourse but also of legally enforceable censorship. Who will judge morality? Who, finally, will control the very language of judgement? Indicative of this new engagement is Wilde's promulgation of a new category, 'criticism', where previously art alone would do.

The dialogue swarms with cultural allusions, to the great and the near-great, the famous, the infamous, and the vaguely remembered; but its dazzle of quotation and allusion amounts to more than saturation name-dropping. For all its professed quietism, it is a power-play, aggrandizing Wilde by making him heir to an ancient and honourable tradition of his own creation: 'The one duty we owe to history', as Gilbert says, 'is to rewrite it' (127). The essay's original title alludes to Matthew Arnold's essay 'The Function of Criticism at the Present Time' (1865). Wilde's spokesman, Gilbert, quotes or echoes Arnold to make some of his most important points, but so too does Ernest, who exists to be corrected. To make some of those corrections, Gilbert quotes or echoes Pater, but Pater's ideas are also under revision. And running throughout the essay is the dialogue with Whistler. The proposition that 'to do nothing at all is the most difficult thing in the world' (167) is historically overdetermined: behind the neat point of the paradox is the long tradition of Christian contemplation, but so too is 'the almond-eyed sage of the Yellow River, Chuang Tsu' (179), whose injunction to contemplative self-culture (in Wilde's redaction) chimes perfectly with Emerson's.[3] And then there is 'Plato, with his passion for wisdom' and 'Aristotle, with his passion for knowledge' (167). And 'Browning felt something of this' (173), as did Darwin, Renan, and Walter Savage Landor (211–12). Out of such literary bricolage Wilde creates a world and then takes personal possession of it.

The technique of allusive dialogue makes 'The Critic as Artist' hard to summarize, hard even to follow as a series of logical propositions. But it is not obfuscation. Wilde harnesses the prestige of culturally remarkable individuals—all those names, Greek and Roman, Renaissance, modern—in order to empower the self-credentialled aesthetic critic. He puts himself in the line, not of figures in the landscape of Victorian professional scholarship, but of personalities who made their own greatness.[4] Compared to 'The Decay of Lying', 'The Critic as Artist' digresses, repeats, and accretes, as Wilde's speakers try to capture all of history in order to win their own day. Wilde had to respond to attacks from the philistine right at the same time that he had to respond to attacks from the aesthetic left, as represented by Whistler. The technique of allusive dialogue allows him to claim allies in improbable places. The dialogue turns allusion into paradox and epigram in order to assert a series of apparently perverse propositions about the cultural work it calls 'criticism', and all of them crown the Wildean critic as newly acknowledged legislator of the world. The best critic, says Gilbert, rather than explaining the work of art, 'may seek rather to deepen its mystery', and 'the true critic is unfair, insincere, and not rational'. According to Gilbert, 'the highest criticism is that which reveals in the work of Art what the artist had not put there'. Such criticism 'treats the work of art simply as a starting-point for a new creation'; it 'is itself an art', and of all the arts it is 'the purest form of personal expression'. As pure creation and personal expression, criticism's responsibility 'is to see the object as in itself it really is not'. Inaccurate and insincere, yet perfectly expressing the critic's moods, 'Criticism . . . makes culture possible'. It 'will annihilate race-prejudices' and 'give us the peace that springs from understanding'. Therefore, 'It is to criticism that the future belongs.'

But not without a struggle. The hostile reviews of *Dorian Gray*, and Wilde's responses to them suggest what is at stake in the attempt to wrest the future for the critic-as-artist. I say 'suggest', because the reviews employ a polemical variant of the inexpressibility topos, always implying that the worst they say is still not the worst that could be said. Wilde and his critics are in a sort of conspiracy of excitingly expressive silence. In the novel, for instance, Basil Hallward is incapable of saying

exactly what Dorian does that is so disastrously and con-
tagiously wicked: 'Why is it, Dorian, that a man like the Duke
of Berwick leaves the room of a club when you enter it? Why is
it that so many gentlemen in London will neither go to your
house nor invite you to theirs?'[5] Hallward begins to list the
young men to whom Dorian's 'friendship [has been] so fate-
ful' (1890; 'fatal' 1891): there was 'that wretched boy in the
Guards who committed suicide', and 'Sir Henry Ashton, who
had to leave England', and Adrian Singleton and Lord Kent's
youngest son and the young Duke of Perth. Dorian stops Basil
in mid-recitation, and—in the *Lippincott's* version of 1890—
leaves the suggestion that the list stretches out to the crack of
doom. This is one of the passages Edward Carson questioned
Wilde about at the trial. It is probably the passage Wilde
alluded to when he rejected Carson's accusation that the 1891
version was 'purged'; rather, says Wilde, 'I made an addition'
after Pater 'pointed out . . . that a certain passage was liable to
misconstruction' (*Trials*, 124). The addition is a paragraph in
which Dorian denies responsibility for the young men's now
specified, non-homosexual problems (1891, p. 118); but the
specificity after-the-fact cannot stop the rhetorical leakage
caused by Basil's damagingly vague accusations. And in the
controversy that erupted with the magazine version, Wilde's
tu quoque—'Each man sees his own sin in Dorian Gray. What
Dorian Gray's sins are no one knows. He who finds them has
brought them' (*Letters*, 266)—does nothing to staunch the
flow.

The reviews to which Wilde responded in the summer of
1890 employ a rhetoric of the inexpressible for their own purposes.[6] The *St James's Review* hinted at a subtext in the novel,
but only by way of refusing to specify it: 'Not being curious in
ordure, and not wishing to offend the nostrils of decent persons, we do not propose to analyse *The Picture of Dorian Gray*:
that would be to advertise the developments of an esoteric
prurience' (*Heritage*, 68). The *Daily Chronicle* almost exhausted
the thesaurus: the novel is unclean, poisonous, mephitic,
effeminate, vulgar, cheap, insincere, squalid; but still there
remains 'every form of secret and unspeakable vice' (*Heritage*,
72). And the *Scots Observer* tried to turn the metaphorically
unspeakable into a legally enforceable silence with its

assertion that 'The story . . . deals with matters only fitted for the Criminal Investigation Department or a hearing *in camera*'.

The obvious conclusion—that the unspeakable thing is the usual suspect, sodomy—is not so much wrong as incomplete. Overdetermination, rather than indeterminacy, is the crucial point. The language is so savagely, inordinately hostile precisely because the physical fact a reader might find lurking under those splendid folds of implication simply does not measure up to the critics' sense of the novel's offence. The reviews, like the novel, are clearly located at the transitional moment when, as Alan Sinfield has pointed out, a modern notion of homosexual identity emerges from a dense nexus of cultural codes.[7] In that nexus, the crime for which Wilde was ultimately convicted is only a part. Unmistakably it is there in the *Scots Observer*'s crack that Wilde 'can write for none but outlawed noblemen and perverted telegraph boys, [and] the sooner he takes to tailoring (or some other decent trade) the better for his own reputation and the public morals'. But even in this allusion to the Cleveland Street scandal of the previous year, the sexual offence bleeds into a class offence (noblemen and telegraph boys), and class is an issue in the suggestion that Wilde take up the traditionally 'effeminate' trade of tailoring.

The reviews accuse Wilde, not of being queer, but of all the things queerness implies when the queer is 'a young man of decent parts, who enjoyed (when he was at Oxford) the opportunity of associating with gentlemen' (*St James's Gazette: Heritage*, 69). The language of the reviews is rife with words of downward social mobility: 'vulgar', 'vulgarity', 'squalor', 'grubbing in muck-heaps'. (In 'The Critic as Artist' Wilde was returning the compliment: journalism 'justifies its own existence by the great Darwinian principle of the survival of the vulgarest' (109)). The surplus of vitriol flows in part from the transgression of social rank by a young man (Wilde or Dorian) whose presumably sexual associations level class distinctions and (however improbably) threaten English society itself. When the *Daily Chronicle* accuses Dorian of 'defiling English society with the moral pestilence which is incarnate in him' (*Heritage*, 73), the accusation of what is technically a sexual offence (which modern readers will extrapolate from the context of a modern and actual pestilence) is being located in a much wider field of threats to established society. Dorian Gray's 'pretty face, rosy with the loveliness that endeared youth of his odious type to the paralytic patricians of the Lower Empire' (*Heritage*, 73), is as fatal to his society as Helen of Troy's was to hers. The *Daily Chronicle*'s reference to 'paralytic patricians', crippled by their soft passions and rendered unfit for the business of class governance, expresses that fear of social decline, loosely labelled 'effeminacy', which Linda Dowling has analysed in *Hellenism and Homosexuality in Victorian Oxford*. It is a decline from ideals of manly productivity and social control traditionally associated with the class of 'gentlemen' which Wilde is supposed to have betrayed.

According to the *St James's Gazette*, the pleasure Wilde 'derives . . . from treating a subject merely because it is disgusting', his 'Puritan prurience', allies his story with two other offenders in the wider field of implication, Tolstoy's *The Kreutzer Sonata* and W. T. Stead's journalistic exposé 'The Maiden Tribute of Modern Babylon'. The linking of Wilde's story, on the one hand to Tolstoy's modern classic and, on the other, to a product of ephemeral journalism, may seem bizarre. What Wilde's co-conspirators have in common, which overrides the distinction between the high seriousness of book publication and the sensationalism of newspaper or pamphlet exposé, is an itch to reveal unwelcome facts about the social organization of sexuality. Tolstoy's story has a kind of madly lucid misogyny: the reader recognizes the speaker's excessiveness but also the power of his vision of women as the tormentors of men whose sexual desire turns female slaves into unappeasable mistresses. His satire of sexual obsession is both 'Puritan' and 'prurient' because it makes public what a gentleman would relegate to the privacy of the bedroom. Stead's articles, published in 1885 in his newspaper, the *Pall Mall Gazette*, were sensational propaganda for the Criminal Law Amendment Act, intended to combat child prostitution by raising the legal age of consent for girls from 13 to 16. 'The Maiden Tribute' was a tremendous *succès de scandale*; circulation of the *Pall Mall Gazette* went through the roof. The articles were attacked by almost every other London newspaper, and members of Parliament urged legal action against Stead rather than against brothel-keepers and their clients. Class issues overlap the narrowly sexual and suggest why the St James's Gazette could associate Stead's sensational campaign with Wilde's novel. Stead's articles pointed the prophetic finger of scorn at the entrenched representatives of wealth and privilege who, in his lurid version of events, preyed on the virginal poor. 'The Maiden Tribute' was 'indecent', 'obscene' and 'calculated to debauch' young people, not only because it told some steamy facts (and fantasies) about sex but also because it created an image of class war.

Wilde's letter to the St James's Gazette expresses pleasure in being associated with 'that great and noble artist Count Tolstoi' (Letters, 259). It says nothing about the association with Stead, despite or because of the fact that Wilde himself had regularly contributed reviews to Stead's newspaper. Under Stead's leadership, the Pall Mall Gazette, if it did not quite invent, most successfully packaged what Matthew Arnold derisively called 'the New Journalism'.[8] Arnold, whose voice is contested at the same time that it lends authority to 'The Critic as Artist', attacked Stead's New Journalism in an article in the Nineteenth Century ('Up to Easter', 1887), as part of his attack on the Irish Home Rule policy of another Nineteenth Century contributor, Gladstone. The complexity of Wilde's own antagonism towards journalism in 'The Critic as Artist' and 'The Soul of Man Under Socialism' is evident in this configuration. He apparently enlists as an Arnoldian enemy of the New Journalism. In a passage added to 'The Critic as Artist' for Intentions, he says that the 'new Journalism . . . is but the old vulgarity "writ large"' (190): it is a moment of characteristically dense dialogism, as Arnold's attack on the democratizing New Journalism is invoked to rewrite Milton's defence of freedom of conscience ('New Presbyter is but old Priest writ large'). Wilde appears to be an enemy of what Arnold calls 'feather-brained' democratic journalism. Yet the reviews of Dorian Gray were at that very moment claiming that Wilde was an ally of the New Journalism's proprietor, Stead.

The confusion arises from Wilde's utopian desire to level all authority. In 'The Critic as Artist' and more so in 'The Soul of Man Under Socialism' he attacks the 'authority' of journalism as a subclass or symptom of the 'authority' of 'the People' or (borrowing Arnold's label) 'the democracy'; but in pursuit of a world where artists are answerable only to their own individuality, he makes a distinctly un-Arnoldian move: *'All modes of government are failures. . . . for all authority is quite degrading. It degrades those who exercise it, and degrades those over whom it is exercised'* ('Soul of Man', 293–4; italics in original here and below). Authority of any sort opposes individualism, and *'Art is the most intense form of individualism that the world has ever known'* ('Soul of Man', 300). Therefore anybody who proposes to exercise authority over the artist—politician, journalist, or 'that monstrous and ignorant thing that is called Public Opinion' ('Soul of Man' 310)—must be resisted. In his fourth letter to the *St James's Gazette* he quotes Renan's saying 'that he would sooner live under a military despotism than under the despotism of the Church, because the former merely limited the freedom of action, while the latter limited the freedom of mind' (*Letters*, 262). An emended version of the saying appears in 'The Soul of Man Under Socialism':

There are three kinds of despot. There is the despot who tyrannises over the body. There is the despot who tyrannises over the soul. There is the despot who tyrannises over the soul and body alike. The first is called the Prince. The second is called the Pope. The third is called the People. (323)

In the name of a radically anti-authoritarian ideal Wilde takes a hard anti-democratic stand. His old argument of the One against the Many crystallizes, in 'The Soul of Man Under Socialism', in the epigrammatic identification of 'Public Opinion', government, and journalism as the united forces of 'authority'. The epigrams are brilliant, but the violent physicality of their metaphors—stoning, nailing, torturing, warping reveals the intensity of Wilde's own pain in the journalistic aftermath to *Dorian Gray*:

It was a fatal day when the public discovered that the pen is mightier than the paving-stone, and can be made as offensive as the brickbat. They at once sought out the journalist, found him, developed him, and made him their industrious and well-paid servant. . . .In old days men had the rack. Now they have the press. . . . In centuries before ours the public nailed the ears of journalists to the pump. That was quite hideous. In this century journalists have nailed their own ears to the keyhole. That is much worse. English public opinion . . . tries to constrain and impede and warp the man who makes things that are beautiful in effect, and compels the journalist to retail things that are ugly, disgusting, or revolting in fact . . . ('Soul of Man' 311–14)

Wilde never solved a basic problem of political science, that efforts to secure freedom in one area tend to create dangers to freedom in another. At times he gets no further than supporting one authority over another. In 'The Critic as Artist' he comes close to endorsing Arnold's chilling proposition (itself a quotation from Joubert) that 'Force and right are the governors of this world; force till right is ready. . . . and till right is ready, force, the existing order of things, is justified, is the legitimate ruler.'[9] Wilde softens it by casting it in the negative: 'There is only one thing worse than Injustice, and that is Justice without her sword in her hand. When Right is not Might, it is Evil' (208). In 'The Soul of Man Under Socialism' Wilde disguises the dilemma under the banner of Utopia. In 'The Critic as Artist' it is more difficult to finesse, because the reception of *Dorian Gray* was currently making it so.

Wilde had to contest the reviews of *Dorian Gray*. Not only did they counter his self-fashioning as the contemplative, detached critic; they went beyond the desirable point of advertising *Dorian Gray* and raised, instead, the spectre of legal action. Fresh in the public mind was the example of Zola's English publisher, sentenced the previous year to three months in prison, and of Stead himself in 1885, in the fallout from 'The Maiden Tribute' also given three months. There was something seriously chilling in the *St James's Gazette*'s question, '[w]hether the Treasury or the Vigilance Society will think it worthwhile to prosecute Mr. Oscar Wilde or Mssrs. Ward, Lock & Co. . . . ' (*Heritage*, 68–9). At the same time that 'The True Function and Value of Criticism' is promulgating the future rule of Wilde's sublimely aloof (read 'effeminate', 'paralysed') critic-as-artist, the guardians of the regnant ideology of manly productivity are threatening to roll out the power of government in defence of their status quo.

Wilde's replies were written literally overnight. They are a triumph of tone: restrained, humorous, but appropriately indignant. They are also, like the essays in *Intentions*, full of those contradictions or paradoxes by which Wilde tries to have things both, or all, ways. The contradictions gather around the proposition, in his first letter to the *St James's Gazette,* that 'The sphere of art and the sphere of ethics are absolutely distinct and separate' (*Letters,* 257). Wilde would repeat the phrase when he revised 'The True Function and Value of Criticism' into 'The Critic as Artist' (188). He needs the separation of art from ethics to preserve the privileged space of Art; the ringing declaration of separate spheres has a strategic aim in Wilde's attempt to create the conditions for his cultural empowerment. But repeatedly, in his letters and in 'The Critic as Artist', the separate spheres merge (as they must) when art's superiority to morals becomes, itself, a moral issue.

His first letter to the *St James's Gazette* merely asserts the doctrine of separate spheres and then wittily objects, not to the review, but to the magazine's posters, 'on which was printed in large letters: MR OSCAR WILDE'S LATEST ADVERTISEMENT; A BAD CASE'. '[O]f all the men in England', Wilde protests, 'I am the one who requires least advertisement' (*Letters,* 257). The second letter steps up the counter-attack on journalism: 'To say that such a book as mine should be "chucked into the fire" is silly. That is what one does with newspapers' (*Letters,* 258). And it begins to make explicit the seriousness with which he takes the threat of censorship: 'The poor public, hearing from an authority so high as your own, that this is a wicked book that should be coerced and suppressed by a Tory Government, will, no doubt, rush to it and read it.' And then a neatly papered-over attempt to have things both ways: the poor public will find that 'it is a story with a moral. . . . Is this an artistic error? I fear it is. It is the only error in the book' (*Letters,* 259). Still, the spheres of art and of ethics have for a moment come very close to merging.

And in his third letter Wilde completes that merger. He pounces on a tactical error: the editor had denied that his paper ever suggested the book 'should be "suppressed and coerced by a Tory Government"' (*Letters,* 260). The denial lets Wilde return to the attack. And the artist's absolute right to free expression becomes (as such assertions inevitably do) a right guaranteed under a limits-on-government clause that is assumed to exist in the sphere of ethics:

What is of importance is that the editor of a paper like yours should appear to countenance the monstrous theory that the Government of a country should exercise a censorship over imaginative literature. . . . any critic who admits the reasonableness of such a theory shows at once that he is quite incapable of understanding what literature is, and what are the rights literature possesses. A Government might just as well try to teach painters how to paint, or sculptors how to model, as attempt to interfere with the style, treatment, and subject-matter of the literary artist . . . (*Letters*, 260)

Of course governments *have* taught painters and sculptors how (and what) to paint and model. But that is not a precedent which the editor of a newspaper aimed at the higher bourgeoisie of a democratic country will want to embrace. The editor of the *St James's Gazette* is trapped by Wilde, and with Wilde, in the moral, or ethical, assumption that goverment's intervention in individual expression must be strictly limited. The editor has tried to control the damage by 'proposing that [only] the subject-matter of art should be limited' (*Letters*, 261). In response to that editorial wiggle Wilde made an addition to `The Critic as Artist' when he revised it for *Intentions*: 'Who can help laughing when an ordinary journalist seriously proposes to limit the *subject-matter* at the disposal of the artist' ('Critic as Artist', 189; my italics); instead he suggests that 'Some limitation might well, and will soon, I hope, be placed upon some of our newspapers and newspaper writers' (189). Newspapers should be controlled because they belong to the sphere of action; but art belongs to the sphere of thought 'and [he tells *The St James's Gazette*] even the editor of a London paper has no right to restrain the freedom of art in the selection of subject-matter' (*Letters*, 261).

Art is not a form of action but the highest mode of thought. In the Preface to *Dorian Gray* Wilde repeats his declaration of artistic independence from the laws of action and ethics: 'There is no such thing as a moral or an immoral book. Books are well written, or badly written. That is all.' The idea appears again in moments of wilful miscomprehension at Wilde's first trial. Carson asks whether one of the 'Phrases and Philosophies for the Use of the Young' is 'moral or immoral'. Wilde replies, 'There is no such thing as morality or immorality in thought.' About *Dorian Gray* Carson asks whether 'a perverted novel might be a good book?' 'I don't know what you mean by a "perverted" novel.' Carson continues to probe the semantic divide with a paradox of his own: 'An illiterate person reading *Dorian Gray* might consider it [a perverted] novel?' Wilde answers that 'The views of illiterates on art are unaccountable. I am concerned only with my own view of art. I don't care twopence what other people think of it' (*Trials*, 123–4). Taking his case to court, Wilde asks that his life be judged as if it were a literary text. The critic-as-artist knows that such a life belongs to the sphere of art, not of ethics, action, morality. But in 1890/1 Wilde was talking to journalists, and in 1895 he was talking to the judge; for neither of them was the argument from separate spheres even comprehensible.

The definition of the critic-as-artist depends on the definition of the critic-as-journalist: you can know the one because he is not the other. But it was in fact very hard, in 1890 as it is now, to draw the line between the journalistic reviewer and the—what? aesthetic critic, literary critic, cultural critic? 'The Critic as Artist' attempts to create a distinct category which will allow the differentiation of two otherwise similar functions. From 1885 to 1891 Wilde himself could have passed as a journalist. Most of his (at least) ninety reviews in the *Pall Mall Gazette* are unsigned. Anonymity in periodical publication contributes to the idea of a homogeneous class of writers whose work is a commodity; signed articles (like those which became the essays in *Intentions*) advertise the writer's possession of his words and ideas, spinning the writer toward the area where, in Wilde's realignment, 'criticism' and 'art' come together in opposition to 'journalism'. In the *Dorian Gray* controversy Wilde had to guess at the authorship of the hostile reviews: perhaps 'there have been really only two people engaged in this terrible controversy, . . . the editor of the *Scots Observer* and the author of *Dorian Gray*' (*Letters*, 271). The reviewers are anonymous, their work as indistinguishable as it is undistinguished; the author of *Dorian Gray*, whose name is attached to his book and his letters, makes everything he touches his own, the unalienable work of a critic-as-artist.[10]

Wilde had models for his attempt to upgrade the critic's job description, and in 'The Critic as Artist' he does nothing to hide them. His revisionary appropriation of Matthew Arnold and Walter Pater—their public roles as well as their ideas—is well known, because he virtually advertised it. According to Matthew Arnold, the function of criticism is to prepare a current of fresh ideas with which the creative artist can work. Although it is not the equal of creation, criticism under certain historical conditions makes progress possible, by avoiding the practical view and remaining, instead, 'disinterested'. And 'the aim of criticism is to see the object as in itself it really is'. Wilde's spokesman, Gilbert, quotes Arnold's line but calls it 'a very serious error', because 'Criticism's most perfect form . . . is in its essence purely subjective . . . the highest Criticism deals with art not as expressive but as impressive purely' (139). Gilbert's example of 'impressive' criticism is Pater's essay 'Leonardo da Vinci'. Gilbert does not care whether Leonardo put into the painting what Pater finds there, since 'criticism of the highest kind . . . treats the work of art simply as a starting-point for a new creation'.

Pater himself, in the Preface to *The Renaissance*, had emended Arnold: 'the first step toward seeing one's object as it really is, is to know one's own impression as it really is'. Wilde takes the progression from Arnoldian disinterestedness to Paterian impressionism—from the object to the subject, from a stable and knowable out-there to an always changing receiver of impressions—a step further: now the critic must 'see the object as in itself it really is not' (144), in order to escape the prison of the already constructed, to be creative instead of imitative. The Wildean critic neither knows nor feels the world, but makes it.

Of the three positions, Arnold's is the most paradoxical: in order not to be affected by or to affect the thing they see, disinterested critics have to lift themselves by the intellectual bootstraps and, from that gravity-defying position, perceive objects unchanged by the angle of perception.[11] (But in 1995 a reviewer in the London *Times* wrote that he prefers a book by an amateur critic to the work of virtually all 'modern literary scholarship' because, unlike the professionals' books, 'it is in the great tradition of criticism which attempts to see the object as in itself it really is'.)[12] By contrast, Wilde's way ('to see the object as in itself it really is not') is almost commonsensical: it preserves the object (which must *be* in order to be misperceived) and makes a virtue of necessary subjectivity. But, as we saw in 'The Decay of Lying', Wilde pushes the matter further, to claim for art a self-referentiality and for the artist an ahistorical autonomy which is, by that token, in danger of irrelevance or solipsism.

Wilde revels in the contradictions he causes to bubble in his stew of Paterian sensation and Arnoldian disinterestedness: the more inconsistent he is, the more, he claims, he is himself.[13] So he can indulge the language of decadent aestheticism to define 'the true critic' as 'he who bears within himself the dreams, and ideas, and feelings of myriad generations, and to whom no form of thought is alien, no emotional impulse obscure' (172), and pass untroubled from it to the language (actually quoted) of Arnold's liberal empiricism: 'the true man of culture . . . develops [the] spirit of disinterested curiosity . . . [and learns] "the best that is known and thought in the world"' (173). In the debate between critic and creator, Wilde can seem to stand squarely with the critic. He gives to the corrigible Ernest the Arnoldian opinion that 'the creative faculty is higher than the critical', and lets Gilbert amend it: 'the highest Criticism, being the purest form of personal impression, is in its way more creative than creation, as it has least reference to any standard external to itself, and is, in fact, its own reason for existing . . . ' (137). He thereby valorizes criticism—a word, if not, as he uses it, an activity, associated with Arnold—by aesthetic standards more appropriate to Pater's ideal of art. The trick is to collapse the categorical distinction between criticism and creation by defining one as a form of the other while simultaneously keeping the nominal distinction so that criticism can be regarded as superior: Wilde's 'criticism' needs something to be superior to even if that something is the thing it represents in its most perfect form. Gilbert goes on speaking as if there were a difference, and as if creation (which is blindly active) is running out of raw material while criticism, which 'creates fresh forms' (123), is getting up a new head of steam (204–5); but his examples of critics who are at the present time replenishing creation's supplies are Kipling, Browning, and Meredith (203–4).[14]

Wilde's yoking together of disparates serves other ends than inconsistency. The prestige of Arnold's voice underwrites the socially central, indeed legislative, function Wilde assigns to his aesthetic critic-as-artist. Assuming Arnold's authority, he gives the critic an active role in the formation of culture: 'It is Criticism, as Arnold points out, that creates the intellectual atmosphere of the age' (205); 'Criticism . . . by concentration, makes culture possible' (206). But Wilde's 'culture' is profoundly different from Arnold's. It is to politics what the anti-mimeticism of 'The Decay of Lying' is to aesthetics: a form of representation in which the individual subsumes the general. 'Individualism' will be the key word in 'The Soul of Man Under Socialism'; but Wilde had already reached the political conclusion of that essay—that 'All modes of government are failures' (293–4)[15]—by the time of 'The True Function and Value of Criticism'. In 'The Soul of Man Under Socialism' Wilde would draw on Chuang Tsu to underwrite his visionary individualism. And in 'The Critic as Artist' he draws on Chuang Tsu (as, however improbably, he also does on Arnold) to help him move the aesthete from the margin of society to a redefined centre. Chuang Tsu preached `the great creed of Inaction, and . . . the uselessness of all useful things'.[16] In 'The Critic as Artist', 'to do nothing at all' becomes the most difficult and intellectual thing in the world, and the non-productive dandy becomes the critic who is dedicated to self-culture and has 'that serene philosophic temper that loves truth for its own sake' (209).

Wilde's transvaluation of criticism into the highest form of creativity—or the most irresponsible self-indulgence, depending on your point of view—follows upon his rejection of the transcendent object, whether it goes by the name of 'history', 'culture', or 'nature'. Partly for that reason, not all critics welcome his effort to save them from secondariness. The valorization of criticism by conflation with art threatens to efface criticism as a profession with its own history, standards for membership, and rules of behaviour. Wilde's critic-as-artist reads (*inter alia*) Flaubert, Baudelaire, and Mallarmé, and in response writes an essay called *Salomé*. Unchecked, such practices could lead to the worst excesses of what the next century was to call 'theory'—and we know what that unfortunate movement led to. With that danger in mind, René Wellek, the New Critical historian of criticism, writes that 'the idea of "creative criticism" propagated by Oscar Wilde . . . spell[s] the breakdown or even the abolition of all traditional literary scholarship and teaching'.[17] But Wellek is prematurely apocalyptic. Wilde's essay breaks down the traditional distinctions not in order to create a playground for a free-for-all but to elevate the 'critic' to a position of moral, even legislative authority.

Wilde's long-running and very public controversy with the exquisitely competitive Whistler was, on its comic surface, an argument about who said what *originally* in a situation of such dense intertextuality that it has, strictly speaking, no beginning. Simple chronology fails to capture the affair: an accusation which was an offence in the present refers to an accusation made years before, which was an offence both then and now. One of the texts under contention was 'the definition of a disciple as one who has the courage of the opinions of his master'. That was Wilde's rough requotation of a phrase from 'The Decay of Lying' which Whistler claimed he originated but which Wilde said 'is really too old even for Mr. Whistler to be allowed to claim . . . '.[18] In strict chronology, Whistler, twenty years Wilde's senior, was the master aesthete to Wilde's disciple. In 1882 Wilde lectured in America from texts which unabashedly aimed to spread Whistler's gospel. (But those lectures also echoed voices, some of them French, which Whistler himself was echoing; and, as the subsequent controversy made clear, they also contained heresy.) And on 30 June 1883 Wilde lectured to the art students of the Royal Academy: 'There is a man living amongst us', he told them, 'who unites in himself all the qualities of the noblest art, whose work is a joy for all times, a master of all time. That man is Mr. Whistler' (*Misc.* 319–20).

The praise did not mollify Whistler: 'we who are working in art' (*Misc.* 311) was Wilde's way of addressing the art students, and the master was having none of the pronoun. Whistler's declaration that he would not let Wilde's 'we' usurp his 'I' came in a letter to the editor of the *World* in which he dizzily piled text upon text. It reports 'A supposititious conversation from *Punch* brought about by the following interchange of telegrams.' In the first of these Wilde is supposed to say, '"*Punch* too ridiculous—when you and I are together we never talk about anything except ourselves"', and in the second Whistler corrects him, 'when you and I are together, we never talk about anything except me'.[19] Five years later Whistler published a letter in which he claimed prior possession of all the ideas in Wilde's lecture to art students: 'Oscar— the amiable, irresponsible, esurient Oscar—with no more sense of a picture than of the fit of a coat, has the courage of the opinions . . . of others!'[20] Thus Whistler put into play the accusation of plagiarism he would later accuse Wilde of plagiarizing in 'The Decay of Lying'.

From the beginning it should have been obvious that there could be no peace between them. In 1878, while Wilde was at Oxford, Whistler's enemy had been Ruskin. In a pamphlet that followed the Pyhrric victory of his libel suit against Ruskin, Whistler thundered: 'Let work . . . be received in silence, as it was in the days . . . when art was at its apogee. . . . let there be no critics! they are not a "necessary evil," but an evil quite unnecessary, though an evil certainly.'[21] (The words are still echoing in 'The Critic as Artist': Ernest asks, 'what is the use of art-criticism? . . . in the best days of art there were no art-critics' (100, 104), to which Gilbert replies, 'I seem to have heard that observation before, Ernest. It has all the vitality of error and all the tediousness of an old friend' (105).) In February 1885 Whistler delivered his 'Ten O'Clock Lecture'. The lecture and Wilde's review of it in the *Pall Mall Gazette* (21 February 1885) made clear that there wasn't room in London for two top aesthetes. The points of contention in 1885 would help to shape 'The Critic as Artist' in 1890.

It was literally a question of who should speak for art. Whistler had in effect outflanked Wilde on the issue of art's autonomy and freedom from historical determination: art refers only to itself, and therefore no one but the artist (in the narrow sense now of practitioner) can judge it, not a dress-reformer or any other pretender to knowledge of beauty. To salvage a role for himself, Wilde had to temper his own anti-historicism, as he did in his review of the 'Ten O'Clock': 'An artist is not an isolated fact; he is the resultant of a certain

milieu and a certain *entourage* . . .'.[22] Mainly he had to defend
words over paint: 'the poet is the supreme Artist, for he is the
master of colour and form, and the real musician besides, and
he is lord over all life and all arts . . .'.[23] In 'The Critic as Artist',
Wilde transmutes this battle for turf into a theoretical claim for
the foundational force of language in culture; and he goes
beyond even a defence of written language to the claim that
'writing has done much harm to writers. We must return to the
voice' (114).

Two separable issues intertwine in the controversy. One, the
question of who has the bigger art, the poet or the painter, has
an ancient pedigree but remains irredeemably petty. The other,
who has the authority to speak for art, has at least a practical
urgency. In an unsigned review in 1887, Wilde claimed, with
direct reference to Whistler, that the painter is limited because
'it is only through the mask of the body that he can express the
mystery of the soul'. Tied to 'physical equivalents', the
painter's domain can never extend as far as the poet's, to
whom 'belongs Life in its full and absolute entirety; not only
the world that men look at, but the world that men listen to
also', the worlds of feeling, thought, passion, and 'the spiritual
development of the soul'.[24] Painting is limited by its materiality but words create thought, and thought is free. ('Do you
wish to love?' Gilbert asks. 'Use Love's Litany, and the words
will create the yearning from which the world fancies that
they spring' (198).)[25] Gilbert's claim that 'Literature is the
greater art' (140) is immediately followed by his question,
'Who . . . cares whether Mr. Pater has put into the portrait of
Mona Lisa something that Leonardo never dreamed of?' The
painter, like the rhapsode in Plato's *Ion*, is the instrument of his
art, the played-upon rather than the player: 'The painter may
have been merely the slave of an archaic smile' (140). The real
creator of the Mona Lisa is the aesthetic critic.

Wilde is playing several sides of the street on the currently
hot topic which a reviewer of *Intentions* characterizes as `the
fundamental *unity of the arts*, which it is now the fashion, following Mr. Pater, to introduce with a specious languor into the
criticism of any subject'.[26] Wilde sometimes sounds like a
spokesman for unity, a position which can translate insti-
tutionally into a kind of aesthetic free market, without

boundaries between professional and amateur, practitioner and critic: `there are', he wrote in his review of Whistler's 'Ten O'Clock Lecture', 'not many arts, but one art merely—poem, picture, and Parthenon, sonnet and statue—all are in their essence the same, and he who knows one, knows all' (*Pall Mall Gazette*, 21 February 1885: *Misc.* 66). But he sounds that way only when it is tactically useful, for instance in the competition with Whistler, and his purpose is as territorial as Whistler's. Even in Pater's *locus classicus*, the synthesis of the arts is the result of hierarchy and competition: though 'each art may be observed to pass into the condition of some other art', '*All art constantly aspires to the condition of music*' (Hill, 105–6; italics in original). Whistler's so-called symphonies and nocturnes seem to acknowledge painting's aspiration towards another art's condition, but *The Gentle Art of Making Enemies* records his absolute faith that only a painter has the equipment to hear a painter's notes. Whistler's artist works in a closed shop.

In order to open a space where his personality will secure the benefits of the professionalism it banishes, Wilde revises the assumption that the least discursive art is the highest art. Words have music, colour, and plastic form, and 'thought and passion and spirituality are theirs also, and theirs indeed alone' (119). (*Salomé* is there to demonstrate his point.) His sarcastic review of Selwyn Image's lecture on 'the absolute unity of all the arts' mocks the assumption that 'The lofty spiritual visions of William Blake, and the marvellous romance of Dante Gabriel Rossetti, can find their perfect expression in painting.'[27] But simply elevating the poet at the expense of the painter will not satisfy Wilde's expansive social desire. Ernest, wrong as usual, wonders whether 'the poet is the best judge of poetry, and the painter of painting' (200). The answer is that 'Art does not address herself to the specialist.' Indeed an artist can never judge another artist's work and sometimes not his own, because 'concentration of vision' and 'energy of creation' get in the way: 'It is exactly because a man cannot do a thing that he is the proper judge of it. . . . for creation limits, while contemplation widens, the vision' (202). Only 'the aesthetic critic . . . can appreciate all forms and modes. It is to him alone that Art makes her appeal' (202). In 'The Critic as Artist', partly to *épater* Whistler, Wilde takes the view that all art constantly aspires to the condition of criticism: the critic, whose mode is 'never imitative' and who creates mystery as well as meaning, 'solves once for all the problem of Art's unity' 'by transforming each art'—including, we must add, his own— 'into literature' (148).

7 'The Soul of Man Under Socialism'

QUEENSBERRY'S lawyer Edward Carson did not cross-examine Wilde about his fairy-tales. He should have, and not for the sake of an anachronistic pun. I want to begin my discussion of 'The Soul of Man Under Socialism' by way of a digression.

'High above the city, on a tall column, stood the statue of the Happy Prince' (CW 285): a reader would need a heart of stone not to laugh at what happened to him. From a work of art whose gilded perfection gives Charity Children the stuff to dream on, the Happy Prince turns himself into a philanthropist, and from a philanthropist to a martyr. 'The Happy Prince' is the perfect expression of a mood. It is the self-congratulatory mood the Swallow feels when he carries out the first of the Happy Prince's charitable intentions:

'It is curious', he remarked, 'but I feel quite warm now, although it is cold.'
'That is because you have done a good action', said the Prince. (CW 287)

The Swallow's warm feeling is one of the pleasures available to participants in the city's economic system. There are many opportunities for it where the few hold the capital which trickles down to the working poor and is doled out to the mass. A lover says '"how wonderful is the power of love!"', and his beautiful beloved, who wants a new dress in time for the state ball, replies, '"but the seamstresses are so lazy"' (CW 287). These heedless lovers are employers and consumers of others' labour, and the Happy Prince supplies the ideological mystification ('"There is no Mystery so great as Misery"' (CW 290)) which permits the inequity, and he is himself that ideology's most efficacious symbol ('"He looks just like an angel", said the Charity Children as they came out of the cathedral in their bright scarlet cloaks and their clean white pinafores' (CW 285)). The Swallow flies from the cathedral and the palace to the places of labour—the ships on the river, the ghetto, the seamstress's house. With the Swallow's help, the Happy Prince mutilates himself to help a struggling playwright, a match-girl, all the city's poor. But his charity changes little. A statue of the Mayor will replace the statue of the Happy Prince. The philanthropists lose one city of gold ('"the living always think that gold can make them happy"' (*CW* 290)) only to gain another. In the tale's bleak final line, God tells His Angels the fate of 'the two most precious things in the city': '"in my garden of Paradise this little bird shall sing for ever-more, and in my city of gold the Happy Prince shall praise me"' (*CW* 291).

Obviously this is not the only way to read 'The Happy Prince', even if you read it (as I have done) in light of 'The Soul of Man Under Socialism'. The story's meaning is that of which the opposite is also true: the meltingly erotic sentimentality yields its own legitimate pleasure, without the sub-Blakean twist I have given it.[1] But the politically ironized reading is a plausible one which does little violence to the evidence of Wilde's intentions. 'The Soul of Man Under Socialism', although written five or six years after Wilde conceived the story, supplies all the terms of the analysis: 'The majority of people spoil their lives by an unhealthy and exaggerated altru-ism. . . . [W]ith admirable but misdirected intentions, they very seriously and sentimentally set themselves the task of remedy-ing the evils they see. But their remedies do not cure the dis-ease: they merely prolong it. Indeed their remedies are part of the disease. . . . *The proper aim is to try and re-construct society on such a basis that poverty will be impossible.* . . . It is immoral to use private property to alleviate the horrible evils that result from the institution of private property.'[2]

A later story, 'The Young King', is more explicit (and, as fairy-tale, less successful) in its social commentary: 'This is a parable on the capitalist system', writes George Woodcock, 'as severe as anything in William Morris, and it can stand beside the grimmest passages of Marx as an indictment of the kind of horrors which, Wilde was fully aware, were inflicted on the toilers of this world for the benefit of the people he satirised in his plays'.[3] But Woodcock is as unfair to Wilde as he is to Marx and Morris. He underrates the extent to which Wilde's 'par-able' invites readings that comfort as well as indict—even as

'The Happy Prince' indicts what it also makes comfortable. The phenomenon is common in Wilde's work, and not just in the fairy-tales. 'The Portrait of Mr W. H.' denies what its readers make it affirm. *The Picture of Dorian Gray* condemns the hedonism its readers (not only of the prosecutorial sort) claim that it promulgates. In his society plays Wilde satirized a world he was simultaneously recuperating by the glamour of its appearance on stage at the St James's or the Haymarket Theatre. And in 'The Young King' the horrors of alienated labour that are revealed to the hero in his dreams are recuperated—or at least recuperable—for existing social conditions by a narrative coup of ostentatiously mystified hierarchy:

He stood there in the raiment of a king, and the gates of the jewelled shrine flew open, and from the crystal of the many-rayed monstrance shone a marvellous and mystical light. . . . And the people fell upon their knees in awe . . . And the young King came down from the high altar, and passed home through the midst of the people. But no man dared look upon his face, for it was like the face of an angel.

The Young King refuses to don his robe of tissued gold and is rewarded by more gold and more power. It is the kind of rhetorical situation which gives ascetics their heavenly crowns and brides of Christ their ecstasies. We know the difference, but the words are the same.[4]

In Wildean paradox, too, the ironized new meanings of words are only realizable in relation to their old meanings, which the paradox, for its subversive purpose, keeps in circulation. Regenia Gagnier finds a similar rhetorical principle at work in 'The Soul of Man Under Socialism'; she claims that Wilde's method, like Engels's, is 'to subvert the speech of his adversaries', a 'dialogical' process of deconstructing 'bourgeois categories of thought': 'Like Bakhtin's double-voiced words, Wilde's epigrams and paradoxes exploit the self-critical possibilities of Victorian language and thought patterns.'[5] I would add, however, that Wilde's double-voicing here is more duplicitous—or, rather, less univocal in its political meaning —than Gagnier implies. Wilde finds his semantic 'adversaries' among the socialists as well as among the soulful. As his title warns,[6] directness is not the essay's primary virtue: its terms —individualism, socialism, and (expectably) personality—

shimmer with the ingenious instability of paradox. As in 'The Portrait of Mr W. H.' an appropriated language—here, the discourse of contemporary political theory—tries to communicate a personal meaning, which is no party's line. 'The Soul of Man Under Socialism' rewrites the history of the future on Wilde's terms: it proposes the abolition of private property in order to invest the individual with the right of total self-possession.

Throughout the essay, Wilde defamiliarizes words in order to defamiliarize the world they supposedly represent. He enacts the arbitrariness of language, as he does in *The Importance of Being Earnest*, to rediscover the arbitrariness of supposedly 'natural' social arrangements. Here, not only poverty but 'Charity creates a multitude of sins' (275); yet the 'sins' that poverty creates—ingratitude, discontent, disobedience, and rebellion—are also virtues: 'Disobedience in the eyes of any one who has read history, is man's original virtue. It is through disobedience that progress has been made, through disobedience and rebellion' (279). What distinguishes 'The Soul of Man Under Socialism' is the explicitness of its lexical manoeuverings. Much of the essay is taken up with redefining, by expansive analysis as well as by the compaction of paradox, such words as 'immoral', 'morbid', 'exotic', 'selfish' —and, of course, 'Socialism, Communism, or whatever one chooses to call it' (276). Wilde's linguistic imperiousness makes him the Lady Bracknell of political theory. Lady Bracknell's fiat can move a house to the fashionable side of a square, or alter the fashion in sides. It can make smoking a suitable occupation for an eligible young man and elevate ignorance into 'a delicate exotic fruit' which keeps Grosvenor Square from acts of violence. The essay is not always up to Lady Bracknell's aphoristic and punning self-confidence. She knows that 'between the duties exacted of one during one's lifetime and the duties exacted from one after one's death, land has ceased to be either a profit or a pleasure' (Act 1: *CW* 332). In 'The Soul of Man Under Socialism', Wilde takes this at a more ponderous pace:

Property not merely has duties, but so many duties that its possession to any large extent is a bore. It involves endless claims upon one, endless attention to business, endless bother. If property had simply pleasures we could stand it; but its duties make it unbearable. (278)

On other occasions he rises to her level. He appropriates and personalizes the language of politics: 'democracy means simply the bludgeoning of the people by the people for the people. It has been found out' (294). His aphorisms invent a better world by rearranging elements of the old to assert a reasonable primacy for his individual will: *'Selfishness is not living as one wishes to live, it is asking others to live as one wishes to live'* (328).

But there are some houses and some squares that words cannot alter. And there is a fine line, which 'The Soul of Man Under Socialism' occasionally crosses, between paradox and platitude, satire and silliness. The essay is an epitome of Wilde's career. At times it makes you want to cheer, and at times to cry. It is wise, it is good, it is quotable, but it can also be breezily inconsequential or demonstrably wrong. It dismisses 'public opinion' as a thing 'of no value whatsoever', but (as we have seen) the essay came into being as part of Wilde's passionate campaign against the power of a hostile journalistic press. Wilde tries to enlist Jesus and Chuang Tsu, Emerson and William Morris, to help underwrite his utopian vision of the 'calm and self-centred' man, the individualist 'complete in himself', who knows that 'The things people say of a man do not alter a man. He is what he is' (290). But this bland hymn to the *integer vitae* concludes with a proposition which the authority of his own life converts to pathos: 'Even in prison, a man can be quite free. His soul can be free. His personality can be untroubled. He can be at peace' (290–1).

Yet for all its blindness, its manifest special pleadings and momentary failures, the essay works. The evidence is its enemies: more even than 'The Critic as Artist' it provokes its critics' apocalyptic strain. Their anxiety is the index to what is so powerfully right about it. More than a century after its publication, the American political scientist Christopher Lasch worries because Wilde's 'religion of art has survived the collapse of the Marxist utopia'. It is, he says, 'the most durable—in its own way the most seductive and insidious' of the nineteenth century's 'secular religions'.[7] 'Seductive' is Lasch's keyword. It calls to mind Mr Justice Wills's description of Wilde at the centre of a circle of extensive corruption among young men, except that now the Wildean blandishment is not only sexual: Wilde seduces the modern intellectual with the vision of a life founded on joy rather than pain, on possibility rather than renunciation. Wilde says that Christ's message was '"Be Thyself"'; Lasch replies that 'In place of self-denial and self-control, [this message] offered the seductive vision of selfhood unconstrained by civic, familial, or religious obligations' (232). The pariah of 1895 becomes in Lasch's neo-conservative vision the potent Lucifer of the next century's radicalism. Lasch claims that Wilde's call for artistic individualism was taken up in the 1960s by 'revolutionary students [who] adopted slogans much closer in spirit to Wilde than to Marx: "All power to the imagination" [Lasch forgets 'Power to the People']; "It is forbidden to forbid"' (234). But Lasch's real concern is not the bygone student movement but its supposed rebirth in the academic and cultural unsettlings of the 1980s and 1990s. Like the Victorian MP warning against the spread of pernicious literature, Lasch warns against the staying-power of what he balefully calls 'The Soul of Man Under Secularism': 'The continuing appeal of such ideas . . . should be obvious to anyone who casts an eye over the academic scene and the media' (234).

Lasch compliments Wilde by taking his ideas seriously as a threat to order. He was anticipated in a much more subtle essay by the sociologist Philip Rieff. In what American academics called 'Moratorium Year', 1970, in the same issue of *Encounter* which carried Robert Brustein's report of a Black Panther rally before 4,500 students at Yale, Rieff wrote about the 'psychiatric and historical fact [that] it is *No*, rather than *Yes*, upon which all culture, and inner development, depends'.[8] Rieff chose to designate Wilde, rather than a more current opponent of the cultural *No* (say, Herbert Marcuse or Abby Hoffman) as one of the 'great commanders in the forces' of the revolution. Like Marx and Nietzsche, Wilde tells us that 'men need not submit to any power—higher or lower—than themselves' (37). Rieff uses one of Wilde's own tactics, the redefinition of basic terms, to oppose Wilde's sublime anti-authoritarianism. 'Culture', says Rieff, is the name for that 'deeply installed' authority to which we must submit in order to survive 'the assault of sheer possibility'. Wilde's claim that the artist can 'express everything', and that everyone can be an artist, is destructive in an especially acute way: the flood of 'everything' is precisely what the walls of 'culture' are there to protect against:

the claim to express everything exacerbates feelings of being nothing. In such a mood, all limits begin to feel like humiliation. Wilde did not know that he was prophesying a hideous new anger in modern men, one that will render peaceable existence even more Utopian than before. (44)

The limitless permission of the Wildean Yes, like the pleasure principle, tempts us to our doom.

It didn't happen. Berkeley survived the free speech movement, and authority lives. But Rieff identifies a real threat to order posed by 'The Soul of Man Under Socialism', and (incidentally) reveals its continuity with the rest of Wilde's work, including the *The Importance of Being Earnest*. 'When authority becomes external it has ceased to be authoritative' (41), he writes in an epigram worthy of Wilde; and he analyses what is really meant by the '"depth" of character' Wilde famously lacked: 'By the grace of his opposition to militant truths Wilde helped lead an aesthetic movement away from the dominance of inwardness and towards an externalisation that works against all received conceptions of character' (42). Repression, sublimation, character are the property of culture; masks, surface, personality are the gifts of what Wilde strangely calls *both* socialism and its opposite, individualism.

Wilde had written previously on the subject of left-wing politics but what he wrote would not have been very threatening to anyone but himself. He is interested in the *idea* of revolution, and in the idea's interesting effects upon himself. In *Vera, or The Nihilists* (privately printed 1880, performed 1883) he combined Jacobean pastiche with old-fashioned nineteenth-century melodrama to create a play in which love conquers revolutionary sentiment. Vera Sabouroff has taken the nihilist oath:

To strangle whatever nature is in us; neither to love nor to be loved, neither to pity nor to be pitied, neither to marry nor to be given in marriage, till the end is come; to stab secretly by night; to drop poison in the glass; to set father against son, and husband against wife; without fear, without hope, without future, to suffer, to annihilate, to revenge. (CW 653)

This is asking for trouble since one of her fellow conspirators is the Czarevitch, Alexis, lightly disguised but still good-looking. Nihilists don't love, but Vera loves Alexis (who reciprocates), and love makes Vera into a royalist even before she knows Alexis's identity: 'Why does he make me feel at times as if I would have him as my king, republican though I be?' (CW 658). Alexis, whose nihilism is indistinguishable from a liberal Englishman's regard for reform, becomes Czar after his father's assassination (tableau, act drop), and Vera must now oppose her fellow conspirators' plan to assassinate Alexis. 'He is no tyrant', she protests, 'He loves the people'; and a benevolent despot is necessary: 'The people are not yet fit for a republic in Russia' (CW 678). In Act 4, Alexis and Vera (who has been sent to assassinate him) acknowledge their love ('I am no king now' he says, 'I am only a boy who has loved you' (CW 687)). The Nihilists, realizing that Vera hasn't been doing her job, make threatening offstage noises ('Conspirators *murmur outside*'). Vera gives the Nihilists the sign that saves Alexis: stabbing herself, she throws the bloody dagger out of the palace window, and in her dying line tells the young Czar, 'I have saved Russia' (tableau, curtain).

To the actress Marie Prescott, who played Vera during its run in New York (21–8 August 1883), Wilde wrote that 'I have tried in it to express within the limits of art that Titan cry of the peoples for liberty . . . ' ([?July 1883]: *Letters*, 148). But there are no Titans in his play and the threat of political instability is summoned into being only to be disarmed. Wilde's letter goes on to disavow any political intent:

it is a play not of politics but of passion. It deals with no theories of government, but with men and women simply; and modern Nihilistic Russia, with all the terror of its tyranny and the marvel of its martyrdoms, is merely the fiery and fervent background in front of which the persons of my dream live and love.

In both the letter and the play Wilde is trying to make his own flesh crawl; his nihilists will seem fiery and fervent, their martrydoms marvellous, only to someone for whom a little revolution would go a very long way.

Poems (1881) contains several sonnets on the subject of his lack of commitment to the cause. The book's second poem (after the waverings of 'Hélas!') is 'Sonnet to Liberty', four-teen lines of ambivalence and torn syntax, beginning with a negative:

> Not that I love thy children, whose dull eyes
> See nothing save their own unlovely woe,
> Whose minds know nothing, nothing care to know,
> But that the roar of thy Democracies,
> Thy reigns of Terror, thy great Anarchies,
> Mirror my wildest passions like the sea
> And give my rage a brother—! Liberty!
> For this sake only do thy dissonant cries
> Delight my discreet soul, else might all kings
> By bloody knout or treacherous cannonades
> Rob nations of their rights inviolate
> And I remain unmoved—and yet, and yet,
> These Christs that die upon the barricades,
> God knows it I am with them, in some things.

This is less interesting as poetry than as a symptom which demands 'The Soul of Man Under Socialism' for cure. The poet's soul is 'discreet'—a fastidious centre, and also 'dis-crete', as fearing merger with other, less discreet, souls, such as the dull-eyed children of Liberty with 'their own unlovely woe'. The 'dissonant cries' of Liberty 'delight' him only because they create images sufficiently awful to mirror his own soul which, like Liberty's democracies, reigns of terror, and great anarchies, is full of 'wildest passions' and 'rage'. If it were not for the ambiguously narcissistic 'delight' he takes in seeing his reflection in the uncontrollably populous vastness called Liberty, the poet would 'remain unmoved' at its repres-sion by kings' knout or cannonades. 'And yet, and yet', the poem concludes, with an unintentionally comic anticlimax of further ambivalence, 'I am with them, in some things'.

The ambivalence goes both ways: the poet has mixed feel-ings about Liberty because he has mixed feelings about his own 'passions', and vice versa. The more frightened he is of his inner anarchy, the more frightened he is by—yet possibly almost in love with—Liberty.

Liberatory politics scare him in another sonnet, 'Libertatis Sacra Fames'. It too begins in negation:

> Albeit nurtured in democracy
> And liking best that state republican
>   Where every man is Kinglike and no man
>   Is crowned above his fellows, yet . . .

Speranza's son is to the revolutionary manner born, but the effects of his nurture frighten him:

>   yet I see,
> Spite of this modern fret for Liberty,
>   Better the rule of One, whom all obey,
>   Than to let clamorous demagogues betray
> Our freedom with the kiss of anarchy.

In preference to a stew of alternatives he vaguely denominates as democacy, republicanism, and anarchy, he chooses 'the rule of One, whom all obey'. The sestet tries to explain this apparent sell-out but only comes up with a cliché about the effects of Liberty on a series of equally unresonant abstractions:

> Wherefore I love them not whose hands profane
>   Plant the red flag upon the piled-up street
>   For no right cause, beneath whose ignorant reign
> Arts, Culture, Reverence, Honour, all things fade,
>   Save Treason and the dagger of her trade,
> And Murder with his silent bloody feet.

Panic overwhelms the poet's tepid 'liking' of democracy when culture's *No* is threatened by the murderous *Yes* of anarchy.

Mixed feelings—about sexuality, religion, politics—is the subject and mode of much of *Poems*. That inauspicious volume is only a few years but otherwise a world away from the paradoxical tricks and Hegelian turns which, in *Intentions* as in *The Importance of Being Earnest*, allow him to turn ambivalence into liberation. In the poems, choosing is an agony, for poet and reader; in the prose, where paradox is the master trope, there are no choices to be made, and all of them are right. The real achievement of 'The Soul of Man Under Socialism' is not as theory or manifesto but as realization and demonstration: it is the prose equivalent of a world where the conditions which produce the poetry's agony of choice have already been overcome, a political revelation at the level of style.

According to Wilde's own account, it was Pater who made the excellent suggestion that he should turn away from poetry and try the 'much more difficult' medium of prose (22 March 1890: *Rev.* 538). The prose of *Intentions* accommodates the poetry's self-division without requiring resolution. Now Wilde can be totally committed to a socialism which means exactly what he wants it to mean, including its historical opposites. 'Libertatis Sacra Fames' follows a logic of decline which runs from democracy to demagoguery to anarchy to the loss of 'Arts, Culture, Reverence, Honour'. By contrast, the prose of *Intentions* dismantles the poem's binaries; now you get both 'Art' and 'anarchy' because both foster the individualism which is socialism perfected. The poem is eager to give names to scary abstractions and turn them into minatory signs of necessary limits. 'The Soul of Man Under Socialism' has an easier way with names. 'Socialism, Communism, or whatever one chooses to call it', says Wilde, 'by converting private property to public wealth, and substituting co-operation for competition, will restore society to its proper condition of a thoroughly healthy organism, and ensure the material well-being of every member of the community' (276). Facts do not prove the truth of this proposition, any more than facts disprove the beauty of a lie.

George Bernard Shaw allowed himself the credit for making Wilde a socialist. In his 'Memories of Oscar Wilde' appended to Harris's *Oscar Wilde: His Life and Confessions*, Shaw says that Wilde was immediately inspired to write 'The Soul of Man Under Socialism' after he heard Shaw lecturing on the subject. It is possible that Wilde did hear Shaw's lecture and that the lecture he heard became *The Quintessence of Ibsenism*, which Wilde found 'such a delight . . . that I constantly take it up, and always find it stimulating and refreshing' (23 February 1893: *Letters*, 332). But Shaw's voice was hardly the only one Wilde heard talking about socialism. The subject was all around him. Reviewing a book of poems by Alfred Austin (whom the

Observer had called 'the poet of Nature, of Patriotism'), Wilde asks, 'Is Mr Alfred Austin among the Socialists? Has somebody converted the respectable editor of the respectable *National Review*? Has even dulness become revolutionary?' (24 June 1889: *Rev.* 513). Austin's 'lumbering and pedestrian verses [about] his conception of the ideal state' include the image of young men and women holding 'parley brief or long, / Without provoking *coarse suspicion / Of marriage*', and of a *'poet, dragging / A load of logs along'*, while 'Each one some handicraft attempted' (Wilde's italics). Austin's poem, says Wilde, is 'interesting as a sign of the times' (514). They are times when bourgeois respectability can draw upon the discourse of utopian socialism and a conservative poet and editor unintentionally begins to sound like a second-rate William Morris. In such times even Queen Victoria sees socialism all over the place. She wrote to her Liberal Prime Minister that she would 'welcome warmly any words of Mr Gladstone's which affirmed that liberalism is not socialism and that progress does not mean revolution'. But Gladstone could not deny that '"a disposition to favour" socialism had already "made considerable way with the two chief political parties in the state"'.[9]

As Queen Victoria feared, it had spread; it was, as Wilde knew, not an 'it' at all but a broad term for many different and sometimes contradictory ideas. Reviewing *Chants of Labour*, a volume of socialist poetry edited by Edward Carpenter, Wilde says that 'the first thing that strikes one . . . is the curious variety of [the contributors'] several occupations, the wide differences of social position that exist between them, and the strange medley of men whom a common passion has united for a moment' ([15 February 1889]: *Rev.* 425). The contributors' ideological points of view are similarly diverse: 'This is, on the whole, very promising. It shows that Socialism is not going to allow herself to be trammelled by any hard and fast creed or be stereotyped into an iron formula. She welcomes many and multiform natures. She rejects none and has room for all.' And having gathered everyone under this big tent, Wilde gives a glimpse of the revisionary socialism he will create in 'The Soul of Man': 'She has the attraction of a wonderful personality . . . ' (426). Wilde is drawn to this 'personality' as Basil Hallward is drawn to Dorian Gray's. But Wilde knows, as Basil Hallward does, that there are risks. Basil recognizes in Dorian someone 'whose mere personality was so fascinating that, if I allowed it to do so, it would absorb my whole nature, my whole soul, my very art itself' (CW 21). Much of the energy of 'The Soul of Man Under Socialism' comes from Wilde's effort to dominate, rather than be dominated by, socialism's wonderful personality.

If socialism was everywhere, it was also in some specific places.[10] Wilde dominates his version of socialism—takes possession of the word even as he abolishes the institutions of possessiveness—by moving among these specific places with an appearance of casualness. Elsewhere in *Intentions* he is casual with the minutiae of scholarly citation in his pose as the dandy, disdainful of details. In 'The Soul of Man Under Socialism' he is still the dandy, still the connoisseur; but the object of his discriminating glance is the many-sided personality which, to a less competent eye, might look like a mere confusion of ideologies. He exploits the difficulty of sorting out all those irreconcilable yet supposedly like-minded groups: Fabian from SDP from anarchist from Socialist League from Fellowship of the New Life from, indeed, the Liberal Party. Of course there are limits to what Wilde's anti-authoritarian socialism can tolerate. It cannot tolerate 'an industrial barrack system, or any system of economic tyranny': 'It is to be regretted that a portion of our community should be practically in slavery, but to propose to solve the problem by enslaving the entire community is childish' (281–2). Authoritarian socialism or 'Industrial Tyrannies' would make 'the last state of man worse than the first' (276).

In 'The Critic as Artist' he had referred explicitly to the most immediately prominent of the competing socialisms his language takes into its embracing paradox: 'We are trying at present to stave off the coming crisis, the coming revolution as my friends the Fabianists call it, by means of doles and alms' (176). At the same time that Wilde invokes Fabianism he distances himself from it: they call it revolution, he calls it crisis—and the passage continues in an un-Fabian way:

England will never be civilized till she has added Utopia to her dominions. There is more than one of her colonies that she might with advantage surrender for so fair a land. What we want are unpractical people who see beyond the moment, and think before the day. Those who try to lead the mob can only do so by following the mob. (176)

Making the Fabians the allies of his utopianism is a difficult trick, but no trickier than his whole project: 'to make men Socialists is nothing, but to make Socialism human is a great thing.'[11]

In fact Shaw was the only member of the Fabian Society Wilde could, in even the broadest sense, call 'friend'. The Fabian Society was founded in 1884 and by 1888 it had barely grown to a hundred members, many of them the kind of 'sad vegetarians', the 'men in mackintoshes and women in knitted shawls' Wilde disdained in a typical audience of Ibsenites.[12] Shaw was the house ironist but the rest were pure essence of earnestness. Sidney Webb's gradualist tactic was to over-whelm the opposition with statistics in tract (number 5, *Facts for Socialists*) after tract (number 8, *Facts for Londoners*). But in 1889 the society did something Wilde had to admire: it issued a bestseller, the *Fabian Essays in Socialism*. The first thousand copies of *Fabian Essays*, with contributions by Shaw (two), Webb, William Clarke, Sydney Olivier, Annie Besant, Graham Wallas, and Hubert Bland, sold out in a month. By the end of the year 25,000 copies were in print.[13] (The print-run for *Intentions*, first edition and cheap edition combined, was 2,500.) A preface suggests that the Society's socialist ideology had already been put into practice in the book's joint author-ship: 'Everything that is usually implied by the authorship and editing of a book has in this case been done by the seven essayists, associated as the Executive Council of the Fabian Society. . . . But there has been no sacrifice of individuality.'

Individuality is not necessarily individualism, and indi-vidualism can be construed as the enemy of socialism if the individual's ends conflict with the socialist's means, like state ownership of the means of production. But the terms are almost comically reversible throughout the period. 'Indi-vidualism' could run the semantic gamut from a 'negative [sense], signifying individual isolation and social dissolution . . . [to] a positive, signifying individual self-fulfilment and . . .

the organic unity of individual and society'.[14] This is the kind of contested discourse Wilde negotiates in 'The Soul of Man Under Socialism'. Although Sydney Olivier could write in his contribution to *Fabian Essays* that 'Socialism is merely Individualism rationalised, organised, clothed, and in its right mind' (105), most of the Fabian essayists agree with Webb in making individualism another term for *laissez-faire* capitalism, the sort of thing which 'made possible the "white slavery" of which the "sins of legislators" have deprived us' (41). According to Webb, the organization of municipal services in England already shows the 'unconscious abandonment of individualism' (46); and a good thing too: 'the perfect and fitting development of each individual is not necessarily the utmost and highest cultivation of his own personality, but the filling, in the best possible way, of his humble function in the great social machine' (58).

Wilde's *rapprochement* almost magically reverses the course of Fabian progress: 'Individualism, then, is what through Socialism we are to attain to' (293). First will come socialism, through it individualism, and 'As a natural result the State must give up all idea of government' (293). In the context of Webb's rhetoric of humble functions and social machinery, Wilde's vague programme is, at its worst, no worse. Where no one exercises authority over anyone else, everyone's 'personality' will be perfectly realized. In this perfected state, nature itself is sufficiently recuperated to become a source of metaphors:

It will be a marvellous thing—the true personality of man—when we see it. It will grow naturally and simply, flower-like, or as a tree grows. It will not be at discord. It will never argue or dispute. It will not prove things. . . . The personality of man will be very wonderful. It will be as wonderful as the personality of a child. (287)

Here is the artist as critic as flower-child. For contrast, and as a reminder of the non-utopian conditions under which Wilde actually writes, we can remind ourselves of Dorian Gray's discovery that his personality is *not* 'a thing simple, permanent, reliable, and of one essence', that there is (as the narrator of 'The Portrait of Mr W. H.' suspects) 'no permanence in personality', and that, as 'The Critic as Artist' knows, 'we are never more true to ourselves than when we are inconsistent' (182).

Insipid though it is, Wilde's rhetoric of the conflict-free organic personality tacitly acknowledges another improbable presence in the essay. 'My ideal of the society of the future', writes William Morris,

> is first of all the freedom and cultivation of the individual will, which civilization ignores, or even denies the existence of; the shaking off the slavish dependence, not on other men, but on artificial systems made to save men manly triumph and responsibility; and in order that this will may be vigorous in us, I demand a free and unfettered animal life for man first of all: I demand the utter extinction of all asceticism.[15]

Unlike Morris, Wilde, of course, 'demands' nothing. Morris's language of manliness, vigour, and 'animal life' is not Wilde's. But Morris's optimistic impatience with existing conditions can recall Wilde in his Lady Bracknell vein. In Morris's society of the future, 'vicarious servanting, sewer-emptying, butchering, letter-carrying, boot-blacking, hair-dressing, and the rest of it, will have to come to an end' (460). Wilde, though he explicitly rejects Morris's Luddite tendency, can be at least as imperious about nasty occupations: 'To sweep a slushy crossing for eight hours a day when the east wind is blowing is a disgusting occupation. . . . All work of that kind should be done by a machine' ('Soul of Man', 297).

News from Nowhere, Morris's great 'Utopian Romance', was published in the same year as 'The Soul of Man Under Socialism'. But it had previously appeared in instalments in Morris's magazine *Commonweal*, from January to October 1890, and so, as J. D. Thomas points out, 'was almost certain' to have been read by Morris's long-time admirer.[16] It is as contemptuous of the machinery of liberal democracy as Wilde is. From the point of view of the socialist future, the Parliament of the present is 'a dung-market'.[17] Morris's time-traveller asks his native informant Hammond, '"How do you manage with politics?"' Hammond, smiling, claims he is the only man in Nowhere who could even understand the question: '"we are very well off as to politics,—because we have none"' (116). The question and brief answer comprise, at Hammond's request, a chapter by themselves. But Morris supplies something Wilde cannot: his astonishing long chapter on 'The Change' is an unillusioned 'history of the terrible period of transition from commercial slavery to freedom' (133). Wilde can look at the world as it is and as it might become, but he cannot, like Morris, look without flinching (as he does in the 'Sonnet to Liberty' and 'Libertatis Sacra Fames') at the revolutionary interval of pain and death, General Strike and civil war.

Instead Wilde negotiates the interval by renovating the language of the present with paradox. Paradox may point towards a perfected future but it can never rest in it. It is impossible, without laughing, to imagine Wilde in the England of Morris's anarcho-socialist future, where all is 'trim and neat and pretty' (105) and the inhabitants have no use for lies or paradoxes. With nothing to oppose, there can be no Wildean paradox, with no law there can be no subversion. Wilde's antinomianism is only expressible oppositionally; unlike Morris's socialism, it requires the condition it seeks to eliminate. For Wilde, Utopia is a place to leave, a staging-ground for the next revision: Utopia is 'the one country at which Humanity is always landing. And when Humanity lands there, it looks out, and, seeing a better country, sets sail. Progress is the realisation of Utopias' (299).

The in-your-face first sentence of 'The Soul of Man Under Socialism' begins the essay's work of linguistic renovation: 'The chief advantage that would result from the establishment of Socialism is, undoubtedly, the fact that Socialism would relieve us from that sordid necessity of living for others which, in the present condition of things, presses so hardly upon almost everyone.' What is called altruism is in fact sentimental self-martyrdom, like the Happy Prince's, a futile if understandable response to finding ourselves 'surrounded by hideous poverty, by hideous ugliness, by hideous starvation' (274). Authority, in the form of possessiveness, produces the social ills which warp the language and thereby keep us from knowing our own, and therefore everyone else's, best interest: 'a community corrupted by authority [cannot] understand or appreciate Individualism'; it alienates the best interests of its

members through the institutions of government and journalism, and spawns that 'monstrous and ignorant thing that is
called Public Opinion' (310).

This is the nexus of concerns that brings the journalist and
the artist into collision in 'The Soul of Man Under Socialism'
and makes the polemic on Public Opinion more than an over-
flow of hurt feelings at the hostile reviews of *Dorian Gray*. I discussed that occasional aspect in the previous chapter; here I
only add that Wilde's self-defence in the essay repeats the
offence insofar as several of its best lines were originally
spoken by Lord Henry Wotton in the novel.[18] 'The Soul of Man
Under Socialism' is beyond the letter-writing stage of answering accusations point by point. Instead, Wilde explains that his
opponents—Art's opponents—cannot know what they are
talking about because they use a language debased by authority. '[T]he very limited vocabulary of art-abuse that is at the
disposal of the public' (309) is the discourse that makes every
manifestation of 'the new' into a symptom of *le fin*; and 'The
Soul of Man Under Socialism', like 'The Critic as Artist', is
Wilde's explicit attempt at reappropriation.

The public, speaking against their individual best interests,
'say a work is grossly unintelligible', but what 'they mean [is]
that the artist has said or made a beautiful thing that is new;
when they describe a work as grossly immoral, they mean that
the artist has said or made a beautiful thing that is true' (306).
'Morbid' is one of the words the public use 'very vaguely, as
an ordinary mob will use ready-made paving stones' (306).
But the morbid, in its true meaning, is 'a mood of emotion or
a mode of thought that one cannot express'; on the Lord Goring principle that 'Fashion is what one wears oneself', Wilde
explains that 'The public are all morbid, because the public can
never find expression for anything. *The artist is never morbid.
He expresses everything*' (307–8; Wilde's italics). Groping to say
what it thinks it means, public opinion uses the words
'unhealthy' and 'exotic': 'The latter merely expresses the rage
of the momentary mushroom against the immortal, entranc-
ing, and exquisitely lovely orchid' (309); while 'a healthy work
of art is one whose style recognises the beauty of the material
it employs . . . [and] has both perfection and personality' (309).
(Apparently public opinion is incorrigible: a reviewer wrote

that Wilde's 'article, if serious, would be thoroughly unhealthy'.)[19]

The keyword, a semantic philosopher's stone that will lead to the recovery of all true meanings, is, of course, Individualism. Individualism will bring a renovated language, because it will mean the end of authority's distortions: 'Under Individualism people will be quite natural and absolutely unselfish, and will know the meaning of the words . . . ' (329). Individualism is the end to which socialism is the means or, better, it is the right name of any right socialism; for 'the State must give up all idea of government. It must give it up because, as a wise man once said many centuries before Christ, there is such a thing as leaving mankind alone; there is no such thing as governing mankind' (293). The 'wise man' of Wilde's socialism is neither Marx nor Herbert Spencer but the sage Chuang Tsu speaking in his avatar as an Irishman, a sexual dissident, an artist and a critic. Wilde's 'socialism' is ahistorical, or it exists after history's end, when ideology in no way mediates either individual existence or relationships between individuals. 'The Soul of Man Under Socialism' refuses to accede to any shaping force beyond the individual—a site or personified abstraction it can believe in when belief in anything else is impossible or inimical. In Wilde's anarcho-socialist utopia, artists will be responsible only to themselves, unmolested by governments, by wage-hungry journalists, or by a badly brought up public.

I acknowledged at the start of this book that Wilde largely failed in his project of renaming the world in order to make himself. The equivocal proof of that failure, I said, was his fame—the fame, or infamy, which displaces the individual and puts in his place the alienated figure which, however great, is the public's revenge on the artist who would be himself alone. Oscar Wilde intended to live into history on his own terms—a paradox history will not allow. My book about Wilde's *Intentions* wants to pay tribute to the greatness of his failure, to the rightness and, as most readers of 'The Soul of Man Under Socialism' will feel, the goodness of the effort. Like all Wilde's best prose, the essay's epigrammatic surface tempts me to quotation, to laughter and applause. And as Oscar Wilde once said, 'The only way to get rid of a temptation is to yield to it.' Therefore, from 'The Soul of Man Under Socialism': 'a community is infinitely more brutalised by the habitual employment of punishment than it is by the occasional occurrence of crime' (294); 'Selfishness is not living as one wishes to live, it is asking others to live as one wishes to live' (328); 'Pleasure is Nature's test, her sign of approval. When man is happy, he is in harmony with himself and his environment' (334).

Notes

INTRODUCTION

1. H. Montgomery Hyde, *The Trials of Oscar Wilde* (London, 1948). Subsequent references to this book appear parenthetically in the text as *Trials*.
2. Letter to Max Beerbohm [28 May 1897], in *The Letters of Oscar Wilde*, ed. Rupert Hart-Davis (New York, 1962), 576. Subsequent references to this volume appear parenthetically in the text as *Letters*. In this letter, Wilde objects to the title of Beerbohm's satire, *The Happy Hypocrite*.
3. See Jeff Nunokawa, 'Oscar Wilde in Japan: Aestheticism, Orientalism, and the Derealization of the Homosexual', *positions: east west cultural critique*, 2 (1994), 44–56, on Wilde's 'voluntarism' and what Nunokawa calls 'desire lite'.
4. Ricketts designed an unusual cover for *Intentions*: 'bound in dull green cloth [it] bore the titles of the four essays in hand-drawn lettering based on Rossetti's version of William Blake's script' (Stephen Calloway, *Charles Ricketts: Subtle and Fantastic Decorator* London, 1979, 14). The American edn. by Dodd, Mead and Co. had a different binding. An American reviewer, over the top with enthusiasm about everything else, deplored only the cover: 'it is bound in that execrable tint of half rose which seems to be their [*sic*] present fad, and which one might believe would make Wilde himself howl with rage' (*Photo American Review* (June 1891), 160).
5. As published by Heinemann & Balestier (Leipzig, 1891) for sale in Europe outside Great Britain, the volume's contents are identical to the English and American first edns.
6. See Ed Cohen, 'Writing Gone Wilde: Homoerotic Desire in the Closet of Representation', *PMLA* 102 (1987); 801–13.
7. This is only a small part of the list given by Holbrook Jackson, *The Eighteen Nineties* (1918; repr. New York, 1966), 21.

CHAPTER 1

1. It also sounds like a more significant volume than either of those: *Keynotes* (1893) by the feminist 'George Egerton'.
2. *Seven Men* (New York, 1920), 17
3. Regenia Gagnier, *Idylls of the Marketplace* (Stanford, 1986), uses the word 'dialogical' in its Bakhtinian sense to characterize Wilde's way of making words 'double-voiced' (31–2). I prefer to leave 'paradox' as the rhetorical term for that feature of Wilde's rhetoric. Patricia Clements, *Baudelaire and the English Tradition* (Princeton, 1985), adapts a term from Harold Bloom to characterize Wilde's relations to other writers as 'anthological'. This comes closer to my sense of Wilde's dialogue with his sources.
4. *The Autobiography of William Butler Yeats* (New York, 1938), 114.

5. *The Vanishing Subject: Early Psychology and Literary Modernism* (Chicago, 1991), 29.
6. 'From Pater to Wilde to Joyce: Modernist Epiphany and the Soulful Self', *Texas Studies in Literature and Language*, 32 (1990), 417–45: 420.
7. Perry Meisel, *The Absent Father: Virginia Woolf and Walter Pater* (New Haven, 1980), notices another, related, conflict in Pater's idea of selfhood: 'Despite its status as an ontological given from which artistic work pro-ceeds . . . [Paterian selfhood] is less a natural object than a well-wrought vessel'; it is 'already the kind of thing it is supposed to produce' (104–5).
8. Cf. McGowan, 'From Pater to Wilde to Joyce': 'Wilde . . . was torn from the start between a belief that the self is a fiction that can be reinvented in each successive moment and more traditional notions of destiny and identity that were grounded on a belief in an essential character or soul possessed by each individual' (426).
9. 12 May 1891, in Karl Beckson (ed.) *Oscar Wilde: The Critical Heritage* (London, 1970), 91; subsequent references to this book are given as *Heritage*.
10. In order, the adjectives are from the *Spectator* (11 July 1891), the *Athenaeum* (6 June 1891), the *Nation* (New York, 9 July 1891).
11. See below, Ch. 6, for a discussion of the reviews and Wilde's response.
12. Cf. the *Pall Mall Gazette*: 'Mannerism apart, there is much excellent matter in Mr. Wilde's dialogues and essays . . . with more common sense . . . than he would perhaps care to be accused of'; the *Graphic*: 'Mr. Wilde is always worth reading', but he would be more welcome 'could he dispense with the artificial dialogue form which lends a cumbrousness to his lightest essays'; the *Athenaeum*: Wilde 'has something to say . . . in spite of his showy paradoxes'; *The Times*: Wilde has a 'very pretty turn for epigram', which means that 'those who are not repelled by his rather obtrusive affectations will find his volume very entertaining reading'; *Andover Review*: when Wilde leaves off 'the extravagant paradox and its luscious development', we discover in his 'plain prose' that 'he has after all some-thing important or interesting to tell us'.
13. [W. L Courtney], *Daily Telegraph*, 19 May 1891, p. 6. This brief review is not listed in E. H. Mikhail, *Oscar Wilde: An Annotated Bibliography of Criticism* (Totowa, NJ, 1978). Wilde wrote to Courtney, 'I think I detected your pleasant friendly touch' in the *Daily Telegraph* review, and asked if Courtney would also 'notice' *Dorian Gray*: 'when it first appeared it was grossly and foolishly assailed as an immoral book, and I am anxious to have it treated purely from the art-standpoint . . .' ([c. 19 May 1891], *More Letters of Oscar Wilde*, ed. Rupert Hart Davis (London, 1985), 97); subse-quently cited as *More Letters*.
14. The list included the memoirs of a New England nun, a book about explorers in the Middle East, and four volumes by Count von Moltke, the recently deceased Prussian hero. Osgood died in the second year of the firm's existence. I do not know how Wilde became involved with Osgood—whose 20-cent. biographer, in the course of 282 pages, never mentions Wilde's name (Carl J. Weber, *The Rise and Fall of James Ripley Osgood* (Waterville, Maine, 1959)). For publishing conditions generally and information on the Bodley Head, see James G. Nelson, *The Early Nineties: A View from the Bodley Head* (Cambridge, Mass., 1971); Jerome

McGann, *Black Riders: The Visible Language of Modernism* (Princeton, 1993).

15. Stuart Mason (ed.), *Bibliography of Oscar Wilde* (London, 1914), 355–8. Of the 1st edn., 600 were issued in America under the Dodd Mead imprint; of the 'cheap edition', Dodd Mead took 500.

16. But Charles Ricketts, explaining his reluctance in 1895 to enter into a publishing scheme with Wilde, says, 'if his plays enchanted the public, his books were far from being successful' (*Oscar Wilde: Recollections by Jean Paul Raymond and Charles Ricketts* (London, 1932), 41).

17. *The Oxford Book of Modern Verse*, 'chosen by W. B. Yeats' (New York, 1936), pp. vii–viii.

18. Weber, *Rise and Fall of James Ripley Osgood*, 252–4. Hardy told Osgood 'how the editor of the *Graphic* had called on him to substitute a rickety wheelbarrow for Angel Clare's strong arms in the scene in which Clare carries the three dairymaids across a flooded lane' (254–5). See also Michael Millgate, *Thomas Hardy: A Biography* (New York, 1982).

19. 'Jude the Obscene' was the title of reviews in both the *Guardian* and the *Pall Mall Gazette*; 'Hardy the Degenerate' was supplied by the *World*.

20. Ricketts, *Recollections*, 30.

21. 'The English Renaissance in Art', a lecture delivered in America in 1882, in *The First Collected Edition of the Works of Oscar Wilde*, ed. Robert Ross, 14 vols. (London, 1908; repr. 1969), xiv. 277. Subsequently cited as *Misc.*.

22. Walter Hamilton, *The Aesthetic Movement in England* (London, 1882), 110. Hamilton is enthusiastic about Wilde, antagonistic towards the 'eccentric' Whistler, and in several minds about Ruskin. His quirky jumble of a book is intended as a response to the satires in *Punch*, and to Gilbert and Sullivan's *Patience* and F. C. Burnand's *The Colonel*.

23. The situation was similar in France. The preface to Théophile Gautier's novel *Mademoiselle de Maupin* can be heard echoing in the epigrams that make up the Preface to *The Picture of Dorian Gray* and in the subtitle ('The Importance of Doing Nothing') to 'The Critic as Artist'. But Gautier's novel was published in 1835; his poems, *Émaux et Camées*, were published in 1852. Baudelaire, who died in 1867, published *Les Fleurs du mal* in 1857.

24. Beerbohm's essay was originally called 'A Defence of Cosmetics'. It was retitled 'The Pervasion of Rouge' for publication in *The Works of Max Beerbohm* (London: 1896).

25. *A Peep into the Past and Other Prose Pieces*, ed. Rupert Hart-Davis (Brattleboro, Vt., 1972), 7.

26. Lord Alfred Douglas, *Oscar Wilde and Myself* (New York, 1914), 35–6.

27. On the tactical advantage of turning aestheticism to dandyism, see Alan Sinfield, *The Wilde Century: Effeminacy, Oscar Wilde, and the Queer Movement* (New York, 1994), 98

28. Clements, *Baudelaire and the English Tradition*, 142, echoing Harold Bloom's characterization of Wilde's poetry in *The Anxiety of Influence*.

29. On Wilde's attempt to create 'an audience for art and life', see Gagnier, *Idylls of the Marketplace*, 19–47.

30. For Wilde's legal team, this established a fallback position. At it turned out, they asked Queensberry to accept a verdict of not guilty 'having reference to the word "posing," and to Dorian Gray and the epigrams in the *Chameleon*. Nothing would then be conceded about Wilde's acts of

sodomy as itemized in the plea of justification' (Richard Ellmann, *Oscar Wilde* (New York, 1988), 452, subsequently cited as Ellmann). The defence would not co-operate, and Wilde's lawyer 'had to consent that Queensberry was justified in calling Wilde a sodomite in the public interest' (ibid. 452).

31. Stuart Mason, *Art and Morality: A Record of the Discussion which Followed the Publication of 'Dorian Gray'* (London, 1907; rev. edn. 1912), 22.
32. Cohen, 'Writing Gone Wilde' writes that 'the aftermath of Wilde's trials has left no doubt in the critical mind that the "immorality" of Wilde's text paralleled that of his life. Yet this critical reflection has never directly addressed the question of how Wilde's "obviously" homoerotic text signifies its "deviant" concerns while never explicitly violating the dominant norms for heterosexuality' (805). The figuration of 'effeminacy' is central to the question Cohen raises.
33. Justin McCarthy, *Gentleman's Magazine* (Apr. 1892): *Heritage* 131.
34. *Oscar Wilde: His Life and Confessions* (1916), repr. as *Oscar Wilde (Including 'My Memories of Oscar Wilde' by George Bernard Shaw)*, ed. Lyle Blair (East Lansing, Michigan, 1959), 53.
35. Hugh Kingsmill, *Frank Harris* (1932; rev. edn. London, 1987), 70–1. For Beerbohm's caricature, see my *Max Beerbohm and the Act of Writing*, 162 and fig. 19.
36. *A Peep into the Past and Other Prose Pieces*, 7.
37. 'The unspeakable one' is the epithet Henry James used for Wilde in a letter about the opening of *Lady Windermere's Fan* (quoted in Ellmann, 367). Unspeakably vulgar, one supposes, but also unspeakable in the way that psychic threats in James's own work are often unspeakable. The governess in 'The Turn of the Screw' forces Miles to name the ghostly menace, and in speaking it he dies.

CHAPTER 2

1. This is a fragmentary manuscript of leaves which did not become part of the printer's copy for the first magazine edition. I am grateful to its owner, Lady Eccles, for permission to see it. I have not been able to locate the complete manuscript which was used as printer's copy. That manuscript is described by Stuart Mason, *Bibliography of Oscar Wilde* (London, 1914); I have traced it as far as a sale at Sotheby's in 1934.
2. *The Memoirs of John Addington Symonds*, ed. Phyllis Grosskurth (Chicago, 1984), 99.
3. *Hellenism and Homosexuality in Victorian England* (Ithaca, 1994), 73.
4. In his *Autobiography* Yeats mistakenly says that before their first meeting Wilde had reviewed *The Wanderings of Oisin*. He is also mistaken in saying that Wilde 'praised [the book] without qualification' (117). In fact, as of Christmas 1888 Wilde had not reviewed anything by Yeats. Shortly afterwards he did review *Fairy and Folk Tales of the Irish Peasantry* (*Woman's World*, Feb. 1889: *Rev.* 406–11), and he reviewed *The Wanderings of Oisin* twice: in *Woman's World* (Mar. 1889), a condescending review which says that Yeats has 'a quality not common in the work of our minor poets . . . the romantic temper', and predicts future work of 'high import'

from a poet who 'has been merely trying the strings of his instrument, running over the keys' (*Rev.* 437–9), and again in *Pall Mall Gazette* (12 July 1889), this time censuring 'strange crudities and irritating conceits' but 'recklessly pronouncing a fine future' for an author who 'is very naïve and very primitive and speaks of his giants with the air of a child' (*Rev.* 523–5).

5. 'Tradition and the Individual Talent' (1917), in *Selected Essays* (London, 1932), 21.

6. *Gaudier-Brzeska: A Memoir* (London, 1916), 98.

7. *Idylls of the Marketplace: Oscar Wilde and the Victorian Public* (Stanford, 1986), 134. Gagnier argues that Wilde satirizes the dandiacal figures his audience thought he was endorsing. Drawing on Debord's commodity theory, she claims that Wilde 'exploited the society he criticized'. But she is driven to create a two-level model for Wilde's work, like the one which claims that Shakespeare wrote one play for the groundlings and another for the discerning few. It is hard to see how a critique of society can function effectively if the society critiqued is merely amused.

8. Arnold, *The Complete Works*, ed. R. H. Super, v: *Culture and Anarchy* (Ann Arbor, 1965), 141–2.

9. Ibid., ch. 3.

10. Cf. 'Cigarettes have at least the charm of leaving one unsatisfied' ('Critic as Artist', 119).

11. Quoted in Priscilla Metcalf, *James Knowles: Victorian Editor and Architect* (Oxford, 1980), 299. I am indebted to Metcalf for much of the information in this paragraph.

12. *Sexual Dissidence* (Oxford, 1991), 14.

13. Quotation from Lyn Pykett, 'Representing the Real: The English Debate About Naturalism, 1884–1900', in Brian Nelson (ed.), *Naturalism in the European Novel* (New York, 1992), 171. Pykett discusses the professionalization of a discourse on 'the feminine', but what she says holds for the emerging idea of a homosexual identity as well.

14. *Realism* (Harmondsworth, 1971), 36.

15. Robert Y. Tyrrell, '*Robert Elsmere* as Symptom', *Fortnightly Review*, NS 45 (1889), 727–31: 727.

16. Smith's speech and the replies to it come from *Hansard*, as repr. in the National Vigilance Association pamphlet *Pernicious Literature* (London, 1889), itself repr. in George J. Becker (ed.), *Documents of Modern Literary Realism* (Princeton, 1963), 350–82. Quotations here and below are from pp. 352–5.

17. Ibid., 371.

18. Sales catalogue repr. in A. N. L. Munby (ed.), *Sales Catalogues of Libraries of Eminent Persons*, i: *Poets and Men of Letters* (London, 1971), 376.

19. Cf. Patrice Hannon, 'Aesthetic Criticism, Useless Art: Wilde, Zola, and "The Portrait of Mr W. H."', in Regenia Gagnier (ed.), *Critical Essays on Oscar Wilde* (New York, 1991), 186–201.

20. *Thérèse Raquin* (1867), trans. Leonard Tancock (Harmondsworth, 1962), 63–4; subsequent page references are given in the text.

21. *Nana* (1880), trans. Douglas Parmée (Oxford, 1992); page references are given in the text.

22. Wilde called on Zola in Paris in March 1891. Robert Sherard records

Wilde's ironic agreement with his host's statement that a writer needs to do documentary research: 'In writing *Dorian Gray* I studied long lists of jewelry. The other day I spent hours over a catalogue published by a firm of horticulturalists, to learn the names of various kinds of flowers and their technical descriptions. You cannot write a novel from your brain as a spider draws its web out of its belly' (Ellmann, 323 n.).

23. 'Reticence in Literature', *Yellow Book*, 2 (July 1894); 259–69: 264.

24. Mrs Humphry Ward's article of 1884, 'Recent Fiction in England and France', published in *Macmillan's*, is quoted by Pykett, 'Representing the Real', 182.

25. In the year of *Intentions*, John Addington Symonds defended Zola in '*La Bête humaine*: A Study of Zola's Idealism', *Fortnightly Review*, NS 50 (1891), 453–62. Symonds shows that *La Bête humaine* (like *Thérèse Raquin*) has the shape of a moral tale, not a scientific experiment.

26. 'The New Naturalism', *Fortnightly Review*, NS 38 (1885), 240–56: 242; subsequent page references are given in the text.

27. Wilde's borrowing from Swinburne is noticed by Patricia Clements, *Baudelaire and the English Tradition* (Princeton, 1985), 145. Swinburne's much-plagiarized footnote occurs on pp. 137–8 of his book (5th impression, repr. New York, 1965).

28. *Realism*, 28.

29. *Literary Opinion* (July 1891), 10.

30. *North American Review* (Jan. 1892), repr. in her *Essays in Miniature* (New York, 1893); also in *Heritage*, 104.

CHAPTER 3

1. 'The New Naturalism', *Fortnightly Review*, NS 38 (1885), 244.

2. *Fortnightly Review*, NS 50 (Oct. 1891), 453–62: 460.

3. George J. Becker (ed.), *Documents of Modern Literary Realism* (Princeton, 1963), 126–8.

4. 'Shakespeare and Stage Costume', *Nineteenth Century*, 17 (May 1885), 800–18: 800. Subsequent references to this article appear parenthetically in the text as 'Stage Costume'.

5. Lord Lytton died 24 Nov. 1891; Wilde dedicated the printed edn. (1893) of *Lady Windermere's Fan* to his 'dear memory . . . in affection and admiration'.

6. Lytton, 'Miss Anderson's Juliet', *Nineteenth Century*, 16 (Dec. 1884), 879–900: 882; subsequent page references are given in the text.

7. *Theatre* (Dec. 1884), 310, quoted in Michael R. Booth, *Victorian Spectacular Theatre 1850–1910* (London, 1981), 33.

8. *Resistable Theatres: Enterprise and Experiment in the Late Nineteenth Century* (London, 1972), 46.

9. Booth, *Spectacular Theatre*, 13, 20.

10. 'Archaeology in the Theatre' *Macmillan's Magazine*, 54 (1886), 126–34: 127. (In the *Wellesley Index*, i (item 2501) the article is attributed to H. B. Simpson.) I owe the reference to Russell Jackson: on the subject of archaeology, see Jackson's articles 'Designer and Director: E. W. Godwin and Wilson Barrett's *Hamlet* of 1884', *Deutsche Shakespeare-Gesellschaft West*

Jahrbuch (1974), 186–200, and 'The Shakespeare Productions of Lewis Wingfield, 1883–90', *Theatre Notebook*, 32 (1977), 28–41.

11. Quoted in Stokes, *Resistable Theatres*, 49.

12. In addition to 'Shakespeare and Stage Costume', Wilde had written two other, briefer, pieces in support of archaeology (and apparently of realism): 'Shakespeare on Scenery', *Dramatic Review*, 14 Mar. 1885 (*Rev.* 6-10), and '*Henry the Fourth* at Oxford', *Dramatic Review*, 23 May 1885 (*Rev.* 22–6).

13. Quoted in Stokes, *Resistable Theatres*, 49.

14. *National Review* (Sept. 1884), 128. Stokes, in *Resistable Theatres*, says that the performance did not actually take place on the Duke of Cambridge's estate at Coombe, but on 'the adjoining grounds of Dr. MacGeagh's hydropathic establishment' (47). Hart-Davis calls it 'Dr. McGragh's hydropathic establishment' (*Letters*, 160 n.). Whatever his or its name, Austin preferred to associate the performance not with hydropathy but with aristocracy.

15. *Resistable Theatres*, 48; subsequent page references are given in the text.

16. When the first Coombe Park *As You Like It* took place in July 1884 Wilde had not yet begun regular reviewing. In Aug. 1884 he was temporary drama critic for *Vanity Fair*, substituting for his brother Willie. The first review Ross collects is dated 7 Mar. 1885; 'Shakespeare and Scenery' is the third.

17. 'Disrupting Sexual Difference: Meaning and Gender in the Comedies', in John Drakakis (ed.), *Alternative Shakespeares* (London, 1985), 180.

18. Rodney Shewan, *Oscar Wilde: Art and Egotism* (London, 1977), discusses Wilde's interest in the androgynous potential of Lady Archie's performance, and claims that it 'must have been one of the principal stimuli for Wilde's two imaginative projections of idealised Shakespearean actors: She is the progenitor not only of Sibyl Vane but also of Willie Hughes [in 'The Portrait of Mr W. H.']' (81–2).

19. From *Poems and Ballads* (2nd ser.), in *The Poems of Algernon Charles Swinburne*, 5 vols. (New York, 1904), iii. 71. Cf. Swinburne's description of *Mademoiselle de Maupin* in his 'Memorial Verses on the Death of Theophile Gautier': 'Veiled loves that shifted shapes and shafts, and gave / Laughing, strange gifts to hands that durst not crave, / Flowers double-blossomed, fruits of scent and hue / Sweet as the bride-bed, stranger than the grave.'

20. 'Mr. Pater's Last Volume', *Speaker*, 22 Mar. 1890: *Rev.* 539.

21. *Mademoiselle de Maupin* (Paris, 1860), 21. Quotations in English, below, are from the translation (New York and London, 1944), introd. Jacques Barzun, which I have compared to the French text; subsequent page references are given in the text.

22. In 'Pen, Pencil, and Poison' Wilde explicitly recalls D'Albert's paean to the hermaphrodite: the artist–criminal Thomas Wainewright was 'with Gautier . . . fascinated by that "sweet marble monster" of both sexes' (68).

23. Gautier's use of the phrase 'third sex' puts him in the historical vanguard of sexological discourse. Beginning in the 1860s, the idea of a third sex was promulgated by writers such as Ulrichs, Krafft-Ebbing, and Havelock Ellis. It was repudiated by Ellis's sometime collaborator, J. A. Symonds (see Alan Sinfield, *The Wilde Century* (New York, 1994), 110).

Gautier's use of the phrase is so emphatic and precise that it suggests a conscious reference to the medicalizing discourse. The idea was inimical to Wilde, but on D'Albert's statement that his desire 'has no name' see below, Ch. 5, on 'The Portrait of Mr W. H.'

24. 'Gendered Space: *The Woman's World*', *Women: A Cultural Review*, 2 (1991), 149–62: 153.

25. 'The Woodland Gods', *Woman's World* (London, 1888), 1–7; cited from vol. i of the facsimile edn. (3 vols.; New York, 1970).

26. *Resistable Theatres*, 47.

27. Katherine Worth, *Oscar Wilde* (London, 1983), 65; Worth quotes Robertson and Ricketts.

28. See Alan Sinfield, '"Effeminacy" and "Femininity": Sexual Politics in Wilde's Comedies', *Modern Drama*, 37 (1994), 34–52, on the 'feminine, leisure class woman' as dandy. Wilde's maxim derives from Baudelaire (see Patricia Clements, *Baudelaire and the English Tradition* (Princeton, 1985), 141, citing *Œuvres Complètes* ii. 494), and suggests again that the 'modernity' of Wilde's position is at least recursive.

29. Ellmann, 366, prints the curtain speech as the actor–manager George Alexander remembered it, and also, in a footnote, the report of the speech that appeared in the *Boston Evening Transcript*. The two versions agree fairly well on the conclusion, about the audience's success, but the *Evening Transcript* version is longer, less insolent, and full of decorous thanks to Alexander and the cast.

30. *Illustrated London News*, 27 Feb. 1892: *Heritage* 124–5. Scott was unusual in his indignation; most critics thought Wilde was only pretending to be serious, in the play and in person.

31. See Sinfield, '"Effeminacy" and "Femininity": Sexual Politics'.

32. *Idylls of the Marketplace: Oscar Wilde and the Victorian Public* (Stanford, 1986), 126,

33. Cf. Jessica R. Feldman, *Gender on the Divide: The Dandy in Modernist Literature* (Ithaca, 1993), 6: 'Dandyism exists in the field of force between two, opposing, irreconcilable notions about gender. First, the (male) dandy defines himself by attacking women. Second, so crucial are female characteristics to the dandy's self-creation that he defines himself by embracing women, appropriating their characteristics.'

CHAPTER 4

1. Frank Harris, *Oscar Wilde: His Life and Confessions* (1916), repr. as *Oscar Wilde (Including 'My Memories of Oscar Wilde' by George Bernard Shaw)*, ed. Lyle Blair (East Lausing, Mich., 1959), 68.

2. Norbert Kohl, *Oscar Wilde: The Works of a Conformist Rebel*, trans. David Henry Wilson (Cambridge, 1989), 118.

3. *Idylls of the Marketplace: Oscar Wilde and the Victorian Public* (Stanford, 1986), 39.

4. *Against Interpretation* (New York, 1966), 288. See also Gregory Bredbeck, 'Narcissus in the Wilde: Textual Cathexis and the Historical Origins of Queer Camp', in Moe Meyer (ed.), *The Politics and Poetics of Camp*, (London, 1994), 51–74.

5. Letter of 21 Sept. 1819, in *Letters of John Keats*, 2 vols., ed. Hyder E. Rollins (Cambridge, Mass., 1958), ii. 167.
6. Wallis's painting is in the Tate Gallery. 'Unrecorded face' is quoted from the sonnet by Rossetti which appears at the end of Wilde's MS essay on Chatterton. See Roger Lewis, 'A Misattribution: Oscar Wilde's "Unpublished Poem on Chatterton"', *Victorian Poetry*, 28 (1990), 164–9.
7. Stuart Mason, *Bibliography of Oscar Wilde* (London, 1914) 13.
8. Small, *Conditions for Criticism: Authority, Knowledge, and Literature in the Late Nineteenth Century* (Oxford, 1991), 92, 112, and *passim*; Gagnier, *Idylls of the Marketplace*, 13.
9. *Shakespeare's Lives* (Oxford 1970), 681.
10. London, 1866; 2nd edn. 1868.
11. *The Poetics of Impersonality* (Brighton, 1987), 16.
12. *The Pathology of Mind* ('Being the Third Edition of the Second Part of *The Physiology and Pathology of Mind*, Recast, Enlarged, and Rewritten') (New York, 1896), 12. To add to the bibliographical confusion, this is a version of the edn. originally published in 1879.
13. Billie Andrew Inman, 'The Intellectual Context of Walter Pater's "Conclusion"', in Philip Dodd (ed.) *Walter Pater: An Imaginative Sense of Fact* (London, 1981), 15, quotes this passage and notices its consonance with the imagery of Pater's conclusion.
14. *OED*, supplement, s. v. 'personality', 3*b*.
15. In his introduction to Wilde's *Works* (1909), quoted by Claude J. Summers, *Gay Fictions: Wilde to Stonewall, Studies in a Male Homosexual Tradition* (New York, 1990), 29.
16. On the relations between aestheticism and commodity culture, see Gagnier, *Idylls of the Marketplace*; Rachel Bowlby, 'Promoting Dorian Gray', *Oxford Literary Review*, 9 (1987), 147–63; Jonathan Freedman, *Professions of Taste: Henry James, British Aestheticism, and Commodity Culture* (Stanford, 1990).
17. Rodney Shewan discusses the personality–perfection nexus in *Oscar Wilde: Art and Egotism* (London, 1977), 20–2; this quotation is from p. 77.
18. This is the passage as revised for book publication.

CHAPTER 5

1. Harris, *Oscar Wilde: His Life and Confessions* (1916), repr. as *Oscar Wilde (Including 'My Memories of Oscar Wilde' by George Bernard Shaw)* ed. Lyle Blair (East Lausing, Mich., 1959), 68–9. Harris claims that he was abroad when the article arrived at the *Fortnightly* office and that 'much to my chagrin, my assistant [John Stuart Verschoyle] rejected it rudely' (69).
2. Charles Ricketts, *Oscar Wilde: Recollections by Jean Paul Raymond and Charles Ricketts* (London, 1932), 30.
3. Both are quoted in Horst Schroeder, *Oscar Wilde, 'The Portrait of Mr W. H.': Its Composition, Publication and Reception* (Braunschweig, 1984), 14. This, with its companion volume *Annotations to Oscar Wilde, 'The Portrait of Mr W. H.'* (1986) are invaluable resources, and I gratefully acknowledge them here.

4. Repr. and identified in Stuart Mason, *Bibliography of Oscar Wilde* (London, 1914), 6.

5. John Addington Symonds, *A Problem in Greek Ethics* (1883), in *Male Love*, ed. John Lauritsen (New York, 1983), 80.

6. Jeffrey Weeks, *Coming Out: Homosexual Politics in Britain, from the Nineteenth Century to the Present* (London, 1977), 1–55.

7. I cite the revised, expanded text as edited by Vyvyan Holland (London: Methuen, 1958), 16. Future page references appear parenthetically in the text. Holland's text is accurately derived from the first printing of the expanded text, by Mitchell Kennerley (New York, 1921). For purposes of comparison, I will occasionally indicate, parenthetically, that a passage appears in the revised version, not *Blackwood's*: the unrevised *Blackwood's* text is reprinted in *Lord Arthur Savile's Crime and Other Prose Pieces*, vol. vii of *The First Collected Edition of the Works of Oscar Wilde*, ed. Robert Ross, 14 vols. (London, 1908; repr. 1969).

8. Cf. Carson's attempt at the first trial to make *Dorian Gray* and 'Mr W. H.' reciprocally reveal each other's sodomitical reality, and to make both of them dependent on Wilde's own sexual nature: Carson quotes from *Dorian Gray* the phrase 'I quite admit that I adored you madly', and asks Wilde, 'Have you ever adored a young man madly?' Wilde replies, 'No, not madly; I prefer love . . . ' Carson: 'Then you have never had that feeling?' Wilde: 'No. The whole idea was borrowed from Shakespeare, I regret to say—yes, from Shakespeare's sonnets.' And this provokes the exchange I quoted earlier: 'I believe you have written an article to show that Shakespeare's sonnets were suggestive of unnatural vice?' (*Trials*, 129).

9. *Sexual Anarchy: Gender and Culture at the Fin de Siècle* (New York, 1990), 176.

10. On the challenge of reading 'The Portrait of Mr W. H.', see Gerhard Joseph, 'Framing Wilde', *Victorian Newsletter*, 72 (1987), 61–3; William A. Cohen, 'Willie and Wilde: Reading *The Portrait of Mr. W. H.*', *South Atlantic Quarterly*, 88 (1989), 219–45; and Kevin Kopelson, 'Wilde, Barthes, and the Orgasmics of Truth', *Genders*, 7 (1990), 22–31.

11. From the first count against Queensberry: *Trials*, 107.

12. Cf. Lee Edelman, 'Homographesis', *Yale Journal of Criticism*, 3 (1989), 189–207, on 'the gay body as text' bearing legible signs of its difference.

13. This account of events is given by Ricketts in *Oscar Wilde: Recollections*. Ricketts's book is in the form of a narrative by a fictitious Frenchman named Jean Paul Raymond and of fictitious letters to 'Raymond' from Ricketts. H. Montgomery Hyde, *Oscar Wilde: A Biography* (New York, 1975), 196, accepts Ricketts's version as fact; Ellmann's biography is silent about it.

14. The expanded version (interleaved and interlineated in a copy of the *Blackwood's* text) was thought to have disappeared from Wilde's Tite Street house on the day of his bankruptcy sale. In 1921 it was published in a limited edn. in New York by Mitchell Kennerley, without any explanation of its provenance. The full history of the manuscript's reappearance is still in doubt, but the available facts are set forth by Schroeder, *Oscar Wilde, The Portrait of Mr. W.H.*, 36–9. The manuscript was bought from Kennerley by A. S. W. Rosenbach and is now at the Rosenbach Museum and Library in Philadelphia.

15. Mahaffy, *Social Life in Greece from Homer to Menander*, 2nd edn. (London, 1875), p. x.
16. Ibid. 308. Ellmann, 29, also identifies this passage as Wilde's.
17. This and other quotations below are from the 1st edn. (London, 1874), 306; they do not appear in the 2nd.
18. *The Memoirs of John Addington Symonds*, ed. Phyllis Grosskurth (Chicago, 1984), 62; subsequent page references are given in the text.
19. See Linda Dowling's extensive treatment of the 'the fatal book' in *Language and Decadence in the Victorian Fin de Siècle* (Princeton, 1986), esp. p. 164.
20. *The Symposium* 182b, in *The Dialogues of Plato*, trans. Benjamin Jowett, 4th edn., rev. (Oxford, 1953), 1: 513.
21. In *Male Love*, 31.
22. *A Problem in Modern Ethics* (1891), in *Male Love*, 80.
23. *A Problem in Greek Ethics* (1883), in *Male Love*, 49.
24. Douglas's poem alludes to Shakespeare's sonnet no. 144, 'Two loves I have, of comfort and despair', but it may also glance at Pausanius' distinction in the *Symposium* between a higher and lower love.
25. *Letters of James Joyce*, 3 vols. ed. Gilbert Stuart (vol. i), Richard Ellmann (vols. ii and iii) (New York, 1966), II. 105 (19 Aug. 1906), quoted by R. B. Kirschner, Jr., 'Artist, Critic, Performer: Wilde and Joyce on Shakespeare', *Texas Studies in Literature and Language*, 20 (1978), 216–29.

CHAPTER 6

1. Letter to the editor of *Truth*, 2 Jan. 1890.
2. The two-part publication was the decision of the editor, James Knowles. After publication of part 1 but before he had received proofs for part 2, Wilde wrote to Knowles: 'It is still a great source of regret to me that the dialogue has been interrupted' (*Letters*, 272). When he received proofs for part 2 he had another disappointment: Knowles had omitted the entire set-piece on Dante (*Intentions*, 159–62). Referring to a previous letter (not extant) about the omission, Wilde apologizes for belonging to 'the *genus irritabile*' but says, 'It seemed to me that the entire passage was essential' (*Letters*, 274).
3. Wilde reviewed a translation of Chuang Tsu in Feb. 1890 (*Rev.* 528–38). See J. D. Thomas, '"The Soul of Man Under Socialism": An Essay in Context', *Rice University Studies*, 51 (1965), 83–95, and Isobel Murray, 'Oscar Wilde and Individualism: Contexts for "The Soul of Man"', *Durham University Journal*, 52 (1991), 195–207
4. On the professional critic versus the sage or man of letters, and their respective institutions, see R. J. Green, 'Oscar Wilde's *Intentions*: An Early Modernist Manifesto', *British Journal of Aesthetics*, 13 (1973), 397–404; and esp. Ian Small, *Conditions for Criticism: Authority, Knowledge, and Literature in the Late Nineteenth Century* (Oxford, 1991).
5. I quote here from the 1890 *Lippincott's Magazine* text, which is printed, along with the 1891 Ward, Lock and Co. text, in *The Picture of Dorian Gray*, ed. Donald L. Lawler (New York, 1988). This quotation is from p. 257 (ch. x in the 1890 version, ch. xii in the 1891 version).

6. The first of the reviews to which Wilde responded appeared in the *St James's Gazette*, 24 June 1890. Wilde's letters appeared on 26, 27, and 28 June. The *Daily Chronicle* weighed in on 30 June, and Wilde's response (written the same day) appeared on 2 July. Finally, the *Scots Observer* published a singularly nasty one-paragraph notice on 5 July and Wilde responded to the review and its epistolary aftermath in the issues of 12 July, and 2 and 16 August. These and other pieces of the record were published by Stuart Mason, *Art and Morality* (London, 1907; rev. edn. 1912). I quote from Karl Beckson, *Oscar Wilde: The Critical Heritage* (London, 1970), here as elsewhere, because it is more widely available.

7. *The Wilde Century: Effeminacy, Oscar Wilde, and the Queer Movement* (New York, 1994); cf. Ed Cohen, 'Writing Gone Wilde: Homoerotic Desire in the Closet of Representation', *PMLA* 102 (1987), 801–13.

8. On Stead and the New Journalism, see Raymond L. Schults, *Crusader in Babylon: W. T. Stead and the Pall Mall Gazette* (Lincoln, Nebr., 1972), 28–65, 128–211; Laurel Brake, *Subjugated Knowledges: Journalism, Gender and Literature in the Nineteenth Century* (Basingstoke, 1994), 83–103.

9. *The Complete Prose Works*, ed. R. H. Super, 11 vols. (Ann Arbor, 1960–77) iii. 265–6.

10. See Brake, *Subjugated Knowledges*: 'The terms "critic" and "criticism" functioned as our terms "reviewer" and "review", with no special association with what we have since defined as "literature"' (2). This is slightly misleading: the category 'literature' is not a post-19th-cent. formation, although the contents of the category may have shifted; and the distinction between reviewer and critic is still unfixed, except, possibly, for academic critics.

11. See Wendell V. Harris, 'Arnold, Pater, Wilde, and the Object as in Themselves They See It', *Studies in English Literature 1500–1900*, 11 (1971), 733–47.

12. Stephen Logan, 'Shakespeare is Not Just for Dons', *The Times*, 9 Feb. 1995, p. 38.

13. '[E]ach mode of criticism is, in its highest development, simply a mood, and . . . we are never more true to ourselves than when we are inconsistent' (182).

14. For other purposes he can collapse the distinction: 'The antithesis between them [creative and critical faculties] is entirely arbitrary' (120).

15. Five months before the appearance of the first part of 'The True Function and Value of Criticism', in his review ('A Chinese Sage') of Herbert Giles's translation of Chuang Tsu, he had written that 'All modes of government are wrong' (*Rev.* 531).

16. 'A Chinese Sage', 8 Feb. 1890: *Rev.* 529.

17. 'Destroying Literary Studies', *New Criterion*, 2 (1983), 1–8, quoted by Zhang Longxi, 'The Critical Legacy of Oscar Wilde', *Texas Studies in Literature and Language*, 30 (1988), 88. By contrast, Longxi cites Northrop Frye, who called 'The Decay of Lying' 'the beginning of a new kind of criticism' and 'the herald of a new age in literature' (1977), because Wilde makes language sovereign rather than servant of a prior, non-linguistic, truth.

18. Whistler's letter was published in *Truth* on 2 Jan. 1890, Wilde's response on 9 Jan. 1890 (*Letters*, 253–4). All the correspondence was reprinted by

Whistler in *The Gentle Art of Making Enemies*, enlarged edn. (1892; repr. New York, 1967). The contested phrase in 'Decay of Lying' has nothing to do with disciples; rather, it is 'the modern novelist' who 'has not even the courage of other people's ideas' (8).

19. Published in the *World*, 14 Nov. 1883, and repr. in *Gentle Art*, 66.
20. *World*, 17 Nov. 1888, repr. in *Gentle Art*, 164; ellipsis points in original.
21. 'Whistler v. Ruskin: Art and Art Critics' (1878), in Whistler, *Gentle Art*, 30.
22. *Gentle Art*, 161: *Misc.* 65.
23. *Gentle Art*, 161: *Misc.* 66.
24. 'The Butterfly's Boswell', *Court and Society Review*, 20 Apr. 1887, p. 378; not in *Rev.*, but repr. in *The Artist as Critic: Critical Writing of Oscar Wilde*, ed. Richard Ellmann (Chicago, 1968).
25. Cf. 'Mr W. H.': 'It is never with impunity that one's lips say Love's Litany. Words have their mystical power over the soul, and form can create the feeling from which it should have sprung' (63). This passage was added (in MS) to 'Mr W. H.' sometime between 1889 (when the magazine version appeared) and 1893, so it is impossible to say whether 'Critic' is repeating 'Mr W. H.' or vice versa.
26. *Andover Review*, 16 (1891), 570; my italics.
27. *Pall Mall Gazette*, 12 Dec. 1887: *Misc.* 88. Cf. 'The conception of the unity of the arts is certainly of great value but in the present condition of criticism it . . . would be more useful to emphasise the fact that each art has its separate method of expression' ('Mr. Symonds' History of the Renaissance', *Pall Mall Gazette*, 10 Nov. 1886: *Rev.* 108).

CHAPTER 7

1. *The Happy Prince and Other Tales* was published in 1888, but Wilde had told the title story to friends at Cambridge in 1885. See Ellmann, 269, who takes the story unironically, although he notices the homoeroticism (and cross-speciesism) of the Prince's relationship with the Sparrow: 'They are transfigured and borne off to God's hand'. Robert K. Martin, 'Oscar Wilde and the Fairy Tale: "The Happy Prince" as Self-Dramatization', *Studies in Short Fiction*, 16 (1979), 74–7, finds a more explicitly sexual and biographical meaning.
2. The essay was published in Harris's *Fortnightly Review* in Feb. 1891, a few months before the appearance of *Intentions* but too late to be included in it. I use the text supplied in *Intentions* and *The Soul of Man Under Socialism* vol. viii of *The First Collected Edition of the Works of Oscar Wilde*, ed. Robert Ross, 14 vols. (London, 1908; repr. 1969). These phrases all come from the first three pages of the essays (273–5). Wilde italicized some sentences or phrases, on no clearly identifiable grounds, throughout the essay. In cases not otherwise specified, the emphases are Wilde's, not mine.
3. George Woodcock, *The Paradox of Oscar Wilde* (London, 1949), 145.
4. Woodcock notices that 'This story, exposing the evils of monarchy, capitalism and imperialism, Wilde dedicated, surely in irony, to a minor ruling princess whose wealth had been derived from colonial exploitation, the Ranee of Sarawak' (145). This too, then, is an irony which manages to have its cake and eat it. In 1896 Wilde wrote to More Adey from Reading

Prison: 'Lady Brooke [the Ranee of Sarawak] has influence with my wife. Could she be asked from me to suggest to my wife not to trouble me or distress me any more till my release? We were great friends once' (*Letters*, 417).

5. *Idylls of the Marketplace: Oscar Wilde and the Victorian Public* (Stanford, 1986), 31–2.
6. The essay was 'privately reprinted' in book form in 1895 under the title *The Soul of Man*. I find no evidence that Wilde himself approved the shortened version of the title.
7. *The Revolt of the Elites and the Betrayal of Democracy* (New York, 1995), 231.
8. 'The Impossible Culture: Oscar Wilde and the Charisma of the Artist', *Encounter*, 35 (Sept. 1970), 33–44: 40.
9. George Watson, *The English Ideology* (London, 1973), 221.
10. See J. D. Thomas's witty essay, '"The Soul of Man Under Socialism": An Essay in Context', *Rice University Studies*, 51 (1965), 83–95. Thomas establishes contexts but warns against any effort to pin Wilde down to a particular source or influence. According to Philip E. Smith II and Michael S. Helfand, in their edn. of *Oscar Wilde's Oxford Notebooks* (New York, 1989), 'Wilde's political and cultural theories . . . developed directly from the synthesis of Hegelian idealism and evolutionary theory sketched in [Wilde's college] notebooks' (82). But as they also say, 'Throughout the eighties Wilde had moved freely in radical, socialist, and anarchist circles and had participated in or otherwise supported their causes' (81). 'The Soul of Man Under Socialism' is Hegelian in practice—as a work of synthesis—rather than coherently in theory.
11. Review of *Chants of Labour*, 15 Feb. 1889: *Rev.* 426.
12. Letter to Mrs W. H. Grenfell, [late Apr. 1891]: *More Letters*, 96, describing the audience at a performance of *Hedda Gabler*.
13. Margaret Cole, *The Story of Fabian Socialism* (Stanford, 1961), 25.
14. Steven Lukes, *Individualism* (Oxford, 1973), 22. See also Isobel Murray, 'Oscar Wilde and Individualism: Contexts for "The Soul of Man"', Durham University Journal, 52 (1991), 195–207.
15. 'The Society of the Future' (lecture, 1885), in May Morris, *William Morris: Artist Writer Socialist*, ii: *Morris as a Socialist* (Oxford, 1936), 457.
16. Thomas, '"The Soul of Man Under Socialism"', 86.
17. Morris, *News from Nowhere and Other Writings* (1890), ed. Clive Wilmer (Harmondsworth, 1993), 107; subsequent page references are given in the text.
18. For instance, '"The mutilation of the savage has its tragic survival in the self-mutilation that mars our lives"' (*CW* 29); cf. 'self-sacrifice . . . is merely a survival of savage mutilation' ('Soul of Man', 326); '"Pleasure is Nature's test, her sign of approval. When we are happy we are always good, but when we are good we are not always happy"' (*CW* 69); cf. 'Pleasure is Nature's test, her sign of approval. When man is happy, he is in harmony with himself and his environment' ('Soul of Man', 334).
19. *Spectator*, 7 Feb. 1891, quoted in Stuart Mason, *A Bibliography of Oscar Wilde* (London, 1914), 73.

Bibliography

1. EDITIONS OF WILDE'S WORKS

The Artist as Critic: Critical Writings of Oscar Wilde, ed. Richard Ellmann (Chicago, 1968).

The Complete Works of Oscar Wilde, introd. Vyvyan Holland (London, 1948; new edn. 1966).

The First Collected Edition of the Works of Oscar Wilde, ed. Robert Ross, 14 vols. (London, 1908; repr. 1969).

Intentions (London, 1891).

The Letters of Oscar Wilde, ed. Rupert Hart-Davis (New York, 1962).

More Letters of Oscar Wilde, ed. Rupert Hart-Davis (London, 1985).

Oscar Wilde's Oxford Notebooks, ed. Philip E. Smith II and Michael S. Helfand (New York, 1989).

The Picture of Dorian Gray, ed. Donald L. Lawler (New York, 1988).

The Portrait of Mr W. H., ed. Vyvyan Holland (London, 1958).

2. OTHER SOURCES

ANDERSON, PERRY, *Arguments within English Marxism* (London, 1980).

ANON., review of *Intentions*, *Athenaeum*, 6 June 1891, p. 731.

ANON., review of *Intentions*, *Graphic*, 12 December 1891, p. 706.

ANON., review of *Intentions*, *Literary Opinion*, (July 1891), 10.

ANON., review of *Intentions*, *Nation*, 9 July 1891, pp. 34–5.

ANON., review of *Intentions*, *Observer*, 14 June 1891, p. 7.

ANON., review of *Intentions*, *Pall Mall Gazette*, 12 May 1891, p. 3.

ANON., review of *Intentions*, *Photo American Review*, (June 1891), 160.

ANON., review of *Intentions*, *Punch*, 30 May 1891, p. 257.

ANON., review of *Intentions*, *Spectator*, 11 July 1891, p. 56.

ANON., review of *Intentions*, *The Times*, 7 May 1891, p. 4.

ARNOLD, MATTHEW, *The Complete Works*, ed. R. H. Super, 11 vols. (Ann Arbor, 1960–77).

BASHFORD, BRUCE, 'Oscar Wilde and Subjectivist Criticism', *English Literature in Transition*, 21 (1978), 218–34.

BECKER, GEORGE J. (ed.), *Documents in Modern Literary Realism* (Princeton, 1963).

BECKSON, KARL (ed.), *Oscar Wilde: The Critical Heritage* (London, 1970).

BEERBOHM, MAX, *The Works of Max Beerbohm* (London, 1896).
—— *Seven Men* (New York, 1920).
—— *A Peep into the Past and Other Prose Pieces*, ed. Rupert Hart-Davis (Brattleboro, Vt., 1972).
BEHRENDT, PATRICIA FLANAGAN, *Oscar Wilde: Eros and Aesthetics* (London, 1991).
BELSEY, CATHERINE, 'Disrupting Sexual Difference: Meaning and Gender in the Comedies', in John Drakakis (ed.), *Alternative Shakespeares* (London, 1985).
BOOTH, MICHAEL R., *Victorian Spectacular Theatre 1850–1910* (London, 1981).
BOWLBY, RACHEL, 'Promoting Dorian Gray', *Oxford Literary Review*, 9 (1987), 147–63.
BRAKE, LAUREL, 'Gendered Space: *The Woman's World*', *Women: A Cultural Review*, 2 (1991), 149–62.
—— *Subjugated Knowledges: Journalism, Gender and Literature in the Nineteenth Century* (Basingstoke, 1994).
BREDBECK, GREGORY, 'Narcissus in the Wilde: Textual Cathexis and the Historical Origins of Queer Camp', in Moe Meyer (ed.), *The Politics and Poetics of Camp* (London, 1994), 51–74.
BRISTOW, JOSEPH, 'Dowdies and Dandies: Oscar Wilde's Refashioning of Society Comedy', *Modern Drama*, 37 (1994), 53–70.
BRITAIN, IAN, 'A Transplanted Doll's House: Ibsenism, Feminism and Socialism in Late Victorian and Edwardian England', in Ian Donaldson (ed.), *Transformations in Modern European Drama* (London, 1963), 14–54.
BUCKLER, WILLIAM E., 'Building a Bulwark Against Despair: "The Critic as Artist"', *English Literature in Transition*, 32 (1989), 278–89.
CALLOWAY, STEPHEN, *Charles Ricketts: Subtle and Fantastic Decorator* (London, 1979).
CARPENTER, G. R., 'Three Critics: Mr Howells, Mr Moore, and Mr Wilde', *Andover Review*, 16 (1891), 568–76.
CHAMBERLIN, J. E., *Ripe Was the Drowsy Hour* (New York, 1977).
CLEMENTS, PATRICIA, *Baudelaire and the English Tradition* (Princeton, 1985).
COHEN, ED, 'Writing Gone Wilde: Homoerotic Desire in the Closet of Representation', *PMLA* 102 (1987), 801–13.
—— 'Legislating the Norm: From Sodomy to Gross Indecency', *South Atlantic Quarterly*, 88 (1989), 191–217.
—— 'Laughing in Earnest: The Trying Context of Wilde's "Trivial" Comedy', *LIT* 3 (1991), 57–64.
COHEN, WILLIAM A., 'Willie and Wilde: Reading *The Portrait of Mr W. H.*', *South Atlantic Quarterly*, 88 (1989), 219–45.
COLE, MARGARET, *The Story of Fabian Socialism* (Stanford, 1961).

COURTNEY, W. C., review of *Intentions*, *Daily Telegraph*, 19 May 1891, p. 6.

CRACKANTHORPE, HUBERT, 'Reticence in Literature', *Yellow Book*, 2 (July 1894), 259–69.

CRAFT, CHRISTOPHER, 'Alias Bunbury: Desire and Termination in *The Importance of Being Earnest*', *Representations*, 31 (1990), 19–45.

D'AMICO, MASOLINO, 'Oscar Wilde Between "Socialism" and Aestheticism', *English Miscellany*, 18 (1967), 111–40.

DANSON, LAWRENCE, *Max Beerbohm and the Act of Writing* (Oxford, 1989).

DELLAMORA, RICHARD, *Masculine Desire: The Sexual Politics of Victorian Aestheticism* (Chapel Hill, 1990).

DOLLIMORE, JONATHAN, *Sexual Dissidence* (Oxford, 1991).

DOUGLAS, LORD ALFRED, *Oscar Wilde and Myself* (New York, 1914).

DOWLING, LINDA, 'Imposture and Absence in Wilde's "The Portrait of Mr W. H."', *Victorian Newsletter*, 58 (1980), 26–9.

—— *Language and Decadence in the Victorian Fin de Siècle* (Princeton, 1986).

—— *Hellenism and Homosexuality in Victorian Oxford* (Ithaca, 1994).

EDELMAN, LEE, 'Homographesis', *Yale Journal of Criticism*, 3 (1989), 189–207.

ELIOT, T. S., *Selected Essays* (London, 1932).

ELLMANN, MAUDE, *The Poetics of Impersonality* (Brighton, 1987).

ELLMANN, RICHARD, *Eminent Domain* (Oxford, 1965).

—— *Golden Codgers* (New York, 1973).

—— *Oscar Wilde* (New York, 1988).

FELDMAN, JESSICA R., *Gender on the Divide: The Dandy in Modernist Literature* (Ithaca, 1993).

FINZI, JOHN CHARLES, *Oscar Wilde and His Literary Circle: A Catalogue of Manuscripts and Letters in the William Andrews Clark Memorial Library* (Berkeley, 1957).

FOULKES, RICHARD, (ed.), *Shakespeare and the Victorian Stage* (Cambridge, 1986).

FREEDMAN, JONATHAN, *Professions of Taste: Henry James, British Aestheticism, and Commodity Culture* (Stanford, 1990).

GAGNIER, REGENIA, *Idylls of the Marketplace: Oscar Wilde and the Victorian Public* (Stanford, 1986).

—— (ed.), *Critical Essays on Oscar Wilde* (New York, 1991).

GAUTIER, THÉOPHILE, *Mademoiselle de Maupin* (Paris, 1860); English trans. *Mademoiselle de Maupin*, introd. Jacques Barzum (New York and London, 1944).

GODWIN, E. W., *Dress and Its Relation to Health and Culture*, International Health Exhibition Handbooks (London, 1884).

GRAHAM, WALTER, *English Literary Periodicals* (New York, 1930).

GREEN, R. J., 'Oscar Wilde's *Intentions*: An Early Modernist Manifesto', *British Journal of Aesthetics*, 13 (1973), 397–404.

GUY, JOSEPHINE M., *The British Avant-Garde* (Hemel Hempstead, 1991).

HAMILTON, WALTER, *The Aesthetic Movement in England* (London, 1882).

HANNON, PATRICE, 'Aesthetic Criticism, Useless Art: Wilde, Zola and "The Portrait of Mr W. H."', in Regenia Gagnier (ed.), *Critical Essays on Oscar Wilde* (New York, 1991), 186–201.

HARRIS, FRANK, *Oscar Wilde: His Life and Confessions* (1916), repr. as *Oscar Wilde (Including 'My Memories of Oscar Wilde' By George Bernard Shaw)*, ed. Lyle Blair (East Lansing, Mich., 1959).

HARRIS, WENDELL V., 'Arnold, Pater, Wilde, and the Object as in Themselves They See It', *Studies in English Literature 1500–1900*, 11 (1971), 733–47.

HAZLITT, W. CAREW, *Essays and Criticisms by Thomas Griffiths Wainewright* (London, 1880).

HEBRON, DUDLEY, *The Conscious Stone: The Life of Edward William Godwin* (London, 1949).

HITCHENS, CHRISTOPHER, 'Oscar Wilde's Socialism', *Dissent*, 42 (1995), 515–19.

HYDE, H. MONTGOMERY, *The Trials of Oscar Wilde* (London, 1948).

—— *Oscar Wilde: A Biography* (New York, 1975).

INMAN, BILLIE ANDREW, 'The Intellectual Context of Walter Pater's "Conclusion"', in Philip Dodd (ed.), *Walter Pater: An Imaginative Sense of Fact* (London, 1981), 12–30.

JACKSON, HOLBROOK, *The Eighteen Nineties* (1918; repr. New York, 1966).

JACKSON, RUSSELL, 'Designer and Director: E. W. Godwin and Wilson Barrett's *Hamlet* of 1884', *Deutsche Shakespeare-Gesellschaft West Jahrbuch* (1974), 186–200.

—— 'The Shakespeare Productions of Lewis Wingfield', *Theatre Notebook*, 32 (1977), 28–41.

JENKYNS, RICHARD, *The Victorians and Ancient Greece* (Oxford, 1980).

JOSEPH, GERHARD, 'Framing Wilde', *Victorian Newsletter*, 72 (1987), 61–3.

JOWETT, BENJAMIN (trans.), *The Dialogues of Plato*, 4th edn. rev. (Oxford, 1953).

KAPLAN, JOEL H. (ed.), 'Special Issue: Oscar Wilde', *Modern Drama*, 37 (Spring 1994).

—— and Stowell, Sheila, *Theatre and Fashion: Oscar Wilde to the Suffragettes* (Cambridge, 1994).

KEATS, JOHN, *Letters*, ed. Hyder E. Rollins, 2 vols. (Cambridge, Mass., 1958).

KINGSMILL, HUGH, *Frank Harris* (1932; rev. edn. London, 1987).

KIRSCHNER, R. B., Jr., 'Artist, Critic, Performer: Wilde and Joyce on Shakespeare', *Texas Studies in Literature and Language*, 20 (1978), 216–29.

KNOEPFLMACHER, U. C., 'Arnold's Fancy and Pater's Imagination: Exclusion and Incorporation', *Victorian Poetry*, 26 (1988), 103–15.

KOHL, NORBERT, *Oscar Wilde: The Works of a Conformist Rebel*, trans. David Henry Wilson (Cambridge, 1989).

KOPELSON, KEVIN, 'Wilde, Barthes, and the Orgasmics of Truth', *Genders*, 7 (1990), 22–31.

LASCH, CHRISTOPHER, *The Revolt of the Elites and the Betrayal of Democracy* (New York, 1995).

LAURITSEN, JOHN (ed.), *Male Love* (New York, 1983).

LEWIS, ROGER, 'A Misattribution: Oscar Wilde's "Unpublished Poem on Chatterton"', *Victorian Poetry*, 28 (1990), 164–9.

LILLY, W. S., 'The New Naturalism', *Fortnightly Review*, NS 38 (1885), 240–56.

LOEWENSTEIN, JOSEPH, 'Wilde and the Evasion of Principle', *South Atlantic Quarterly*, 84 (1985), 392–400.

LOGAN, STEPHEN, 'Shakespeare is Not Just for Dons', *The Times*, 9 February 1995, p. 38.

LONGXI, ZHANG, 'The Critical Legacy of Oscar Wilde', *Texas Studies in Literature and Language*, 30 (1988), 87–103.

LUKES, STEVEN, *Individualism* (Oxford, 1973).

LYTTON, LORD, 'Miss Anderson's Juliet', *Nineteenth Century*, 16 (December 1884), 879–900.

McCORMACK, JERUSHA, 'Masks Without Faces: The Personalities of Oscar Wilde', *English Literature in Transition*, 22 (1976), 253–69.

McGANN, JEROME, *Black Riders: the Visible Language of Modernism* (Princeton, 1993).

McGOWAN, JOHN, 'From Pater to Wilde to Joyce: Modernist Epiphany and the Soulful Self', *Texas Studies in Literature and Language*, 32 (1990), 417–45.

MAHAFFY, J. P., *Social Life in Greece from Homer to Menander* (1874), 2nd edn., rev. and enlarged (London, 1875).

MARTIN, ROBERT K., 'Oscar Wilde and the Fairy Tale: "The Happy Prince" as Self-Dramatization', *Studies in Short Fiction*, 16 (1979), 74–7.

MASON, STUART, [pseud. Christopher Sclater Millard], *Art and Morality: A Record of the Discussion which Followed the Publication of 'Dorian Gray'* (London, 1907; rev. edn. 1912).

—— (ed.), *Bibliography of Oscar Wilde* (London, 1914).

MASSON, DAVID, *Essays Biographical and Critical* (incl. 'Chatterton: A Story of the Year 1770') (Cambridge, 1856).

MAUDSLEY, HENRY, *The Pathology of Mind* ('Being the Third Edition of the Second Part of *The Physiology and Pathology of Mind* [1879], Recast, Enlarged, and Rewritten') (New York, 1896).

MEISEL, PERRY, *The Absent Father: Virginia Woolf and Walter Pater* (New Haven, 1980).

MENAND, LOUIS, 'A Wilde for Our Times', *Partisan Review*, 57 (1990), 255–63.

METCALF, PRISCILLA, *James Knowles: Victorian Editor and Architect* (Oxford, 1980).

MIKHAIL, E. H., *Oscar Wilde: An Annotated Bibliography of Criticism* (Totowa, NJ, 1978).

MILLGATE, MICHAEL, *Thomas Hardy: A Biography* (New York, 1982).

MOORE, GEORGE, *Impressions and Opinions* (London, 1891).

MORRIS, MAY, *William Morris: Artist Writer Socialist*, ii: *Morris as a Socialist* (Oxford, 1936).

MORRIS, WILLIAM, *News from Nowhere and Other Writings* (1890), ed. Clive Wilmer (Harmondsworth, 1993).

MUNBY, A. N. L. (ed.), *Sales Catalogues of Libraries of Eminent Persons*, i: *Poets and Men of Letters* (London, 1971).

MURRAY, ISOBEL, 'Oscar Wilde's Absorption of "Influences": The Case History of Chuang Tzu', *Durham University Journal*, 64 (NS 33; 1971), 1–13.

—— 'Oscar Wilde and Individualism: Contexts for "The Soul of Man"', *Durham University Journal*, 52 (1991), 195–207.

NELSON, JAMES G., *The Early Nineties: A View from the Bodley Head* (Cambridge, Mass., 1971).

NOCHLIN, LINDA, *Realism* (Harmondsworth, 1971).

NUNOKAWA, JEFF, 'Homosexual Desire and the Effacement of the Self in *The Picture of Dorian Gray*', *American Imago*, 49 (1992), 311–21.

—— 'Oscar Wilde in Japan: Aestheticism, Orientalism, and the Derealization of the Homosexual', *positions: east west cultural critique*, 2 (1994), 44–56.

PAGLIA, CAMILLE, 'Oscar Wilde and the English Epicene', *Raritan*, 4 (1985), 85–109.

PATER, WALTER, *The Renaissance: Studies in Art and Poetry, the 1893 Text*, ed. Donald L. Hill (Berkeley, 1980).

POLLARD, DAVID, 'Oscar in the Fantastic Shakespearean Glass', *Proceedings of the 10th International Conference on Literature and Psychology* (1993), 289–98.

POUND, EZRA, *Gaudier-Brzeska: A Memoir* (London, 1916).

POWELL, KERRY, 'Wilde and Ibsen', *English Literature in Transition*, 28 (1985), 224–42.

—— *Oscar Wilde and the Theatre of the 1890s* (Cambridge, 1990).

PYKETT, LYN, 'Representing the Real: The English Debate About

Naturalism, 1884–1900', in Brian Nelson, (ed.), *Naturalism in the European Novel* (New York, 1992), 167–88.

REPPLIER, AGNES, *Essays in Miniature* (New York, 1893).

RICKETTS, CHARLES, *Oscar Wilde: Recollections by Jean Paul Raymond and Charles Ricketts* (London, 1932).

RICKS, CHRISTOPHER, 'Pater, Arnold and Misquotation', *Times Literary Supplement*, 25 November 1977, pp. 1383–5.

RIEFF, PHILIP, 'The Impossible Culture: Oscar Wilde and the Charisma of the Artist', *Encounter*, 35 (September, 1970) 33–44.

ROBINS, ELIZABETH, *Both Sides of the Curtain* (London, 1940).

RYAN, JUDITH, *The Vanishing Subject: Early Psychology and Literary Modernism* (Chicago, 1991).

SCHOENBAUM, S., *Shakespeare's Lives* (Oxford, 1970).

SCHROEDER, HORST, *Oscar Wilde, 'The Portrait of Mr W. H.': Its Composition, Publication, and Reception* (Braunschweig, 1984).

—— *Annotations to Oscar Wilde, 'The Portrait of Mr W. H.'* (Braunschweig, 1986).

SCHULTS, RAYMOND L., *Crusader in Babylon: W. T. Stead and the Pall Mall Gazette* (Lincoln, Nebr., 1972).

SCHWARTZ, SANFORD, *The Matrix of Modernism: Pound, Eliot, and Early Twentieth-Century Thought* (Princeton, 1985).

SHAW, GEORGE BERNARD, (ed.), *Fabian Essays in Socialism* (London, 1889).

SHEWAN, RODNEY, *Oscar Wilde: Art and Egotism* (London, 1977).

SHOWALTER, ELAINE, *Sexual Anarchy: Gender and Culture at the Fin de Siècle* (New York, 1990).

SIMPSON, H. B., 'Archaeology in the Theatre', *Macmillan's Magazine*, 54 (1886), 126–34.

SINFIELD, ALAN, '"Effeminacy" and "Feminity": Sexual Politics in Wilde's Comedies', *Modern Drama*, 37 (1994), 34–52.

—— *The Wilde Century: Effeminacy, Oscar Wilde, and the Queer Movement* (New York, 1994).

SMALL, IAN, 'Semiotics and Oscar Wilde's Accounts of Art', *The British Journal of Aesthetics*, 25 (1985), 50–6.

—— *Conditions for Criticism: Authority, Knowledge, and Literature in the Late Nineteenth Century* (Oxford, 1991).

—— *Oscar Wilde Revalued* (Greensboro, NC, 1993).

SONTAG, SUSAN, *Against Interpretation* (New York, 1966).

STOKES, JOHN, *Resistable Theatres: Enterprise and Experiment in the Late Nineteenth Century* (London, 1972).

—— 'Wilde Interpretations', *Modern Drama*, 37 (1994), 156–74.

SUMMERS, CLAUDE J., *Gay Fictions: Wilde to Stonewall, Studies in a Male Homosexual Tradition* (New York, 1990).

SWINBURNE, A. C., *William Blake: A Critical Study*, 2nd edn. (London, 1868).
—— *A Study of Shakespeare* (London, 1879).
—— *The Poems of Algernon Charles Swinburne*, 5 vols. (New York, 1904).
SYMONDS, JOHN ADDINGTON, *A Problem in Greek Ethics* (1883), in *Male Love*, ed. John Lauritsen (New York, 1983).
—— *The Renaissance in Italy: The Fine Arts* (New York, 1888).
—— '*La Bête humaine*: A Study of Zola's Idealism', *Fortnightly Review*, NS 50 (1891), 453–62.
—— *Memoirs*, ed. Phyllis Grosskurth (Chicago, 1984).
THOMAS, J. D., '"The Soul of Man Under Socialism": An Essay in Context', *Rice University Studies*, 51 (1965), 83–95.
—— 'The Intentional Strategy in Oscar Wilde's Dialogues', *English Literature in Transition*, 12 (1969), 11–20.
TYRRELL, ROBERT Y., '*Robert Elsmere* as Symptom', *Fortnightly Review*, NS 45 (1889), 727–31.
WATSON, GEORGE, *The English Ideology* (London, 1973).
WEBER, CARL J., *The Rise and Fall of James Ripley Osgood* (Waterville, Maine, 1959).
WEEKS, JEFFREY, *Coming Out: Homosexual Politics in Britain from the Nineteenth Century to the Present* (London, 1977).
WEINTRAUB, STANLEY, '"The Hibernian School": Oscar Wilde and Bernard Shaw', *Shaw: The Annual of Bernard Shaw Studies*, 13 (1994), 25–49.
WHISTLER, JAMES ABBOTT MCNEIL, *The Gentle Art of Making Enemies*, enlarged edn. (1892; repr. New York, 1967).
WILLOUGHBY, GUY, 'Oscar Wilde and Poststructuralism', *Philosophy and Literature*, 13 (1989), 316–24.
WILSON, DANIEL, *Chatterton: A Biographical Study* (London, 1869).
WOODCOCK, GEORGE, *The Paradox of Oscar Wilde* (London, 1949).
WORTH, KATHERINE, *Oscar Wilde* (London, 1983).
YEATS, W. B., (ed.), *The Oxford Book of Modern Verse* (New York, 1936).
—— *Autobiography* (inc. *Reveries of Youth and Childhood*, *The Trembling of the Veil*, and *Dramatis Personae*) (New York, 1938).
ZOLA, ÉMILE, *Thérèse Raquin* (1867), trans. Leonard Tancock (Harmondsworth, 1962).
—— *Nana* (1880), trans. Douglas Parmée (Oxford, 1992).

Index